Prosperity with a Purpose:

Exploring the Ethics of Affluence

CHURCHES TOGETHER
IN BRITAIN AND IRELAND

Churches Together in Britain and Ireland
Bastille Court
2 Paris Garden
London SE1 8ND

info@ctbi.org.uk
www.ctbi.org.uk

Prosperity with a Purpose forum address: www.pwap.org.uk

ISBN Paperback 085169 309 1
Large print ISBN 0 85169 312 1
Hardback ISBN 0 85169 313 X

First Published February 2005 by CTBI
Reprinted June 2005

A catalogue record of this book is available from the British Library

Cover design: Nial Smith Design

Contents

Foreword

Ours is a world in which poverty and prosperity exist side by side. That world is increasingly marked by wealth rather than by destitution, though terrible want still ravages the lives of many. How wealth is to be understood and used; whether riches are a blessing for our society or a curse sapping its spiritual strength: these are questions on which vigorous disagreements rage.

Three years ago, the Churches – through their regular meeting of senior representatives of the Churches in Britain and Ireland – commissioned a working group to examine prosperity in the context of poverty, globalization and the threat to the environment. Its work stands in a long line of social comment from within the Churches, speaking prophetically into the political and economic arenas. The group's conclusions are recorded in ***Prosperity with a Purpose: Christians and the Ethics of Affluence*** by Clifford Longley – a companion volume to this.

The essays in this book are published in support of Clifford's work. They take different perspectives and, sometimes, offer contrasting opinions. Each is a personal view, for which its author alone is responsible. Together, they are designed to provoke thought and discussion, and to deepen the quality of reflection ahead of the next United Kingdom General Election.

The writers are all people rooted in the life of the Churches and the Christian faith. Each writes from a conviction that places value on each human person and sees social and economic life as arenas within which God has created the potential for human life to be lived in its fullness. They share the view that prosperity depends on a successful market economy; they explore in different ways what it means to pursue justice and equity in that context.

I am pleased to be able to commend their work. We need a serious and informed debate about economic issues if we are to make sensible judgments on the political choices ahead. Too often debate sinks to an exchange of slogans; these writers deal with serious issues and tackle them in measured ways. They intend to stimulate debate, and that is precisely what they do. We owe it to them to consider carefully what they have to say.

David Goodbourn
General Secretary
Churches Together in Britain and Ireland

Introduction

The Churches' ***Prosperity with a Purpose*** project is designed to provoke discussion of social issues at the time of the next UK General Election. This collection of essays is one element in that process. It forms the basis of a much shorter document, which summarizes the Churches' arguments in order to make the material more cogent and more widely accessible. The essays are by the authors indicated, and express their personal views on the issues raised. The shorter document, ***Prosperity with a Purpose: Christians and the Ethics of Affluence***, has been written by Clifford Longley, the distinguished author, journalist and broadcaster, and it is this paper which carries the commendation of Churches Together in Britain and Ireland. The genesis of the project is described in a note at the end of this introduction.

This volume consists essentially of freestanding essays, though each benefits from the conversations that have taken place between its various authors. These authors want to insist that modern prosperity depends first of all on a successful market economy. The challenge which then follows is to enable that success to be more widely shared. Some of the instruments required to achieve this purpose will seek to stimulate wealth-creation through competitive enterprise; others will create public institutions that serve ends which the market, unaided, cannot. With more difficulty, this quest for equity should be pursued on a global scale. With much more difficulty, that pursuit must be squared with the challenge to protect the environment, vulnerable and certainly under threat from all our plans for improvement.

Those are the purposes of prosperity, but they cannot be achieved simply by reaching for the right combination of policies. They will work only insofar as they are truly desired, and insofar as we are virtuous.

Ian Linden and **John Kennedy** have attempted an overview of the issue of prosperity. They explore the moral realities behind the simple increase in wealth, and ask how economic success translates into greater well-being, into genuine prosperity. There can be no real prosperity without the development of virtue.

'The practice of virtues such as prudence, justice, fortitude and temperance is good in itself. The practice of virtue trains people to choose means that lead to their true well-being. A virtuous society educates, and where necessary, disciplines its members. Thus, virtue forms character and enables people to chart a personal course to human happiness in an ordered and equitable society'.

Such a vision of the common good is a shared inheritance, not an exclusively Christian possession. There can be an argument over what constitutes virtue. However a society where that argument is suppressed may be rich and may be prosperous, but probably neither for very long.

The authors describe the ways in which both market and public institutions can work together to create prosperity, and to spread it wider. They also describe how that ensemble can work badly. They note that one widespread feature of a growing economy is a prevalent anxiety, making many people feel that their well-being is somewhat precarious. They invoke the insights of one of our consultants, Richard Layard, to show that this anxiety is widespread, socially corrosive and largely unnecessary.

They highlight three related concerns that arise as the General Election approaches. The first is what David Marquand has described as "the decline of the public" involving a conflict between government's desire to contain costs, and the desire of the public sector to maintain its professional integrity. Second is the tendency to reduce the relationship between government and media to an aggressive spectator sport, as John Lloyd has suggested. Third, and consequent, is the decline of the public's participation in political life.

Jonathan Lomax presents a discussion of the ***Paradox of Prosperity,*** drawing on studies commissioned by the Salvation Army from the Henley Centre. This valuable empirical material underscores much of what is said elsewhere in these papers. The data describe contemporary life and the changes which can be predicted up to 2010. These indicate a general increase in prosperity, and in genuine well-being, in the near future. There is, however, a tendency for this new affluence to become disengaged from people's real lives. They increasingly express anxiety about their future and about their present quality of life.

Predictably, continuing economic growth has created new levels of inequality. More serious is the seemingly intractable nature of poverty, as the disabilities that attach to it are transmitted down the generations.

Middle-class anxieties are somewhat different. Professional people work ever-longer hours and experience higher levels of stress. The promise of early retirement vanishes as pension prospects worsen. Consequently, even the better off are no longer immune to the threat of poverty.

Family life, for both rich and poor, is likely to follow existing trends. Fewer people will form families, the number of lone-parent families will increase, and problems relating to family breakdown will be exacerbated. Old age will become increasingly difficult for many. All the features of poverty, isolation, loss of support through family breakdown will be felt much more sharply by older people.

Modern prosperity appears to have robbed us of meaning in our lives. Traditional institutions like the Churches have sought to rise to this new situation; but where they have failed, people have been encouraged to seek more widely for satisfying forms of spirituality. This social fragmentation tends to result in what the paper calls the "responsibility gap" – the tendency for people to withdraw from that engagement in civil society which creates much of the social and emotional support that makes life worth living.

Peter Sedgwick reflects on the way that the thinking of the Churches has been shaped by social and especially economic change over the past century. He notes two broad traditions. The first is that of "Christian Realism" shaped by Reinhold Niebuhr, William Temple and Ronald Preston. The second is the tradition of Catholic social thought, arguably beginning with ***Rerum Novarum*** in 1891. Sedgwick then explores the process of changing practice, and of Christian thought, in three areas. These are: the nature of employment; the role of the state and the idea of expanded human needs; and lastly the relationship between poverty, alienation and unemployment.

He too insists that ethical tough-mindedness is essential to any kind of social vision:

"The central task is that of enabling a pluralist, pragmatic society to reflect upon itself, and to accept that talk of judgement is not an alien concept".

He reiterates a central idea of Richard Layard, that happiness is not closely related to growing affluence once a certain level of income is reached:

"What really matters are relationships. The stigma of mental health, the pain of divorce, the benefits of a cohesive community, a satisfying job, freedom and moral values can all be assisted or harmed by government policy".

Ian Linden sets the discussion in the context of globalization, and the challenge that it poses to the Christian vision of social justice. He makes the necessary point that a world economy is no new thing, in fact being a reality for most of the 20th century. However, it is only in recent decades that global interdependency has reached the degree of comprehensive intensity that now exists.

He shows that the forces that shape the increasingly global society are not simply directed from the old imperial nations, but are largely driven by internal dynamics; thus, the burgeoning economies of India and China have as much to do with population increase and urbanization as with the aspirations of the powerful northern nation-states and trans-national companies.

Linden argues that migration policy would benefit from a degree of enlightened self-interest. The ageing West needs new, young people, and should be more relaxed about migration.

He suggests four areas of change. These are: the regulation of corporate power; the regulation of global capital flows; the reduction of rich country protectionism; and the encouragement of good governance in poor countries. This last area involves some unfamiliar ideas. "Good governance" is usually thought of as fostering democracy and competitive markets and curbing corruption. But Linden draws on the work of Hernando de Soto and others to note an unobserved but critical inhibitor of economic and social development. This is the extraordinary fact – that in most poor countries it is enormously difficult for poor people to acquire property rights to the modest premises that they live and work in, and so they find it virtually impossible to expand their businesses.

Linden asks: what kinds of instruments would be required to harmonize the global market, social justice and environmental protection? He then draws on the work of the Commission of the Catholic Bishops' Conferences of the European Union (COMECE) to suggest what institutions would be necessary to shape the global common good.

Finally, Linden asks: how does this mission for justice fit with the present self-regarding and comfortable attitudes and practices of the Churches?

Jennifer Potter reinforces this call to justice in her reflections on the environment. The great challenge is not simply to call for environmental change, it is to reconcile Ian Linden's vision for a just commercial society with the protection of the environment. She is sharply critical of the depredations of the global competitive economy, but recognizes that the collectivist regimes of the Soviet Union and China created more destruction to less purpose. She is adamant that market instruments must be modified to sustain the life of the world. If we don't find ways of making money out of saving the planet, it won't be saved.

She emphasizes that climate change is the most urgent and widely recognized threat to the planet, while acknowledging the qualifications to the case made by the more sceptical.

Niall Cooper outlines the policy issues that arise when social justice is pursued in a market economy. He points out how diverse the social and economic cultures are in the European Union. He contrasts the relative poverty of UK levels of public provision with the much more ambitious achievements of our EU partners, notably France and Germany. But he emphasizes the long-term problems of sustaining (for instance) the French health service and German pension provision. Britain has a long way to go to match its neighbours, but their experience indicates that there are clear limits to what can be done.

That said, there has been a mixed record of achievement in alleviating poverty in Britain since 1997. Policy efforts have been largely, and quite successfully, aimed at stimulating employment, arguing that work is the best route out of poverty. These policies echo much of what the Churches demanded in ***Unemployment and the Future of Work*** (CTBI 1997).

The constraints on future policy, both economic and social, are acknowledged. The Churches have to recognize those constraints, but they may be more challenging than the normal practice of politics allows; and they should affirm the idea that the fostering of competitive enterprise and the pursuit of social justice can be compatible aims.

These social and economic realities are explored in essays on Scotland, Wales, the North-West Region, Northern Ireland and the Republic of Ireland. In those parts of these islands, the prosperous majority enjoy greater wealth often combined with a higher quality of life – that is, genuine prosperity. But these are also places where large minorities suffer from multiple deprivation; the contrasts between rich and poor are frequently sharpest here.

David Sinclair presents an analysis of economic change in Scotland. At a time when most of its people suffered dire poverty,

Scotland was a trading and manufacturing world leader, with Glasgow as the main element in that participation in the global economy up until the beginning of the 20th century. In recent years, investment and employment have stagnated in comparison with the UK as a whole:

> *"Scotland still suffers from a greater concentration of poverty, with long-term unemployment more prevalent, and levels of long-term sickness and disability a third higher than the rest of the UK".*

The Scottish Executive – the Cabinet grouping that constitutes the government of Scotland – has limited instruments at its disposal, but it published in 2002 a policy document called ***Closing the Opportunity Gap***, offering plans to "tackle poverty, build strong, safe communities and create a fair, equal Scotland." These initiatives mirror those which Niall Cooper has described – measures to address debt and financial exclusion, child poverty, fuel poverty, homelessness, community regeneration, active communities and rural poverty. Despite much higher levels of health care expenditure in Scotland compared to the UK, chronic ill-health and premature death are much more prevalent. The Executive recognizes that increasing enterprise is essential to the creation of both wealth and employment, and notes that inward investment appears to be in permanent decline. It is also true that Scotland's population is ageing and virtually static, and that the country would benefit, as would the whole UK, from a more relaxed immigration regime.

A survey of poverty commissioned by the Joseph Rowntree Foundation suggests there has been little improvement in most areas; fewer of those on low income are now unemployed, but the problem of the numbers of working poor remains as great as ever. A cliché of Scottish political debate is "the stubborn refusal" of poverty to respond to policy. Perhaps, therefore, more radical policies are required.

Glasgow, for instance, has huge acreages of derelict land, very much less developed than similar areas of England. In the past, Edinburgh has been redeveloped in ways which fail to address the inequalities of that city, and in ways that have added to car use and its resultant pollution. One suggestion is for fiscal autonomy in Scotland; this is not a crypto-nationalist proposal, but one based in the economic reality of the "chronic underperformance of the Scottish economy".

There is a shrewd discussion about "playing to your strengths" – such as the natural environment and the under-used potential of communities. The Scottish Churches' Inclusion Network has asked that the poor themselves should be the judges of their own situation. They argue that policy should be more orientated towards community than the individual, to redistribution as much as wealth-creation, to creating public value rather than service provision.

Mervyn Phillips and **Robin Morrison** discuss the somewhat similar issues that arise in Wales. The Assembly has already created a stronger Welsh identity and the Churches have been involved in the debate around the extension of its powers. Welsh income levels are lower than the UK average, but the quality of life is in many cases higher. While unemployment is not at present a major problem, the levels of economic inactivity remain a significant challenge – averaging 24% of the working age population. The Assembly has called for "a prosperous Welsh economy that is dynamic, inclusive and sustainable, based on world class competitive business and a skilled, motivated people".

Manufacturing is still important in Wales, counting for 25% of GDP as compared to 18% in the UK as a whole. Inward investment has enjoyed a period of modest increase. Yet small businesses are unable to take up funding support, management capacity is relatively low and business start-up rates – as in Scotland – are low.

The public sector accounts for a very high proportion of employment in Wales. As Ian Linden and John Kennedy have suggested, it is the combination of enterprise and public provision that makes for genuine prosperity. The Welsh Assembly has made particular efforts to create patterns of education and health care that make for greater levels of well-being. Nonetheless, the youth unemployment rate is 27% in Wales, and 33% of the population have no educational qualifications. 28% of adults are functionally illiterate and innumerate.

John Devine emphasizes the ways in which the Churches can engage with regional government to make a valuable contribution to social life. As elsewhere, there is a growing acceptance by government that faith communities are an important social resource. There has been a reappraisal of the value of civil society as a feature of public life, especially in view of the "stubborn refusal" of social ills to respond to official remedies. Faith communities are still the most vibrant and densely organized of any element in civil society, and that has been demonstrated by research in a number of regions.

"A Theology of Partnership must acknowledge a common ethical commitment, non-violence, respect for life, just economic and political order, tolerance and truthfulness, equal rights and partnership between men and women".

This commitment is illustrated with reference to the St Augustine's New Avenham Centre in Preston, and to Operation Eden in Liverpool.

Mgr Devine paints a bleak picture of some aspects of the Region. The North-West enjoys roughly 90% of the level of average national income, but that relatively high figure masks serious inequalities. Indices of Multiple Deprivation measure not just income but employment, health and disability, education, skills and training, housing and access to services – well-being, insofar as that can be measured. According to these more revealing measures, six of the ten most deprived wards and 22 of the most deprived districts are in the North-West.

As in Scotland and Wales, the main policy instruments are managed from Westminster, but Regional Development Agencies have some scope for action. There may soon be elected Regional Assemblies in the three northern regions, and thus the process of development will be brought under political scrutiny. It is widely agreed – again, in concert with Westminster, that work is the key to personal well-being and to community regeneration.

Margaret Burns' material from Ireland throws valuable light on the British discussion. She draws from both the Republic of Ireland and Northern Ireland, using papers presented at two special ***Prosperity with a Purpose*** consultations, held in Dublin and Belfast. The contrasts between these two are salutary.

For more than a decade, the Republic has sought to maximize economic growth, particularly through the stimulus of low taxation. In the meantime, those who have not shared in that burgeoning wealth suffer low levels of social protection and public amenity, with the lowest proportion of national income taken in taxation of any developed country. The paper spelling out these disparities was written by Eithne Fitzgerald, former Minister for Employment.

In the North, on the other hand, economic decline has been accompanied by a dominant public sector. The key feature of all this is, of course, the conflict which has ravaged the Province for thirty years.

The policy recommendations for global growth with equity, and for environmental protection, are those which have been advocated by Churches and global reformers for many years. They simply call upon the movers and shakers on the world economic and political scene to follow through the logic of the new worldwide economy. The free market must be a fair market, and the powerful must submit to something like the same rules that they impose upon the weak.

Similarly, the owners of sophisticated and expensive technologies must shape their economies so that they carry most of the burden of the reduction of CO^2 emissions. This approach is clearly both fair and practicable. What is not clear is whether radical adjustments to the existing economic order can still mitigate disastrous climate change. That is arguably the central moral and political challenge of our age.

Note: The Prosperity with a Purpose Project

Prosperity with a Purpose stands in a long tradition of social comment by the Churches. That process received a powerful recent stimulus from ***Faith in the City***, produced by the Church of England when the effects of the reforms of the Thatcher governments were being felt throughout the country, but especially in urban areas.

In 1996, the Conference of Catholic Bishops of England and Wales produced ***The Common Good***, designed to summarize and mobilize the tradition of catholic social teaching. This too could be seen as a commentary on the radical changes that had taken place in Britain since 1979. Shortly thereafter, the Council of Churches in Britain and Ireland produced its ***Unemployment and the Future of Work***. This document was concerned with what then seemed to be a permanent state of division in British society – between those who were enjoying unprecedented prosperity and those who were condemned to a permanent experience of poverty and exclusion, largely stemming form the then high figures of unemployment. That document enjoyed the benefit of the Churches' increasing capacity for social and economic analysis, and was able to frame some concrete proposals for the wider sharing of prosperity. Many of these were adopted by the incoming Labour administration, and a new consensus began to grow in British politics as to how prosperity might be more widely shared.

Meanwhile, the people of the Republic of Ireland had been riding on the crest of a new wave of prosperity. The Conference of Irish Bishops took note of this new phenomenon, and produced their own discussion paper called, with great prescience, ***Prosperity with a Purpose***. This signalled a new approach to social issues among the Churches. We had in the past tended to concentrate on the plight of the poor, and had failed to see clearly that the great new fact of the day is prosperity. Our thanks are due to our Irish colleagues for their ability to recast the Churches' thinking in this way, and the title of this project seeks to pay tribute to that achievement.

More recently, the Salvation Army produced a stimulating discussion document: ***The Paradox of Prosperity***. This was the first document in which the key issues of modern prosperity were seriously addressed; the project was none the less interesting because the Army has been the biggest agency in Britain to focus on the needs of poor people.

The constitution of the Churches Together in Britain and Ireland enables the two English-speaking member states of the European Union to compare notes. And this new Prosperity with a Purpose is, indeed, the first document on social issues in these islands which has tried, at least in a preliminary way, to take stock of the implications of British and Irish membership of the EU.

The aim of the project is to engage as widely and deeply as possible with the issues of prosperity and poverty in the four nations, examining the connections between them, including the effects on our peoples of an increasingly globalized economy. The participants in the project are the members of the Church and Society Forum of CTBI, and a suitably broad range of expert consultants in each of the four nations. The moderator is David Skidmore, formerly the General Secretary of the Church of England's Board for Social Responsibility.

The guidelines for the project, agreed at the Church Representatives' Meeting in November 2001, are as follows:

The project should:

1. Be informed by the success of ***Unemployment and the Future of Work and The Common Good*** especially to draw widely on the Churches' expertise.
2. Pay attention to existing and future official publications of CTBI members.
3. Be recognized as a modest project, but with the hope of a

substantial final impact; therefore the final document should be short and sharp.

4. Examine the connections between prosperity and poverty rather than simply to limit concern to issues of poverty.
5. Evaluate the moral costs of prosperity.
6. Examine the routes out of poverty.
7. Question fundamental assumptions.
8. Explore the property rights of the poor in the globalization connection.
9. Evaluate the environmental implications of the project.
10. Compare other EU patterns of prosperity and poverty.

The essays which follow attempt to achieve these aims.

1

An Overview: Ian Linden and John Kennedy

Happiness, virtue and the common good

What is prosperity? Is it having three good meals a day? Is it having two cars and family holidays in Spain? Is it having prompt access to reliable medical care? Is it being able to walk the streets without fear? Is it belonging to a just and friendly community? Is it being at peace with God?

Most people would describe prosperity as indicating the opposite of poverty. A significant real increase in household disposable income would generally be agreed to be an important indicator of prosperity, but beyond that we would probably struggle for a clear definition. As an attribute of individuals and countries, the term lacks clarity – though not meaning. In many contexts prosperity has resonances with "success" and "well-being". It may sometimes suggest the consequences of prudent management, growing productivity, or thrift.

Prosperity does not conjure up the idea of a lack of commonwealth as in "private affluence" and "public squalor". Unlike "affluence" it is not a pejorative term – rather the opposite. The values smuggled in with the word "prosperity" need to be addressed in any evaluation of today's prosperity. The values behind the word are not explicit, but they are somewhere there, nonetheless. We might ask God to give us prosperity, even if we would hesitate to pray that we might become rich.

Most people would agree that it is a facile error to think of prosperity only in terms of the accumulation of material things. We would therefore propose a richer definition. In the first instance we would say that prosperity comes from being capable of making effective choices, from having the means to express ones preferences. Prosperity depends on enjoying a variety of freedoms, capabilities and goods. A community of slaves could never be called 'prosperous', even if they were provided with all that their masters thought they should need. And if poverty is the antithesis of prosperity, then it may be because it means lacking a variety of freedoms, capabilities and goods.

We may well believe that freedom is of value in its own right, but that does not mean that it will always be used wisely. So, we may be free and capable, but still not be really prosperous. Having useful possessions does not necessarily lead to a good life. Washing machines, political parties, penicillin, and helicopters are all "goods". But you can kill a cat in a washing machine, use a political party to induce race hatred, sell out-of-date penicillin in poor countries, and strafe innocent civilians with guns while at the same time rescuing them by ambulance helicopter.

The point is that such "goods", freedoms and capabilities are ***means***. They enable us to achieve a variety of ***ends.*** Friendship and good health, for example, are ends; but ends may be good or bad. The individual may misjudge what will make him or her individually happy; what makes the individual happy may be bad for the community as a whole; and what individuals or society as a whole consider to be desirable may actually be damaging to their true prosperity and well-being. Put in another way, in the definition used here, prosperity is the state that results from the successful acquisition of the means to achieve good ends. It is, in other words, an ethical quest – which perhaps accounts for the residual ethical sound of the "secular" ideal of prosperity.

Unfortunately, as experience and history show, human beings are notoriously predisposed to make choices that do not lead even to individual happiness. We may be motivated in our choices by envy, greed or addiction. So simply having goods, capabilities and freedoms does not ensure that people make the choices that, on reflection, they would judge had led to their greater well-being. And even if our choices *do* make us happy, they may not be right in terms of an ethical judgement which might be made by us, by other people, or ultimately by God.

If we are to define prosperity in ethical terms, then we need to include the living of a virtuous life within our definition. The practice of virtues such as prudence, justice, fortitude and temperance is good in itself. It is also directed towards prosperity, and hence towards happiness, properly understood. The practice of virtue trains people to choose means that lead to their true well-being. A virtuous society educates and, where necessary, disciplines its members. Thus virtue forms character and enables people to chart a personal course to human happiness in an ordered and equitable society.

Virtue is not some esoteric 'spiritual' quality but, for example, provides 'what it takes' for people to practise co-operative professions such as teaching and the health service. Health, human development and the acquisition of knowledge are goods that members of the healing and teaching professions ideally all share. The practice of their professions should hold all members to common standards and the shared good of a particular professional excellence. Training and experience in such a profession offers the opportunity to perfect virtues needed for this excellence – such as fairness, temperance, truthfulness, honesty and prudence. Behind government advertisements portraying individuals whose lives have been transformed by good teaching in schools are the stories of the lives of good teachers. In such communities as teaching and the NHS – not particularly small ones – prosperity is the outcome of good lives lived co-operatively and virtuously. In other words the future well-being and happiness of the teacher and the pupil – their prosperity in the most profound sense of the word – is rooted in the successful striving for the shared goods of teaching as a practice and profession. Without a tradition of values in these two communities, without people relating to stories of good teachers, nurses and doctors, successful patients and pupils, this would not be possible.

The state can enhance and encourage such virtue by the way it runs and funds institutions and supports small and large communities, encouraging excellence, or undermining it, providing incentives or disincentives. Where fragmented communities and no tradition exists because of social disintegration, recourse to coercive measures may prove necessary. But legislation against anti-social behaviour and the normal penal apparatus of criminal law must be a last resort after schools, mosques, churches and families have failed. It is self-evident that such apparatus when inadequately staffed and funded and unable to undertake the necessary reform and rehabilitation of people, and return them to gainful employment, well-being and wealth-creation, is itself "anti-social" and in need of urgent legislative reform.

In short, the common good is a core value for both society as a whole and the communities nurturing virtues within it. In each there is an investment of the individual's good in a shared set of values that makes up the common good. The state thus has to find the means to promote all goods, in small or large communities and institutions, that contribute to the common good. In this sense the promotion of citizenship is simply the promotion of that form of serious commitment required for membership of the nation-state and its pursuit of prosperity in a world of poverty.

Such a vision of the common good is the common inheritance

of humanity, not the exclusive possession of Christians or other faith communities, though they will naturally articulate it in religious terms as they seek to contribute towards ethical debate in society at large. From a Christian perspective the vision is a good one because it is pleasing to God. We would maintain that it is the virtuous political and ethical use of freedoms and capabilities that leads to prosperity and that this is the path to happiness. Fundamental to our common humanity is the need to discover meaning, with its associated rights to moral formation and well-being. Or to put it more elaborately, in our view these inalienable rights are part and parcel of being human. And to be human is to be made in the image of God.

The right to meaning relies on people being part of the communities through which they inherit stories about who they are and how they got here, a symbolic universe that conveys these meanings, values, and ideas that derive from it, and some share in the practical wisdom that has come from submitting this tradition to change. The right to religious freedom is one important aspect of this right which is, of course, enshrined in Article 18 of the Universal Declaration of Human Rights. These stories may, of course, be about an absolute individual autonomy, a post-modern moral relativism, and other stories that deny there is any valid story about what it means to be human.

Lives that have lost these capabilities through the social fragmentation attendant on rapid economic growth, or for other reasons, or lives that are experienced as meaningless, are left only "imprisoning" freedoms. One way to attempt to escape alienation is through drugs and other forms of personal recklessness; another is continuing the frantic pursuit of meaning through extreme and totalitarian forms of religion, ideology, nationalism and ethnicity. All these 'freedoms' can have tragic lose-lose consequences – some more than others – as far as the individual and the common good is concerned. A society that generates great wealth but great alienation cannot meaningfully be described as either healthy, stable or prosperous.

For all these reasons, it is quite possible to be rich but not to be prosperous, or, to be more precise, a significant betterment in the economic lot of households can occur with a diminution in their sense of well-being. That is what the Salvation Army in their 1999 Henley Study meant by entitling it 'The Paradox of Prosperity'. The converse is that it is possible to be prosperous without being rich. All one needs is a sufficiency of freedoms, capabilities and goods. If that sufficiency – which different people will assess quite differently – is lacking, then one is experiencing poverty. A few individuals have chosen what they know to be poverty as a willing act of self-sacrifice, but most people's experience of poverty is miserable, and so are its consequences.

Jesus, of course, highlighted the contradictions of our contemporary understanding of prosperity by underlining the problems faced by the rich in reaching true happiness. He excoriated the quest for the exclusive enjoyment of wealth outside the primary Christian economy of 'Give and there will be gifts for you: a full measure, pressed down, shaken together and overflowing' (Luke 6.38). The young man who 'went away sad for he was a man of great wealth' (Matthew 19.22) is the human symbol of this paradox of prosperity.

So prosperity, as conceived and experienced in our countries, is proving an uncertain means to happiness, and is just as much an ethical and political question for Christians as poverty.

Prosperity as experienced today

It is far from clear that the kind of economic prosperity being experienced in Ireland, England, Wales and Scotland is conducive to the realisation of true well-being as we have defined it. The rapid change in economic fortunes has been most notable in Ireland. This is perhaps why the Irish Catholic Bishops' Conference was the first to write about 'Prosperity with a Purpose' in 1999 and to question whether rapid economic growth brought a better quality of life. In short, with a devalued politics and without a usable ethics, real happiness is likely to be elusive and in short supply, even though goods, freedoms and capabilities may be plentiful.

That said, it is important not to underestimate the human liberation afforded by material and social goods in the last half century in Britain, Ireland and other Western countries. Few people would prefer to wash clothes by hand than in a washing machine, have a brutal dictator rather than mediocre political parties, rely on a weakened immune system rather than a course of penicillin, or drown for want of rescue. But many would like to have more time for living and loving outside the work-place, to be free from anxiety and depression, to have secure jobs, affordable housing, affordable dentists, to be able to cross their country and cities as easily as the Victorians did, to have crime-free and clean parks, coastal waters with plentiful fish in them, and not to fear cataclysmic climate change. And Lazarus is always at the gate. Who sits easily with the television screen showing children starving to death as they eat their Christmas dinner?

A much-rehearsed problem of today's economic prosperity is that some publicly provided goods seem to be in short supply, while private goods are relatively abundant. That phenomenon of course presents itself quite differently in rich and poor locations. Almost all developed countries have seen policy changes reducing expenditure in many areas of public expenditure in the last decade. This reflects the fact that public goods – either as a matter of policy or due to the nature of the good – are underpriced to the user, thereby requiring the government or some other agency to ration the available supply of that good.

The public provision of goods is now at the forefront of political debate. Some public provision may be most efficiently supplied by means of contracts negotiated with private companies, and may be paid for either by a mixture of public subsidy and basic access charges, or entirely from the public purse. But in reality public funds are sometimes deployed in the last instance to 'bail out' private contractors of vital public services, or services whose collapse would have catastrophic knock-on effects on national economies or the global economy. The public/private distinction needs careful scrutiny and an avoidance of ideological distortion. The delicate balance between assuring publicly and privately provided goods is part of the art of politics.

The distribution of private incomes and social expenditures is increasingly unequal throughout society and around the world. The consequences have been dire for Africa as failed states have set the four horsemen of the Apocalypse back in the saddle; In the last decade, 3.2 million people died in the Democratic Republic of Congo, unsung and unseen, of disease, famine and war. What have been called the 'global commons' are now supranational goods; air and sea and space are prey to private greed and national belligerence.

On the other hand, developed countries have quite dramatically improved the quality of the air they breathe and the water they drink. Polio, the scourge of 50 years ago, has almost been eliminated. The vast continents and populations of India and China are significantly better off and on the way to becoming 'middle income' countries; increased public revenues and social provision go somewhat hand in hand with rising private affluence. The urbanized modern world has experienced a phenomenal improvement in life prospects in the last century, whereas the rather terrifying urban growth of the past quarter century might have seemed an unmanageable disaster as it got under way.

The language of 'the Common Good' and 'the Global Common Good', with a strong emphasis on public provision, comes from a long Christian tradition. That tradition rarely reflects on the nature of private provision, and upon the relation between the two. So it is necessary to move now from an ethic of the common good, as outlined above, to the mechanics.

Prosperity and the market

Contemporary prosperity depends heavily on the functioning of a successful competitive market economy. Nothing has demonstrated this elementary fact more powerfully than the European experience. Countries that were once miserably poor now enjoy widespread wealth. Such has been the case in the last quarter century in Ireland, Greece, Portugal and Spain. All of these have benefited from the redistributive policies of the EU social and harmonization funds, one of the notable achievements of the member states – now sadly threatened by the parsimonious reaction of the richer countries to enlargement. It is the hope of emulating such success that has driven the countries of Eastern and Southern Europe to seek membership of the European Union.

Most polities are somewhat coy about describing their purposes clearly – an example is the US proclamation of 'life, liberty and the pursuit of happiness' – where the latter objective clearly involves the freedom to make money. The European Union, however, makes a more concrete claim, in the preamble of its draft Constitution:

> *The Union shall offer its citizens an area of freedom, security and justice without internal frontiers, and a single market where competition is free and undistorted.*
>
> *The Union shall work for the sustainable development of Europe based on balanced economic growth, a highly competitive social market economy, aiming at full employment and social progress,*

and with a high level of protection and improvement of the quality of the environment ...

There is a welcome clarity to these aims, but no simple route to their fulfilment, as we shall see when we come to discuss public policy. A quite strong notion of a model of political economy is proposed here as a permanent feature of the Union. It implies that a successful market economy requires an effective and extensive relationship with government.

A successful competitive market requires strong, competent, honest government, for the market works efficiently only if its most powerful actors do that which they least want to do – compete. Many players in the market would set prices if they could. So one very important function of government, acting in the name of consumers and citizens, is to ensure that they do not. It will always be in the interests of producers to combine against the public interest when they can, but with the right kind of regulation they can be compelled to compete in the market-place. That is why one of the greatest challenges in a competitive economy – especially a transnational one like the European Union – is to enforce competition.

Every society is disfigured by poverty, excessive inequality and injustice. But successful market economies have created wealth steadily over such long periods that they offer a possibility which was formerly only dreamed of – the extensive amelioration of these evils. Modern politics has been created largely by the popular demand for social justice to which the powerful have been compelled to respond – with greater or lesser degrees of willingness. Thus, every government in the European Union, in often remarkably different ways, has created complex and hugely expensive systems of public provision. And it is these goods that have the capacity to make a society not only wealthy but also genuinely prosperous. It is the management of the relationship between the dynamic market economy, government and citizens that is one important feature of such potential well-being.

The ensemble can work well or badly. It works well under the following conditions. Innovators in the market-place create successful businesses, which call into being newly prosperous workers and consumers. The revenues generated by this success make possible extensive levels of public expenditure. Democratic politics regulate the market, and set the levels of taxation that are necessary to sustain social progress. The labour market is regulated to permit access without discrimination. Such access is encouraged at as high a level of reward as possible, so that high value added is achieved by ever better equipped workers. Minimum wage levels are set, and levels of benefit agreed for those who have insufficient access to earned income. There is continuous public debate about what constitutes a humane and inclusive society, and how it can be afforded. There is robust conflict between those who see the scandal of remaining injustice, and those who see more clearly the constraints on public policy which circumstances impose. The moral imperative to reduce glaring inequalities in the societies of the European Union remains a pressing duty on member state governments no less than the continued generation of wealth to make this possible.

This is a picture of not merely a rich but (hopefully) a prosperous society, seeing the fulfilment of private interest as only one feature of a shared common good. But it is not a society free from all social problems. Economic prosperity comes at a cost even in the best ordered market economy. The relentless pursuit of economic advantage through innovation and increased efficiency, which is necessary in a competitive world, makes this society an anxious and precarious one.

However, the ensemble can also work badly. The powerful operators in the market-place can dominate politics, and use their power to inhibit competition and to depress social investment. They can collude with government in keeping wages and levels of compensation low. Government may smother the market, destroy its disciplines in the name of social justice, and wind up an inflationary spiral though index-linked salaries and pensions. Politicians may close down ethical and political exchange by imposing unrepresentative, secretive and unaccountable government. Citizens may turn away from public engagement and find satisfaction simply as consumers. The demands of work and obsession with the fulfilment of private desire may suck the spirit out of public life.

Three areas are of particular concern

The first arises from the claim that the institutions of public service are under threat. They are increasingly subjected to the efficiency demands of the market, and so the bonds of professional integrity and public trust are loosened. This argument is countered by the claim that public institutions are required to pursue innovation and efficiency just as urgently as any operator in the market. There is a crucial and little noticed issue at stake here. Wealth increases largely through the perpetual search for productivity gains – more output per person. Where such gains are difficult, if not impossible, to achieve, then the cost of the goods or services delivered automatically increases. It is one of the paradoxes of prosperity that increased wealth makes many vital public services more expensive. The provider of these services is usually government, which has a substantial incentive to contain public service costs. The means by which those costs are to be contained are difficult to devise and to implement. It is essential that there should be public scrutiny of those means, and the consequent pressures on the public service ethos. The issues are discussed at length by David Marquand.

The second area of concern is the manner in which public debate is conducted, and the importance of the print and broadcast media to that debate. The British media are quite distinctive on the world scene. They are much more powerful at national level than in North America and Europe. They are more competitive and more combative than in the media in continental Europe, which are relatively deferential. In this highly market-oriented environment sits the BBC, much the biggest of all media outlets, publicly funded and managed, but with a large degree of independence from the state. It provides a uniquely valuable service in the public interest. But in the media market-place, issues tend to be considered less on their merits than for their entertainment value. The print media allocate a decreasing level of resource to the expensive business of newsgathering, and more to the generation of partisan opinion – columnists as entertainers. Our crucially important informative media are being turned into entertainment products. This is a powerfully contentious question, and centrally relevant to any enriched notion of prosperity. These questions have been raised most recently by John Lloyd. Third, and all embracing, is that the sense of ourselves as public beings is in decline. In a prosperous society, people naturally take charge of wider areas of their own lives. But there is a tendency for those preoccupations to encourage a passive, consumer spectator rather than an active, socially aware citizen. This tendency is enhanced when the public square becomes an arena in which the conflicts between government and the public service, between government and the media, become a spectacle rather than the stuff of shared life.

That, in broad sweep, is an elementary account of how a modern commercial society can hope to be genuinely prosperous and not merely wealthy; a society in which personal wishes are shaped by consent to the pursuit of the common good, not just a stage upon which the affluent can boast of their success and scorn those who are less able, or less fortunate, than themselves. There is a need to refashion a sense of public morality, whose disciplines are essential to the pursuit of genuine prosperity.

2

The Paradox of Prosperity: editor, Jonathan Lomax

The Salvation Army has a long and distinguished track-record of working with some of the most vulnerable people in society. As both a Church and one of the largest charities in the UK it has striven to meet the spiritual and material needs of people for 140 years. In 1999 The Salvation Army, conscious of its unique place at the confluence of many strands of social care, committed itself to looking at some of the key trends in UK society as a way of informing its work and feeding into the wider public policy debate. It commissioned the Henley Centre, a strategic futures consultancy, to produce a study outlining some major societal trends. The report, entitled ***The Paradox of Prosperity***, was warmly received upon publication and articulated trends which other subsequent studies have confirmed. ***The Paradox of Prosperity*** was followed by ***The Burden of Youth*** in 2001, which looked at issues facing children and young people, and by ***The Responsibility Gap*** in 2004, a report looking at the growing deficit of care for vulnerable people and the changing notion of responsibility.

This essay will outline some of the key findings from ***The Paradox of Prosperity*** and ***The Responsibility Gap***.

The Paradox of Prosperity

In ***The Paradox of Prosperity***, the Henley Centre looked at key social, economic and political data and extrapolated trends forward to 2010. They found that:

- Living standards will rise by around 35% between 1998 and 2010.
- This will be tempered by a growing 'paradox of prosperity in which the economic fortunes of many people become decoupled from consumer confidence and quality of life.
- The wealth gap will become more pronounced by 2010 with the forecast that the top 10% of the population would be 10 times richer than the bottom 10%.
- The professional classes are under increasing pressure, working longer hours and suffering higher levels of stress. Life pressures, coupled with increasing job insecurity, will mean that even the

materially privileged will have a reduced immunity from crisis and poverty.

- Increasing working hours will impact upon the family:
- Fewer people will form families
- There will be a 33% increase in lone-parent households and a 55% increase in one-person households by 2011 (measured from 1991)
- By 2010 around 22% of women aged 45 will be childless compared with 16% in 1997.
- Various issues will be linked to the 'ageing population':
- A generation of people currently in midde-age will form a 'care sandwich', which requires them to look after their own children and pay taxes towards their parents' welfare, while also making private provision for their own old age.
- Family breakdown will mean that the traditional support system for elderly people will be lost, resulting in greater social exclusion and loneliness.
- The paradox of prosperity has contributed to a general loss of meaning in our lives. Traditional institutions, including the Church, have found it difficult to tap into this situation and people have cast the net wider in their search for 'spirituality'.

Economic outlook

Figure 1: Real household disposable incomes (index: 1998 = 100)

1958	1978	1986	1998	2010
32.7	57.7	70.1	100	135

In 1998 we were:

- 3 times as well off as we were in 1958
- 70% better off than 1978
- Over 40% better off than we were in 1986
- Living standards forecast to almost double in quarter century to 2010

Source: The Henley Centre

The UK has reached a period of economic development where the majority of households are relatively well-off in terms of basic necessities and consumer durables such as fridges, cookers and TVs. A Gallup poll in

1998 found that 78% of Britons agree that 'there are no material comforts missing from my life'.

According to the psychologist Abraham Maslow, rising consumer affluence should catalyse our progress through a 'hierarchy of needs' – from the satisfaction of basic sustenance needs, to the materialist, status-conscious mid-levels, right up to the highest echelons of personal growth, self-fulfilment, quality and integrity.

Figure 2: Maslow's hierarchy of needs

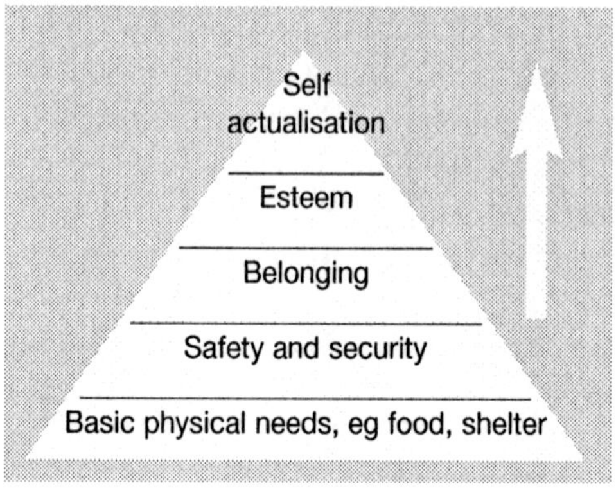

Explaining the paradox of prosperity

Findings from public attitude surveys, when compared against economic trends, reveal an interesting and new phenomenon. Previously, economic upturns or downturns were matched by a corresponding swing in consumer confidence, but for many people the economy has now become 'decoupled' from real life. For a long time in the early 1990s the UK's progress out of recession into positive GDP growth failed to impress consumers. This is partly because, even in a strong economy, low inflation can dampen the impression of prosperity. It holds down wages so that people feel their living standards are not improving and it prevents borrowers from wiping out the value of their debt.

Figure 3: The economy has become decoupled from 'real life'

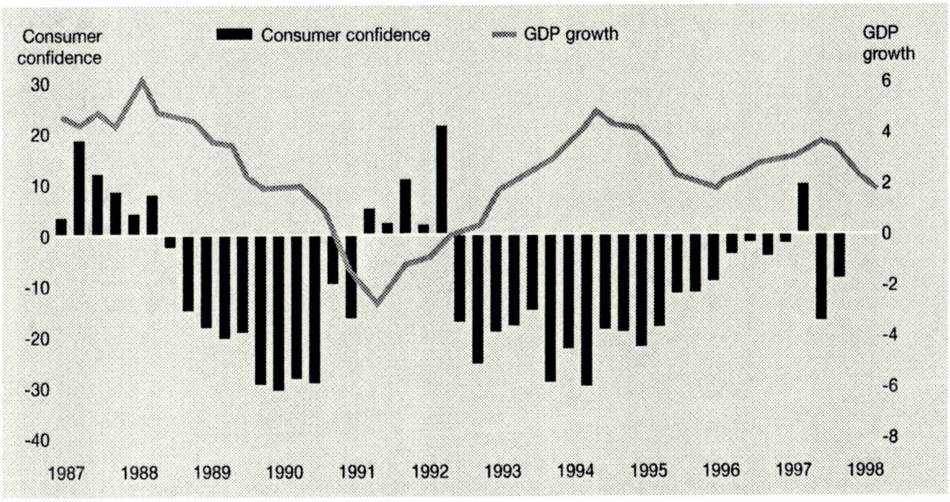

Source: ONS; Gallup; The Henley Centre

However, the 'decoupling' phenomenon is also apparent in a wider context. Concern about issues such as job insecurity, crime and disease is recorded at levels that outweigh the actual risk involved. This shows that the relationship between people's needs and their economic fortunes is actually far more subtle than Maslow's hierarchy might suggest. Long-term economic growth cannot immunize people from some of the shorter-term pressures of living in a modern materialist society.

Figure 4: Which of the following do you feel at risk from? %

Burglary of your home	60
Theft of your property	56
Vandalism of your neighbourhood facilities	44
Youngsters 'hanging around'	42
Drunken drivers	41
Attack on your person	39
Intimidation - eg threat of violence	25
Not being able to pay your bills	23
Undesired urban development	21
Redundancy	16
Obscene telephone calls	15
Sexual discrimination	10

Source: The Henley Centre, Planning for Consumer Change 2000

In many ways present economic circumstances contribute to these pressures. This is the 'paradox of prosperity'. As well as driving value up Maslow's hierarchy of needs, prosperity is, at the same time, driving value back down the hierarchy to the levels of basic physical and security needs. The 'Risk Society' is a theme first coined by the German sociologist Ulrich Beck, and it describes an age in which traditional conventions and directives break down, to be replaced by overwhelming change and choice. Beck proposes: 'Society has become a laboratory where there is absolutely no one in charge.' This results in increased exposure to risk, a 'high stakes' scenario that is manifested in two ways:

1. Inequality

Although the UK has become more prosperous overall, not everyone has enjoyed equal access to its good fortune. Macroeconomic growth figures mask serious inequalities in wealth and prospects.

Figure 5: Inequality is on the rise (% change in incomes by decile, 1979/80-1994/5)

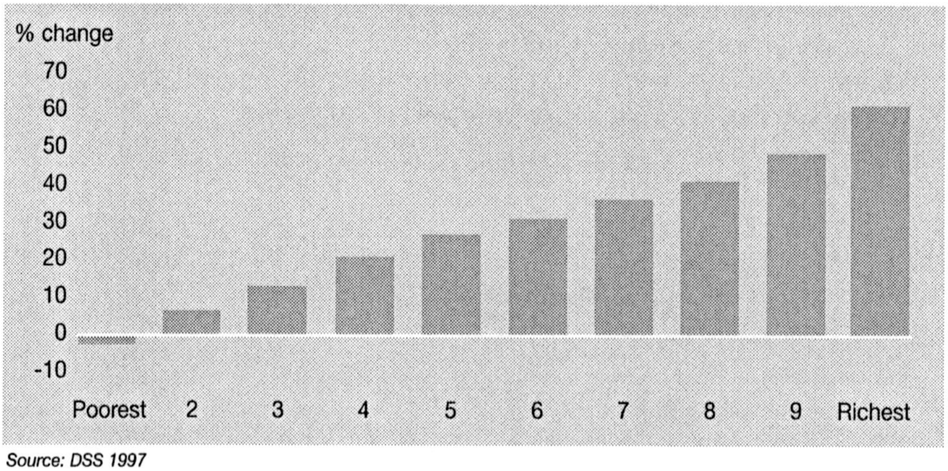

Source: DSS 1997

According to a 1998 Joseph Rowntree Foundation report, income inequality was greater in the mid-1990s than at any time since the late 1940s. And in 1997 the Institute for Fiscal Studies estimated that the richest 10% in the UK had as much income as the whole of the bottom half of the working population. And as we have already seen, the Henley

Centre forecasts that by 2010 the top 10% will be 10 times richer than the bottom 10%.

Income inequality has widespread ramifications, particularly on health and education. In the late 1970s death rates were 53% higher in the lowest socio-economic classes compared with the highest, but by the late 1980s death rates were 68% higher in the poorest groups. According to the British Medical Association children born into poverty are more prone to disease, poor mental and physical development and tend to have markedly poorer diet. Similarly, the worst performing schools in the UK are nearly all located in areas that are classed as economically 'deprived'.

Poverty and deprivation are not simply afflictions of a stable population on 'other people'. Increasingly our lives will resemble a game of 'snakes and ladders' in which those who once enjoyed prosperity and recognized social status suddenly find themselves at the bottom of the pile; redundancy, alcohol and drug problems and family breakdown can all take their toll. Inequality is a universal issue for the reason that it can foster resentment and is often a major cause of crime. It therefore represents a threat to public safety and feeds the fear and concern which reduces the quality of life. Even if actual crime figures do not rise, it is likely that by 2010 people's fear of crime will be higher than ever.

2. *Meaningless prosperity*

The second way in which material wealth is decoupled from personal fulfilment is also a universal issue, perhaps more directly relevant to those who have access to this wealth. Those earning the most money often have the least time to enjoy the fruits of their labour. In other words, high standards of living are not necessarily accompanied by high quality of life. According to the Henley Centre (1999):

- 59% of UK citizens believed 'they never have enough time to get things done' (against a European average of 49%).
- 37% of people felt that their working hours were still increasing and 55% believed that they had been subjected to more pressure at work.
- Working long hours and skipping holiday entitlement exerts huge damage on family life and relationships, but 'downshifting' to a lower paid job with less stress and more free time remains an

option that people are reluctant to take. Though they may aspire to a more relaxed lifestyle they have also become accustomed to the material trappings of the high-powered career. In addition, the need to contribute to pension plans, insurance policies and other areas of private provision may take people beyond the point of no return. Essentially, people have become trapped on a merry-go-round of demands, pressures and expectations, resulting in a constant plateau of stress. Again according to the Henley Centre (2000): 22% of full-time workers would be willing to take a lower-paid job if it meant less stress and more free time, but ...48% of workers say they need more money to keep their quality of life.

Job insecurity is also a growing problem with those over 50 likely to suffer the most. It is estimated that displaced workers (i.e. those who have lost their jobs through redundancy, dismissal or the ending of a temporary contract) lose, on average, 10% in wages in their next job. For workers over 50, however, this loss in earnings rises to 23% (Centre for Economic Performance, 1998).

Many people from all levels of the income scale are reaching crisis point. The number of people visiting counsellors testifies to that. Other, more destructive outlets for stress, such as alcohol and drugs, have also gained ground. Drug abuse has been a particularly malign influence, with growing dependency on sleeping pills, Valium, Prozac or even cocaine among the average working people living middle-class, suburban lives. In 1999 the Chief Medical Officer estimated that one in 28 men and one in 12 women were on antidepressants. As life pressures such as job insecurity, long working hours and private provision continue to exert their influence, it is likely that stress figures will rise along with drug and alcohol dependency.

Family breakdown

The decline of the family as an institution forms one of the primary symptoms of the paradox of prosperity. Significant factors contributing to family breakdown are the growing pressures of work and the pursuit of material gains.

Figure 6: The high cost of work ("What is the single biggest personal sacrifice in your home life you have made in your career so far?" %)

	Men	Women
Missed children growing up	23.7	22.2
Work put before family	23.8	21.3
Moving home for employer	10.8	4
Missed leisure/hobby time	7	15.7
Away from home, short term	8.9	3.1
Divorce/strain on relationship	7.1	7.3
Away from home, long term	4.7	1.3
Time spent on work-related education	2.7	2.5
Not having/postponing children	1.2	1.2
Unable to form relationships	1.2	3.7

Source: WFD/Management Today: The Great Work/Life Debate 1998

In the future, fewer people will form their own families. As well as a fall in marriage in favour of co-habitation, there will be an increasing number of one-person households. More women are also remaining childless – of all women born in 1972, 23% are expected to remain childless at 45 years old (in 2017).

Figure 7: Non-traditional households are showing the fastest growth (% change 1991-2011)

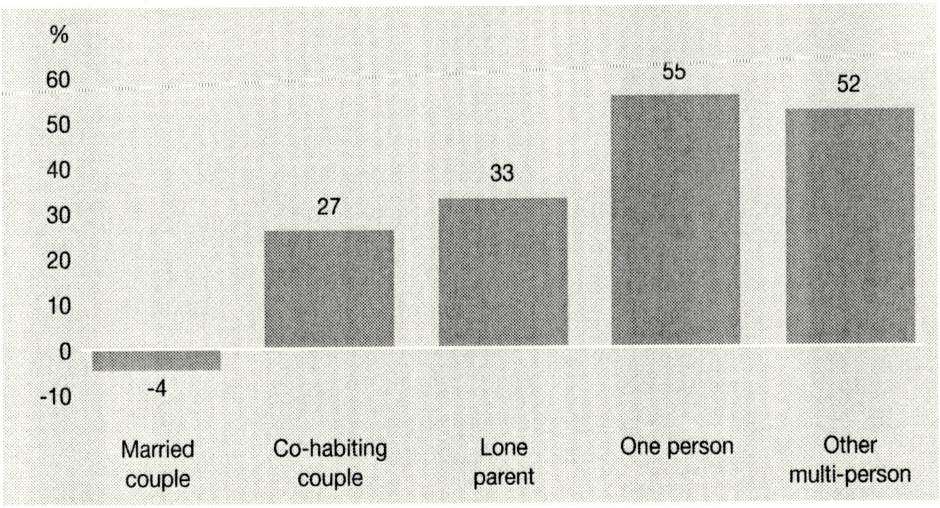

Source: Department of the Environment; The Henley Centre 1999

meaning that this will continue to be one of the major issues facing the UK in the next ten years.

Ageing population

Discussions about the ageing population usually centre on the 'demographic timebomb' which is forecast to cause a pensions crisis from 2020 onwards. By this time those born during the post-war population boom will have reached retirement age, but there will also be a reduction in the number of those in work and paying taxes.

Figure 8: The demographic timebomb (Dependency ratio 1980-2030)

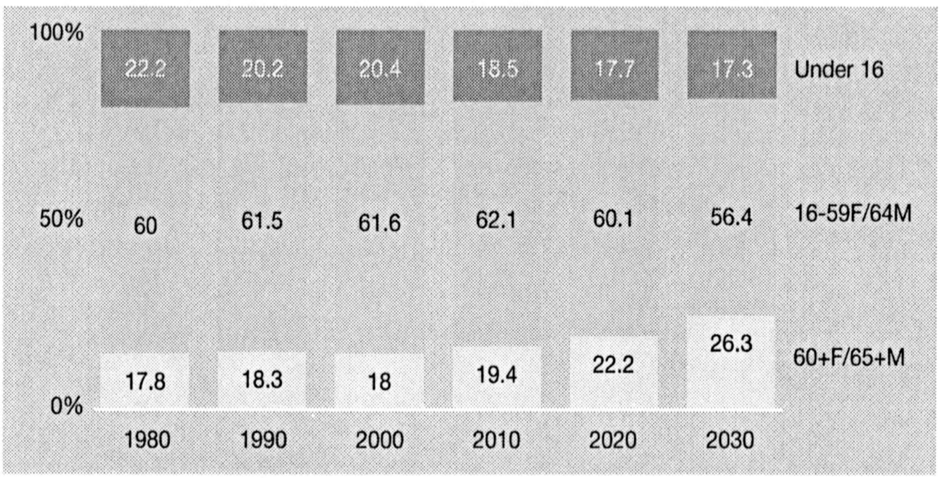

Source: Henley Centre analysis of OPCS data

Although the demographic timebomb will not reach its full impact until 2030 and beyond, long-term care of the elderly will have become a major policy issue well before then, especially as it is estimated that people's current pension contributions fall well below the level required to secure a comfortable future. 55% of people are already worried that they will not have enough money on which to retire. (Henley Centre, 2000)

As with the paradox of prosperity, the ageing population is not simply an economic issue. Those who can afford to take early retirement, the 'young old' as opposed to the 'frail old', may not be ready to enter inactive dependency. These people can and want to continue making a contribution to society. With time on their hands older people can deliver valuable assistance in voluntary services, thereby finding a level of fulfilment that is as important as financial security.

Another issue that impacts disproportionately upon the old is loneliness. This links to the previous discussion of family breakdown and the loss of traditional support networks.

- People may the lack the time or money to look after their parents, especially if they are caught in the 'care sandwich', looking after their own children, making private provision for their future welfare and still paying taxes towards their parents' welfare.
- The geographical dispersal of families, often due to work mobility, can also cause old people to lose regular contact with their families.
- Marriage breakdown will further weaken family ties: will the children of divorced couples stay in touch with their fathers? Will they be prepared to care for their ex-mothers-in-law?
- If people have chosen not to marry and/or have children then family support in old age will not even be an option.

The emergency of new 'spirituality'

The sort of problems associated with family breakdown and the ageing population can be traced back to the competitive materialism by which we live, or to its accompanying inequalities. People are beginning to question whether economic growth engenders equivalent progress in terms of morality or values. There is a growing demand for some sort of alternative approach to life, for new answers to old questions. This has led to the emergence of a renewed emphasis on spirituality. There is recognition that true 'wealth' comes from spiritual as well as material resources and people are drawing up an alternative scale of value that will restore meaning to their lives. However, this is not necessarily a narrowly defined spirituality that adopts the tenets of an organized religion.

- Only 20% of people claim they generally agree with what the Church or religious leaders have to say, a figure lower than that given to radio stations, magazines, books and work colleagues. Only the government scores worse!

The spirituality that is seen as more relevant today is found in a variety of shapes and forms, many of which are directed towards inner development or ethical lifestyles: yoga; self-help and counselling; aromatherapy and feng shui. The search for meaning does not, however, imply that people want a belief system to be dictated to them. The essence of the 'post-modern' age is the denial of a single Truth.

Although the renewed search for meaning represents an opportunity for the Church, it must recognize that it is competing with any number of other options to fill this 'spiritual' gap. Whatever their background, people are now as likely to turn to Buddhism, yoga classes or even self-hypnosis as to organized Christianity. In order to secure a place in people's lives the Church will need to put its credentials on the table, offering a greater degree of flexibility to accommodate people's needs and preferences.

One of the results of the paradox of prosperity has been that the experience of community, the sense of individuality and the notion of responsibility to others have been fundamentally altered. At the same time our expectations of the welfare state have changed. These trends have positive as well as negative impacts but a significant negative consequence is the 'responsibility gap' which has arisen. This refers to the growing deficit of care for vulnerable groups in contemporary British society.

The responsibility gap results from both 'bottom up' changes (to do with the way in which people live their lives) and 'top down' changes (the changing role of government and the economy together with broader demographic shifts). Significantly, it raises questions about the responsibility of government and the role of citizens. It also raises questions about the role of charities and the private sector in the provision of care.

Who cares?

Since the Second World War, responsibility for the vulnerable and needy has lain with the welfare state. Supplementary support has always been offered by charitable organisations and volunteers.

This arrangement is changing. Government still provides the lion's share of funding but is increasingly relying on the private and voluntary sectors to deliver the service provision.

Charities are popular and omnipresent but suffer from the strain caused by a litigious culture, the increased call for professionalism and a growing competitiveness for funding.

Individuals express a great deal of goodwill towards volunteering, but life pressures and subtly changing attitudes to what volunteering should offer them often prevent this goodwill from being translated into action.

New forms of funding, organizing, stimulating and energizing responsibility in society need to be found.

Understanding the responsibility gap

The responsibility gap has its roots in the economic, social and ideological changes that British society has experienced over the last two decades.

The last ten years have witnessed a sustained period of economic growth in Britain. Incomes have increased, unemployment has fallen and markets have expanded. As a result the British public is wealthier today than ever before. This rise in prosperity has not been uniform, however, and income has also become increasingly polarized over this time.

Ideological changes

This affluence has been accompanied by some significant political and ideological shifts. The economic liberalism of the 1980s is the most important of these, when the 'big-state' of the post-war period was rescinded and an emphasis on individual responsibility and consumer choice put in its place. In recent years fewer people have believed that the government should redistribute income to the less well off.

Other ideological shifts, with their roots in the baby boomer generation, have occurred at the individual level. As we discuss later, this group has been at the forefront of the growth in individualism. As it has aged this large cohort has done much to shape society in its own image, emphasizing independence, living for today, rejecting authority and being determined to realize one's own ambitions.

Figure 9: The Government should redistribute income to the less well-off

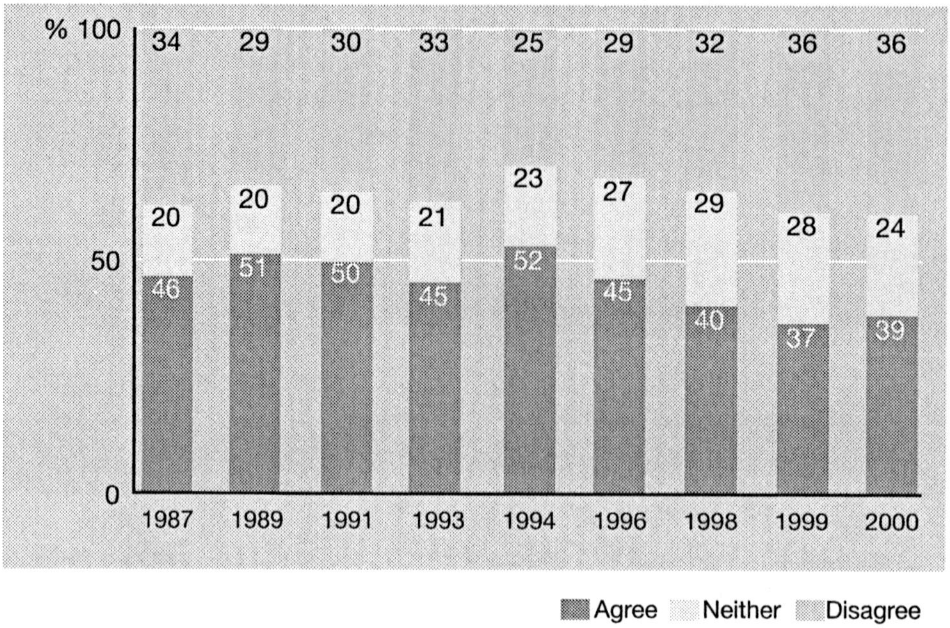

Source: British Social Attitudes: The 18th Report (2001/2002 edition)

Hypermobility

The last 30 years have seen a powerful social drive towards 'hypermobility':

- As a nation we travel more than three times further today than we did in 1952: 720 billion passenger kilometres per year in 1999 compared to 218 in 1952.
- We travel further to work, to school, to shop and to visit friends than ever before.
- The average person makes over a 1,000 journeys per year, totalling nearly 7,000 miles – 2,000 more than in 1975. (Office for National Statistics, Transport Trends, 2001)

Hypermobility is a classic paradox of prosperity; we travel and move house more often because we can afford to and because our lifestyles encourage it. At the familial and community level it has become a factor influencing change in its own right, having a fundamental impact on geographic community and our relationships with our family elders; on our ability to care for our nearest and dearest and, fundamentally, on our perception of who our nearest and dearest are.

Time

The notion of the 'cash-rich, time-poor' society has been well-rehearsed. UK employees work longer hours than those of any other European country. Also, more women of all ages, except those under 19, are in employment and this is a trend forecast to continue over the next decade.

The rise of individualism

The rise of individualism is often used as a synonym for selfishness and is associated with the worst excesses of the 1980s and the 'greed is good' mentality. It is, however, a subtler phenomenon, as much about self-reliance and personal responsibility as it is about egotism.

Figure 10: An increasing proportion of women are in employment

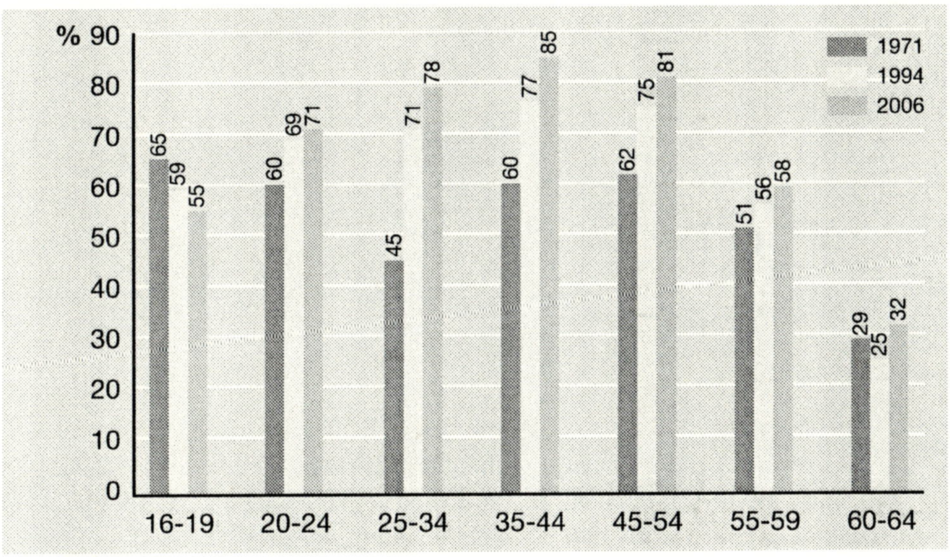

Source: DfES, 2000

Relationships

At its most basic the rise of individualism is literally about people living and acting as individuals rather than as members of any larger group. This is most graphically seen in the rise of single-person households, which numbered around 5 million in 1991 and are expected to increase to 7.3 million in 2011.

Figure 11: Single-person households are projected to increase from 27% to 33% of the total housing stock between 1991 and 2011

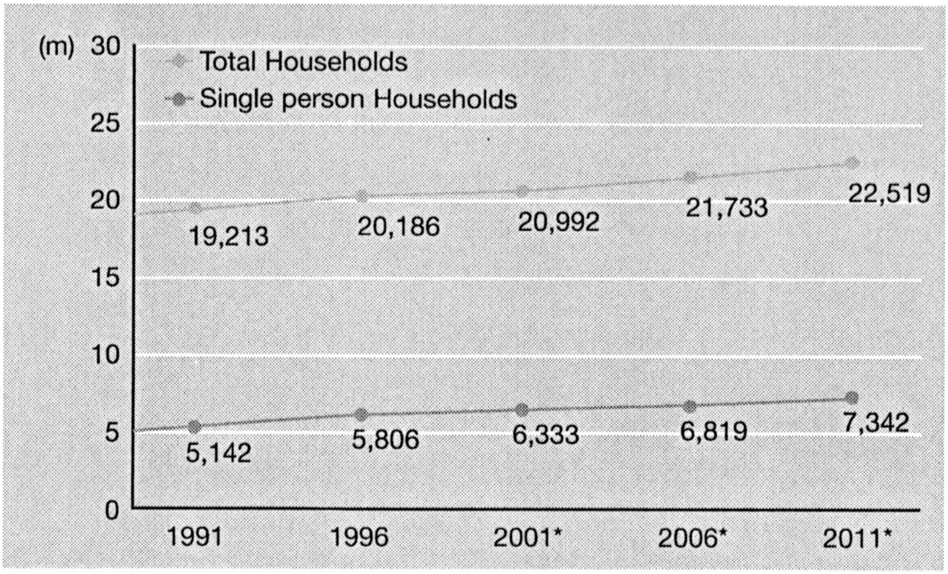

Source: DETR, December 2000

Fewer people are marrying than in previous generations and those that do are marrying later in life. This increasingly irregular marital and relational pattern means that people's lives are no longer shaped by the rigid and permanent relationships of marriage, family and parenting as they used to be. The result of these changes is that people have ever more opportunity to shape their lives according to their own predispositions.

Choice

Since the free-market revolution of the 1980s a huge amount of emphasis has been placed on people's right to choose for themselves. Choice has become central to political rhetoric; it has become the sovereign value in the modern world. So fundamental has the right to choose become in society that we are slowly shifting from an 'off-the-peg' culture, in which we are offered a number of pre-selected options and where we adapt our desires to fit the choices available, to a bespoke one, where solutions are tailored to our requirements and the choices available are adapted to fit our desires.

Shifting priorities

As already observed, individualism has coincided with an increasing resistance to the idea of the redistribution of wealth. It has also paralleled a shifting perception of blame for society's ills.

This ideological shift has been evidenced in research. Over the decades the Henley Centre has been asking people how 'The quality of life can be best improved...' The proportion of people choosing the answer, 'looking after the community's interests rather than simply your own' has been falling since reaching a plateau in the mid-1990s. The proportion of those responding 'looking after ourselves which ultimately raises standards for everyone' has risen dramatically over the same time.

Currently the gap between the two is smaller than at any time since the last Conservative government. Although it is sometimes difficult to admit it, individualism often heralds a more self-interested outlook on life.

The changing nature of community

A great deal has been written about the death of community in Britain. While few people doubt that neighbourliness and community spirit have changed drastically over the last 40 years, the change is again more subtle than commonly presumed. The proportion of people who agree with the statement 'there is a sense of community spirit where I live' has remained constant over the last ten years and has even risen from 38%

in 1995 to 48% in 2001 before falling back to 45% in 2002. (The Henley Centre, Planning for Consumer Change, 1995-2002)

Figure 12: The change in perceptions of why people live in need

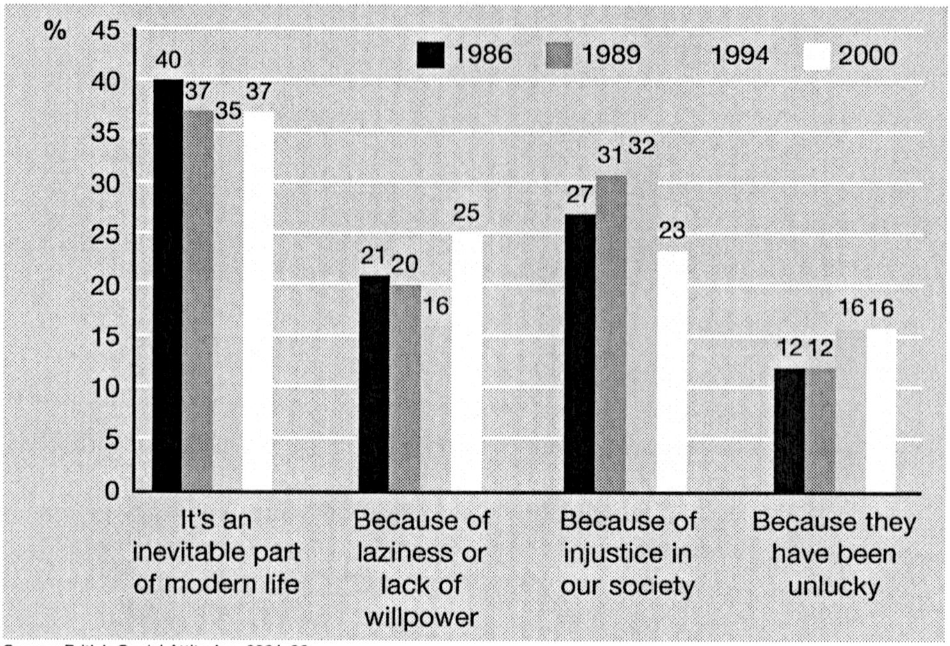

Source: British Social Attitudes, 2001-02

From communities of geography to communities of interest

One of the consequences of the rise of individualism is that more and more people can define themselves according to their pastimes and interests rather than their birthplace, family network or cultural inheritance. This can be most clearly seen in people's perception of with whom they share things in common. (fig 14)

From communities of necessity to communities of choice

The greater mobility afforded by the increase in car ownership allows people to escape their immediate environment and exercise greater choice over where they shop, work, play and generally lead their lives. Cheaper, more efficient and more mobile communications technology now allows people to stay in contact with one another and minimizes the inconvenience that distance once imposed on relationships.

Figure 13: The quality of life can be best improved by...

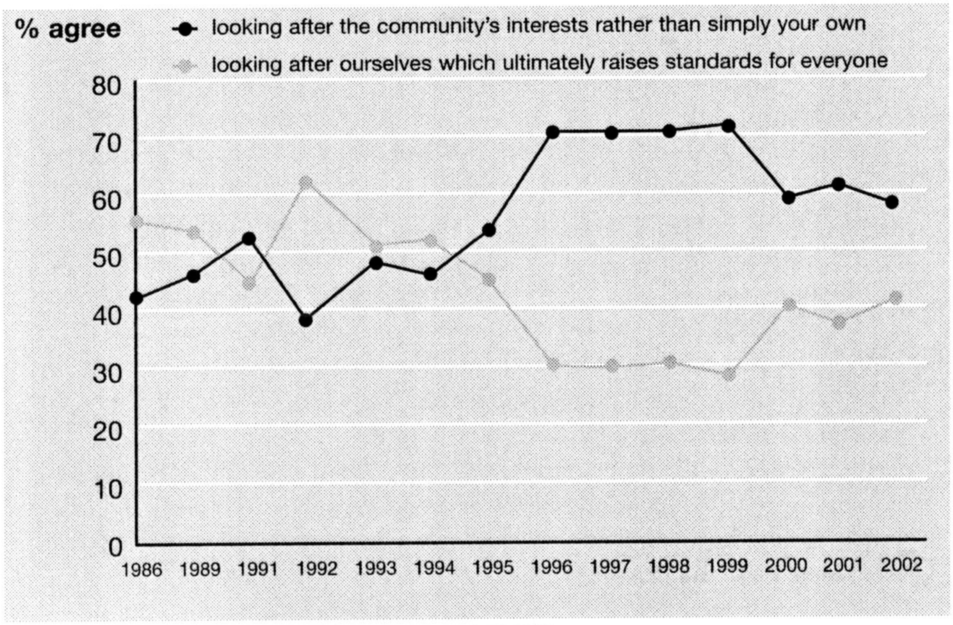

Source: The Henley Centre, Planning for Consumer Change, 1986-2002

The combined result of these factors is a shift from communities in which people associate with people, in places and circumstances that they had not necessarily chosen, to those where they mix with people they have chosen, in locations they prefer and under circumstances which suit them.

From permanent communities to transient communities

The transformation of community life is towards impermanence. The result of this is an upsurge in 'communities' which exist only for a brief period of time. The recent popularity of single-issue groups is an indication of this. The 2002 Countryside Alliance march and the 2003 Stop the War march were two of the largest political demonstrations in British history. While the marches themselves were only communities in the loosest sense of the word, the groups which organized them were more recognizably so. The fact that these communities, being issue-based, are inherently temporary is not an obstacle to the loyalty they provoke or, in some cases, the success they achieve.

The four pillars of care

The Responsibility Gap outlines some of the groups that are being failed by care provision in Britain. It highlights the plight of the elderly, those who rely on childcare, the disabled, substance misusers and carers. Each of these groups has fallen through the gaps in welfare provision.

Traditionally in Europe great emphasis has been placed on the role of the state to care for the vulnerable. The creation of the welfare state in the UK in the post-war period was the biggest single shift of responsibility in the UK in the 20th century and was the most complete expression of this ideal the country had ever witnessed. This role of government was set against a backdrop of strong family and community responsibility. However, as family and community have been renegotiated, we are witnessing a subtle tension over the appropriate balance between the four pillars of care in contemporary British society: the government, charities, individuals and the private sector.

Figure 14: How much do you have in common with the following?

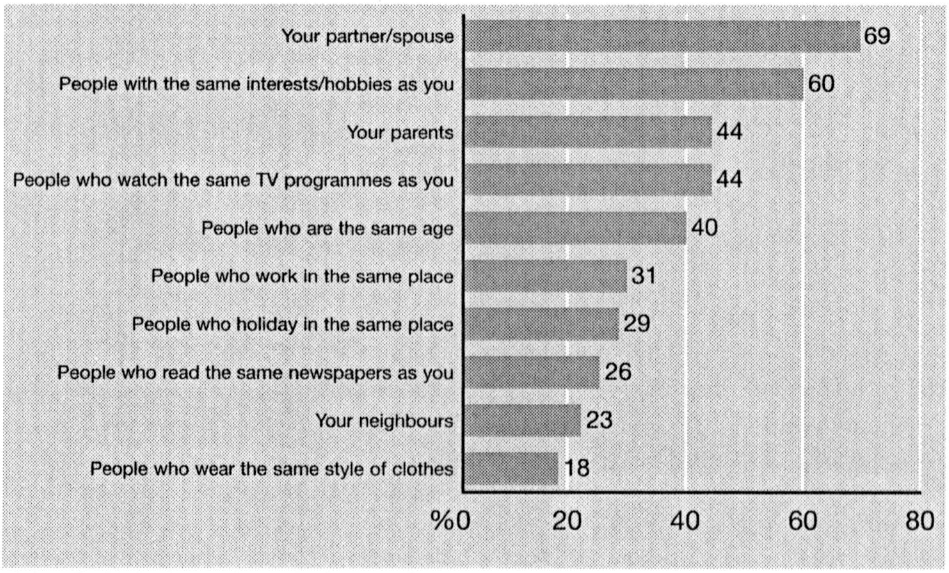

Source: The Henley Centre, Planning for Consumer Change 2001

In 2003 most people seem to view social responsibility as largely dichotomous – that is, those responsibilities which fall outside the (increasingly shrinking) sphere of family are overwhelmingly seen as the responsibility of government.

Figure 15: Who is MOST responsible for looking after/contributing assistance to...

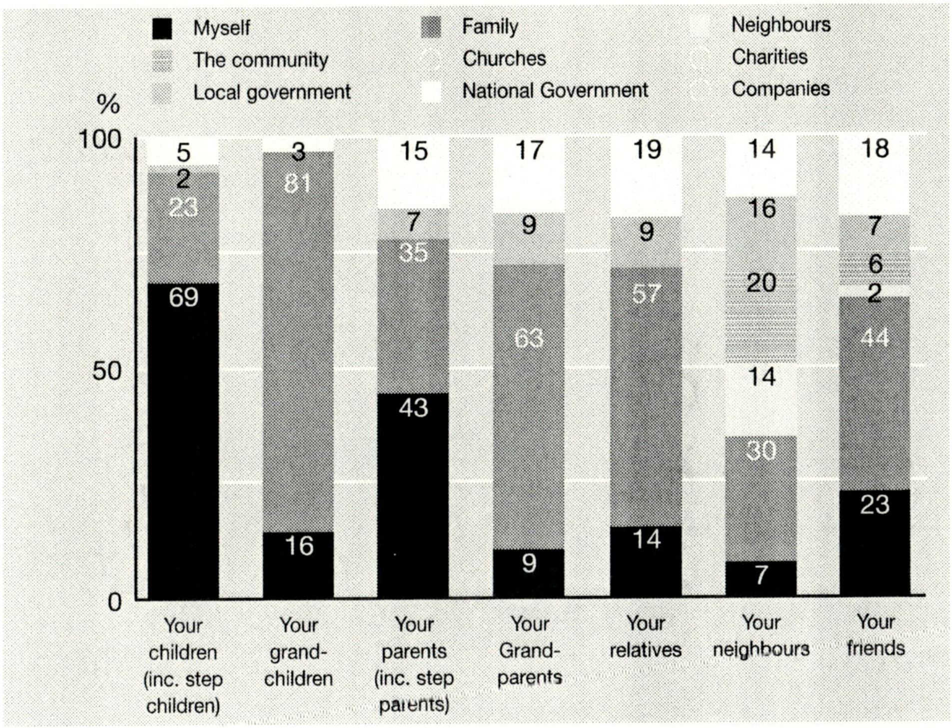

Source: Social Responsibility Omnibus Study, The Henley Centre/The Salvation Army, Fieldwork undertaken 3-7 October 2003

The 'paradox of prosperity' is a social phenomenon that is already having practical effects. ***The Responsibility Gap*** report shows that society is increasingly unsure how to deal with issues of responsibility and community and this is a trend that looks set to continue. The four pillars of care urgently need to find ways of working together. If they do not, it will be the poor and the vulnerable who will pay the price.

Full copies of *The Paradox of Prosperity*, *The Burden of Youth* and *The Responsibility Gap* are available from The Salvation Army. Please call 020 7367 4619 or visit ***www.salvationarmy.org.uk/library***

Figure 16: Who is MOST responsible for looking after/contributing assistance to...

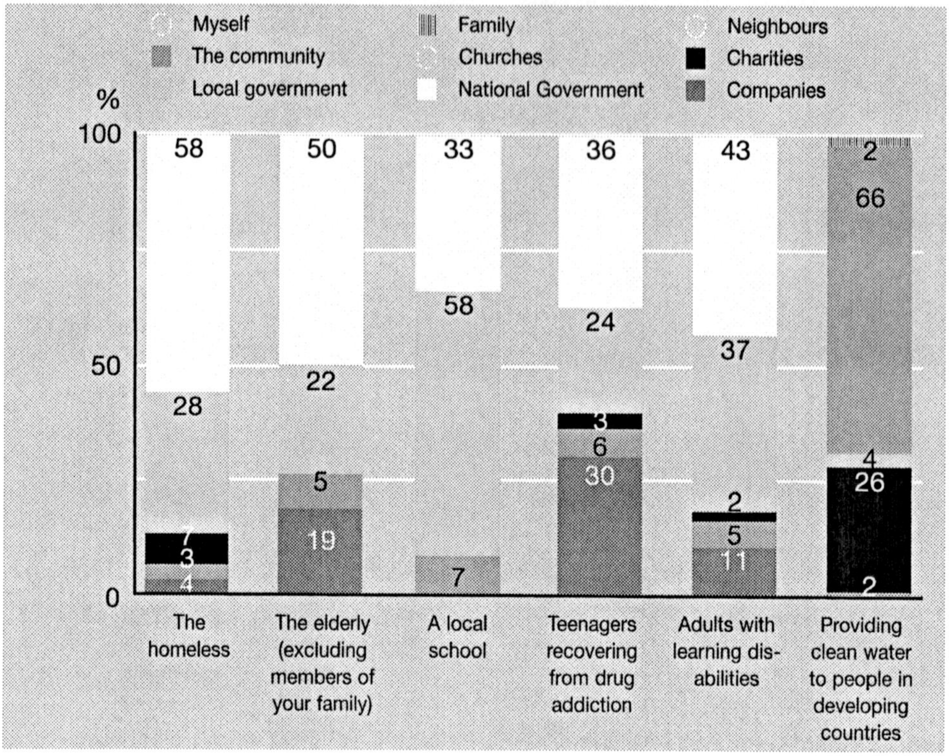

Source: Social Responsibility Omnibus Study, The Henley Centre/The Salvation Army, Fieldwork undertaken 3-7 October 2003

3

A Christian Reflection on Economic Change: Peter Sedgwick

Contemporary society has been largely shaped by the two fundamental economic changes of the last three centuries. In the first industrial revolution, industry and modernity replaced agriculture and tradition. In the second, an economy based upon manufacturing industry was in turn replaced by one in which economic growth and change were driven by information.

Three stages can be identified in the shift from an agricultural to an industrial society as it gradually moved from the early factory system of the 1750s to the situation as it was in 1950. First there was a change in the division of labour with the de-skilling of the worker. Employees were not persons but units of production or 'hands' who used a fairly simple tool, often in their own home. The second stage came when a machine tended by a worker replaced the worker using a tool. The third stage, symbolized by the production line, saw the machine dominating the worker.

All this changed the nature of work. The Churches responded to this new world in a variety of ways: support for secular trade unions; the establishment of Christian trade unions, religious political parties and welfare organizations; the foundation of consumer and producer co-operatives; industrial chaplaincy; worker priests; and the demand for social justice enunciated in many official church documents (from the Roman Catholic ***Rerum Novarum*** in 1891 to the Church of England's ***Men Without Work*** in 1938). This great surge of activity in the nineteenth and early 20th century was accompanied by a great deal of grass roots Christian reflection and action.

The second economic change, after the Second World War, saw an industrial society transformed into an information society. Work came to be based on thought and continuous interpersonal co-operation, though this co-operation was based on work contracts rather than a deepening of personal relationships. This has led to a renewed concern about stress at work, the work/life balance, and the exploitation of workers in new working conditions. Secondly, there is a high degree of employment mobility. Few people expect to do the same job for life or to have the same employer, and certainly not to perform the same tasks at work over a working lifetime. Thirdly, information societies are future oriented. More and more types of jobs are created which were literally inconceivable a decade earlier. For instance a web page designer would have been an unintelligible job description as recently as 1990. It is an open-ended society where the possibilities of change appear unlimited. (This is not to forget, of course, that there are environmental constraints). We have never lived this way before.

The question arises, in a far more fragmented society, as to how both secular and religious bodies should respond to these changes. Of course, as in all human history, much remains of the old order. There are still factories, trade unions, and welfare institutions. But the language of the old industrial era, redolent of worker solidarity and class conflict, does not so easily fit the new individualist service economy. This has left political parties as well as churches across Europe with profound questions about what their social vision should be, and how they should attract and motivate individuals to belong to their cause.

There has been no shortage of Christian debate on these issues. Church reports such as ***Faith in the City*** (1985), ***The Common Good*** (1996), and ***Unemployment and the Future of Work*** (1997), are evidence of the continuing vitality of the tradition of social Christianity. There are a number of sources of that thinking, all of which are reflected to some degree in ***Prosperity with a Purpose***. One is the Anglo-American tradition of William Temple[1] and Reinhold Niebuhr[2], broadly the school of Christian Realism. This mode of thought takes the complexities of modern political and social life as given, though changing in unpredictable ways. Its approach can be summed up in William Temple's remark that public life should be so ordered that self interest serves what social justice requires.

The second source is catholic social teaching, which is set out in the seminal Papal Encyclical ***Rerum Novarum*** of 1891 and develops through to its centennial celebration ***Centesimus Annus*** and other teaching documents from Pope John Paul II and ***The Common Good*** produced by the Roman Catholic Bishops of England and Wales. ***Centesimus Annus*** explored the new situation that arose from the collapse of Communism in Europe, and the apparent triumph of the market. Its main theme is the God-given dignity of humanity. Its economic doctrine, which is highly relevant to an exploration of prosperity and its purposes, might be summarized by saying that while labour is indeed a commodity, people are not things. Other scholars have worked in a framework derived more exclusively from the Bible. Again, a contrast is drawn between human hopes of personal and community fulfilment, and the life to which the gospel calls Christians and the world.

It is difficult to select just a few themes from this rich tradition, but it will be useful to explore theological responses to just three contemporary aspects of prosperity:

- The nature of employment
- The expanding vision of human needs: the role of the state
- Poverty, alienation and unemployment

The nature of employment

The British economy has been changing remarkably fast in the last two decades. Since 1995 real GDP has increased by roughly one fifth, while manufacturing output has hardly risen at all. Only 13% of the work-force is employed in manufacturing and, on present trends, this will fall to under 10% within five years. Despite this, there is relatively low unemployment by European standards and steady growth in total employment. In Germany, by contrast, there are more than four million people unemployed, and renewed recession is possible.

This means that we are a fast changing society. The judgements made by social commentators can quickly become dated and out of touch with lived experience. So what sort of economy are we talking about? 'Modern societies', says Miroslav Wolf, ' are dynamic. A single, permanent, salaried and full-time form of employment has given way to multiple and frequently changing jobs. Such a dynamic society requires a dynamic understanding of work.' [3]

Employment is now understood in different ways. In one working lifetime a person may have several careers. This can feel like liberation because their changing preferences and talents can be fulfilled by new work opportunities. How many school leavers today go into careers knowing what they want to do for the rest of their lives? But it is also the case that if you see relationships more in terms of space than time, a person might do more than one job at a time. So our society has many forms of employment (part-time, multiple, and so on) without regarding one as superior to another, as was the case a century ago.

This has considerable implications for a Christian understanding of vocation. Our grandparents, and generations before them, accepted the idea that they were destined to spend their lives working in one occupation, and perhaps for one local employer. As well as the human qualities of loyalty, integrity and mutual respect between employer and employee, who would often work face to face in the same building, Lutheran theology developed an understanding of the Christian vocation to work that put a great emphasis on stability, constancy and perseverance. The tradition of catholic social teaching, beginning with ***Rerum Novarum,*** developed a remarkably similar account of the Christian vocation in the work-place and argued cogently for a quite new commitment to social justice in modern industrial societies. Archbishop William Temple similarly saw that even in an oppressive setting the vocation to work could be followed faithfully.[4] He also maintained that there was a need for social reform so that workers were not oppressed. However all the changes mentioned so far raise questions about this understanding of vocation.[5] (Most clergy today have spent some years in secular employment, and regard this experience as valuable to their ministry.)

Much recent theological thought has tested the claim that Christianity can still speak of vocation in such a mobile society and economy. The report by Churches Together in Britain and Ireland ***Unemployment and the Future of Work*** published in the run-up to the General Election of 1997 was a significant attempt to answer this question. It appealed for much better working conditions and an expansion of employment.

Other theologians have examined the largely non-economic factors that shape human experience in the work-place[6] – our capacity for creativity, for the fulfilment of inspiration and the enriching of relationships, all within the created order. God does not rule this world without human co-operation, nor is there a pre-ordained plan or blueprint through which all things come to be. Rather, human creativity shapes the destiny of this world in new, unexpected and creative ways. Nowhere is this more so than in technology and the ordering of the economy, for creativity is not only to be found in artistic self-expression. Since the Spirit of God is found in the whole of life, then it makes sense to speak of humanizing the employment process by looking for those actions which reflect the work of the Spirit.

This means that the Spirit of God might call a person to exercise different gifts at different times. As Exodus 35: 2-3 puts it: 'He has filled him with the Spirit of God, with skill, ability, and knowledge in all kinds of crafts, and the ability to teach others.' This work of the Spirit is given for a particular task in which that person's gifts are used both to serve the community and express him or herself, but it does not follow that this task will be the one to which they will be committed for the rest of their life. Such an example links up with Paul's desire that Christians 'excel in gifts (charismata)' in I Cor. 14:2. The Spirit of God is active in sustaining and renewing the whole created order, not just the life of the church, and prepares it for a final transformation into the new creation. Such an understanding of the nature of God fits much better the dynamic nature of the economy today.

Talk of the Spirit of God leads into a discussion of spirituality. Again the spirituality of work has been a central part of the way in which redesigning employment practices has been advocated. Spirituality does not have to be Christian or even religious: its meaning has been widely debated in the last decade. Some companies have paid a great deal of attention to this. This is not the same as happiness at work, but rather relates to a fulfilling environment.[7] One of the main challenges for companies is how competitive working practices can be kept alongside attention to the spirituality of work, and to an office culture where people are able to develop their potential. At the same time this cultural change, much associated with management experts such as Charles Handy, has been seen by some people as putting too much responsibility onto individuals, with a consequent increase in stress and burn-out.

Others have been much more critical of modern employment practices, seeing the use of quasi-religious language (mission statements, personal transformation, etc.) as an improper use of these terms, investing those who use such language with a spurious authority, selling a vision in an aggressive and triumphalist manner. It is certainly true that the prosperity which much employment has brought in recent years also carries a heavy cost in terms of stress and commitment to the organization. Struggling to keep your place in the market makes stress at work virtually unavoidable; some find it stimulating and creative, but for others it results in damage to mental and physical health. Christians will question whether this lifestyle is inevitable or desirable, despite the wealth it brings.[8]

Nevertheless it is clear that all work must be seen as an aspect of service to God and to humanity. This is the overarching reality which unites different understandings of vocation. It might be the case that a person's career is far more flexible and subject to great changes. Flexibility and creativity are the key terms here. It is also the case that 'mission–speak' (the language of corporations and work consultants) can lack integrity. But in all of this what matters is that God is served through daily work. When work is of poor quality, and there is poor service to the public, something fundamental is lost. Poor service, whether in the public or private spheres, undermines the values of compassion and sympathy. It is part of our vocation to humanize work and make it a better experience.

Responding to an expanding vision of human needs: the role of the state

Britain is now enjoying an unprecedented level of prosperity. It is important to affirm the value of prosperity, in spite of reservations expressed later in this essay. Alongside this we need to consider the role of the state and how this will change over the next generation. Ideas about the proper role of the public sector vary, of course, but the similarities are more notable than the differences. Throughout the past century, the dominant idea was the state would always have the ultimate responsibility of ensuring that citizens had access to key services. Spending by the state rose rapidly during two world wars, and yet higher in peacetime, as the state took responsibility for more and more aspects of social life. Governments are now debating whether they should do less and this debate continues in many areas.

The rising expectation of consumers affects this discussion of the nature of the state. In the 1950s, as many films and books from that time show, people were grateful for the welfare state, and felt that they were looked after in a way that they had never experienced before. This was a more deferential society, though, so there was little questioning of what was provided, and people generally accepted social boundaries and hierarchy. Much of the energy of the last fifty years has been expended in allowing women, minority ethnic groups and young people to be treated in a way that respects their needs and a refusal to have those needs predetermined. It can be seen as a fuller vision of human potential and is certainly a consequence of our increased prosperity.

The market has been very successful at responding to this cultural change, so long as those who are the customers in the market-place have the resources to participate in it. There has been a tradition, traceable from the romantic era to the present day, of imagining the self transfigured through literature, art, film, fashion and lifestyle, the aim being to create an existence that reflects the true self, as opposed to the identity imposed by social conditions. This dream of freedom, creativity and self-fulfilment is a prevalent myth of our time, and it is expressed with great power in shopping, advertising, entertainment and sport.

Indeed the search for the new self, made possible by present-day prosperity, is as important as the destination. Or perhaps more accurately, the journey of self-discovery, is one which never ends so long as there is life. Even church life has accepted this change, as demonstrated in the great success of Alpha courses (as a journey of self-exploration in small and welcoming groups which nurture the quest). This relates back to our earlier discussion of spirituality. The old rigid hierarchies of class and status are dissolved into this new world of desire and self-expression.

Once again, this has been a central theme of theology in recent years, with a contrast between the Christian life – as one which is a life of desire for God – and the compulsions of prosperity[9]. However this is to draw too simple a distinction. It is necessary to affirm the secular world alongside the reality of faith, and maintain a tension between them. Belief should not be used to deny what is positive about the experience of modern prosperity and a society in which successful people define themselves in terms of lifestyle rather than their status as producers.

Britain differs in many ways from the rest of Europe. It has already been pointed out that Britain's prosperity and employment pattern is very different now from Germany's. We also consume a higher proportion of our income than other European nations. There is an intense political debate about Britain's longstanding under-investment in public services. But the British financial system makes personal borrowing easier, as does the existence in Britain of owner occupation and (for half the population) an occupational retirement scheme. Many people in Britain, especially the affluent young, now have the self-confidence to enjoy themselves.

All this drives a consumption boom new to the majority of the population. It raises major questions about the level of personal indebtedness, the lack of savings and, above all, about how a renewed self-confidence among the young and affluent is expressed. Individuals increasingly take on debts that they cannot possibly sustain. This also drives what can be called over-consumption and expenditure on conspicuous consumption – goods which are designed to demonstrate the wealth of the purchaser. Examples would be the size of off-road vehicles (which are environmentally damaging) in urban areas, or the manipulation of wants, where affluence and high expenditure is seen as the norm. This consumption can be corrosive of a working identity, as Richard Sennett has shown.[10]

Here we have a stark picture of a materialistic society obsessed with money and goods to the impoverishment of spiritual growth. However it is also possible to see the relationship of prosperity and spirituality in a far more positive way. This prosperity is now expressed in cultural activities that have largely replaced church-going on Sundays over the last fifty years, such as clubbing, shopping, sport, travel and entertainment. Clubbing has become extensively promoted, and is part of the 'commodification' of the leisure industry. Yet at the same time clubbing is an egalitarian activity where class and other barriers are irrelevant.

For the churches there is a particular challenge. Other world faiths may express the cultural and ethnic origin of their adherents, at least partially, through religious worship. The mosque is often at the centre of Asian communities in Britain. This link between cultural identity and the Christian religion is no longer present in many parts of the United Kingdom, and especially not in the affluent south of England. The Christian church faces great challenges to its institutional existence, even as a renewed interest in spirituality also becomes apparent. So one question for the churches must be how they can address this huge cultural change. Prosperity is not simply a question of material wealth and its distribution. It is also a question of cultural meaning. Through prosperity and cultural change there is a new understanding of human needs and personal identity.

One recent and rapidly growing aspect of consumption is ethical consumerism, which can take positive or negative forms. Positive ethical consumers buy or recommend products which are ethically better or less damaging than their competitors. Negative consumerism is driven by protest against the conditions under which the product is made, or the harm that it causes. One of the striking features of the last few decades is the power which ordinary people feel they now have against large corporations through the ethical boycott. Empowering individuals is a key feature of this newfound prosperity.

As we participate in the prosperity and cultural diversity of our fast changing society Christians can feel free to enjoy the riches which this brings. The goodness of creation is encouraged in Matthew 11:19 and 1 Timothy 6:17. The idea of fixed human needs now appears no longer to fit with the plurality of gifts which women, minority ethnic groups and above all young people are both exploring and experiencing for themselves. This often sits ill with the traditional nature of Christian teaching and it requires a re-imagining of what it means to be human in this new world. Indeed at the root of modern economic life lies a permanent rethinking of what it means to be human.

The state has been much less good at achieving this flexibility, as its clientele redefine their needs and seek new ways of being service users, but it has also often failed to provide satisfactory services for those who are in need. This has led to the debate about the role of the state, which has already been mentioned. Sometimes it has seemed that the state has neither afforded satisfaction to those who wanted more flexibility nor cared adequately for those in hardship. It is no surprise, therefore, that one of the great political arguments in the last decade has been about improving public services. Christians will want to affirm the dedication of those who work within public services, often for low pay and in difficult conditions. Many of those in public services have endured much demoralising criticism as they seek to fulfil their vocation in under-resourced jobs. It is important that Christians do not collude with a selfishness that sees no need for public services at all. As we explore later, there are many families whose members are unemployed or receiving low wages. Their plight in retirement is particularly acute. Their income is very low, and they face the prospect of declining health, sub-standard housing and inadequate public services.

For such reasons, Christians may want to voice a preference for urgently needed improvements in some public services over what may seem to be the more trivial aspects of private expenditure on goods and services. ***Unemployment and the Future of Work*** emphasized the central importance of the competitive labour market as the location in which life chances were enhanced. But it also urged the expansion of public services, and looked forward to a consequent increase in public sector employment. The debate about the role of the state and the delivery of public services has already been alluded to. Governments accept that the state will always have the ultimate responsibility to see that citizens have access to key services. The idea of the truly minimal state, providing no more than a safety net, was canvassed in some quarters in the 1980s, but few take it seriously now. By contrast, there is wider recognition that the provision, as distinct from the financing, of social services need not be a function of central government.

There are three reasons for limiting the scale of public spending. Firstly, tax revenues are becoming much more mobile. Highly taxed citizens and companies can move in a global world. Secondly, governments find it hard to respond to changes in consumer demand. Thirdly, there are demographic changes. When each generation was larger than the preceding one, there was sense in putting tax burdens on succeeding generations. Now the population of many European countries is decreasing and, in Britain, population stability is only maintained by immigration. There are fewer taxpayers and more dependants across Europe. How the role of the state will develop in the next fifty years in Europe is one of the hard questions of the 21st century.

The final point to be made in this section returns us to the discussion of what it means to be human, and how the church can interact with the changing cultural understanding of relationships and personal life. At this point it is important to stress that the vision offered by the church of what it means to be human is not endlessly plastic and changeable. The church must resist any idea of humanity which fails to reflect its proclamation of an embodied incorporation into the life of the triune God. Through its sacraments of baptism and the eucharist, in which Christians see themselves as reconciled to God, healed and sent out to the world, the church speaks profoundly of what it means to be human. Such acts of worship are about an understanding of persons who are shaped by their relationships, and reshaped by God's love, mercy and judgement.

There is however also a proper theological emphasis on the place of common grace, and the sustaining power of the divine presence in the midst of the everyday world in which we live. Such a world is often very far from being loving and humane, but it must also be said that the insights of modern culture on human well-being have often been far in advance of the churches. This is the tension with which Christians have lived in the modern world.

Above all, the redemption we are given is one which calls us to take responsibility for the flourishing of our society in profound and far-reaching ways. The need to seek first the Kingdom of God protects us against the endless demand for products (Matthew 6:33). There are enormous implications for the life of the churches: they must minister to the prosperous in our society without being trapped in guilt induced by the adoption of an unrealistic asceticism. Some Christians are truly called to a life of poverty and simplicity. For others, it is good to give thanks to the Lord for his gifts.

When the church performs its sacramental acts of judgement, forgiveness and thanksgiving in this way it expresses a deep faith in God's truth. It holds alongside our society a mirror to other forms of social life, and says that there is an alternative. There is a declaration that human life can communicate God's meaning and, in the Christian view of the good life, solidarity is what matters most. It is possible in the act of worship to look forward (in technical language, to look eschatologically) and to imagine a society characterized by fidelity.

The Christian vision is one of a society where the love of God has overcome all division by the power of the cross and resurrection, and this is a society in which sectional acquisitiveness is limited by the power of mutual solidarity in Christ. This message is highly relevant today for one of the features of contemporary capitalist society is the decline of trust. People trust those whom they know, or with whom they have contractual relationships. There is both an economic and a moral cost to the lack of trust. The economic cost is shown where society spends much time protecting itself against the betrayal of trust by litigation and regulation.

There is however also a moral cost, which can be graphically illustrated by the prevalence of cynicism. Those who live under conditions of deprivation are often made cynical because they find it hard to believe that there is anything that they can trust about people. Those who work with prisoners often find that their greatest challenge is to communicate what trust might mean to someone who has been unemployed and excluded from school, has few if any qualifications and has little experience of a stable and loving home background. Another graphic sign of this lack of trust is the growth of vandalism in deprived areas, sometimes aimed at schools, church buildings and youth clubs. This sober reflection brings us to a discussion of poverty and deprivation.

Inequality and poverty

A third reality, alongside the reality of employment changes, and the nature of prosperity (with the debate about how the state should act), is the harsh persistence of poverty and inequality. It was a constant feature of debates during the 1980s and 1990s that Britain had more children growing up in poverty than any other European country, had a greater rise in income inequality than almost any industrialized nation in the world, and was imprisoning more people (especially young and black people) per head of population than any other nation in the world. Although some progress has been made in the last few years, due to new government initiatives, and while it must be conceded that debate continues about the precise significance of some statistical comparisons, it is nevertheless hard to describe the quality of life for many young people over the last two decades in the old industrialized towns and cities of our nations as anything but bleak.

It is important to notice that the effects of poverty affect personal relationships, attitudes to authority and much else.[11] The complexity of poverty and the multi-faceted nature of deprivation imprison those who are caught within it in the limitations of a world they neither sought nor desired. This sense of captivity and the need for liberation drives the Christian demand so powerfully expressed by Jesus when he declared in his sermon in Nazareth that the spirit of the Lord was upon him and that he was to preach good news to the poor (Luke 4:18).

Financial exclusion is one of the harshest features of poverty[12]. It leads to debt, loan sharks, and even imprisonment for debt. There have been many descriptions of how our society fails its members through low pay, poverty, the awareness of being trapped in poor jobs and without access to credit, and the sense of powerlessness. Any society which changes as fast as ours has, will create many people who do not change, who are left behind and become marginalized. The market is a ruthless means of bringing about change even if planned economies have proved even worse in their inefficiency and corruption. ***Prosperity with a Purpose*** makes a number of recommendations for changes in social and economic policy changes. But, before all else, there is a need to see how this demand for justice fits into the vision of the presence of God in our changing society.

A key concept in the modern study of poverty – always obvious to those who have had to live with it – is the intensity of poverty. Poverty has many facets and income is just one of several dimensions by which poverty can be measured – and experienced. Thus, work is a clear route out of poverty, but workless households will be those most deeply and extensively excluded from the mainstream of prosperity. Similarly, persistent bad housing and accompanying chronic sickness deepen the experience of poverty. It is important to design policies that address not only the simpler forms of income poverty, but also the areas of multiple denials of life chances. Whole neighbourhoods are harmed by the departure of banks, building societies, post offices and supermarkets. This is especially the case in rural areas.

The contrast between credit and debt is an important new feature of poverty. Credit and debit cards enable the management of prosperity for those who are secure within it. But these same facilities also threaten poverty to those who mismanage credit, or who are pitchforked out of normal prosperity by circumstances. The poorer people are, the more expensive credit becomes.

A minority of people live in poverty in Britain – but they include more than a quarter of all children. Only a third of poor people live in areas of multiple deprivation – those 900 wards where unemployment, poor housing, education and health, and fear of crime abound. But intense poverty is also an increasingly rural phenomenon.

Cities have, above all, been places where the chance to exercise capability has been the great attraction for millions of people. Yet millions of them fail to realize their hopes, and become victims of the multiple deprivation which is a central feature of urban life. Even as labour regulation advances in the cause of progress, large numbers of workers are casualized, thus losing the rights that are customary in the mainstream. Thus risk is outsourced to vulnerable workers, who are rendered supplicants rather than partners. The largest single group of poor people now consists of people who are in work. Three and a half million poor people live in working households. There are more working poor than there are unemployed or poor pensioners. People work very hard for long hours, and in the absence of a living wage, still fall below the poverty line.

Asylum-seekers and illegal immigrants, too, frequently endure harsh conditions. At the same time the economy of all the major developing nations has come to depend on their emigrant workers. Their remittances form a substantial part of the earnings of their countries of origin. Churches have taken a lead in the care of asylum-seekers and migrants but their position remains precarious. Ultimately their decision to travel to Britain and Ireland is deeply influenced by global forces, which are discussed later in this report.

Of equal concern is the ending of the culture of thrift that shaped the lives of most people over the age of 50. The arrival of the new prosperity – symbolized perhaps by the slogan 'You've never had it so good' in 1959 – began to erode that careful, often fearful, frugality. Many people no longer felt the need to live in shared communities of need. The new individualism has marked the whole of contemporary life, but its material effects are seen most sharply in poor neighbourhoods. There has been a consequent devaluation of care within the community, care that is usually offered by women and older people. It is important to learn how to evaluate shared quality of life, rather than simply individual income levels. An economy shaped by low inflation and interest rates will begin to produce unfamiliar challenges, and we need to understand that these changes may also bear most heavily on the poor.

Another feature of our society has been the widening inequality between those whose skills are much in demand, and the lower paid. There are powerful moral and practical arguments for adopting policies that end social exclusion, and which include the poor in the mainstream of British life. It is encouraging that there is now something of a political consensus on this issue.

Some questions of inequality are easier to address than others. Much has been made, for instance, of the gross inequalities in remuneration between low paid public service workers and multinational executives. For the latter total pay, including stock options, is sometimes only obscurely related to performance. Successful North European and Scandinavian corporate executives enjoy rather lower levels of pay. There are cases where there is clear need for shareholder action, on prudential as well as moral grounds, because the behaviour of the directors damages the reputation of their companies. In the mainstream of a prosperous economy, however, it is important that the operation of the labour market should be allowed to reward ability and to reveal mediocrity; high pay can be deserved. This leads into the next section, which considers the relationship of levels of pay, wealth and happiness.

Happiness and life satisfaction

It is not clear how far extra income actually contributes to the subjective happiness of those who have enough to live on. Empirical surveys are very inconclusive on this point. As average income rises over time there appears to be no noticeable improvement, in well-being,[13] and indeed in some European countries there is actually a fall in life satisfaction. This is explained if happiness is in fact determined by the rise in income relative to some norm or expectation. If individuals raise these norms as their income rises (which certainly appears to be the case) then we are no better off as a society. Indeed if the motivation for consumer spending is the acquisition of status, then additional consumption by one person can reduce the happiness of those who are unable to match it.

Another aspect of consumption has been the withdrawal of many individuals into protected living places, at the expense of community life. However the increase of prosperity is not to be seen as a 'zero sum game' in which the rich gain at the expense of the poor. Our prosperity today is built on the thrift of previous generations, on their investment in education (human capital), machinery and buildings.

This report will discuss later policy options designed to redistribute income or to enable employees to trade more leisure time for less income. There has been much discussion recently about the relationship of happiness, or life satisfaction, to growth in national income – for example in the Downing Street Strategy Unit[14], in lectures in 2003 by Professor Richard Layard at the London School of Economics,[15] and in the report of the Sustainable Development Commission, chaired by Jonathan Porritt, which advises the Government. Such activity demonstrates that social and economic policy is changing, even if the future direction is not yet clear. Fifty years ago Britain had a far lower standard of living than today, great areas of poverty, and a need to grow economically to sustain the welfare state and to increase standards of living for the general population. Layard demonstrates that the increased standard of living in Britain in the last decade or so is not bringing greater happiness or, to adopt the jargon of social scientists, life satisfaction.

All three reports consider some of the many reasons why this might be so. Clearly genetic inheritance, personality, cultural variations and gender all play a role. But, what is striking is that, taking 1970 as the base point, GDP per capita had nearly doubled by 1997, while life satisfaction remained constant.

What other explanations might be offered? There are economic 'bads' such as rising levels of crime, divorce and separation, declining job satisfaction and higher levels of unemployment. Rising levels of aggregate national income increase life satisfaction but are accompanied by trends which have an offsetting, negative effect.

Secondly, there are relative factors. If an individual's income rises but those of their peers stay the same, the individual may feel better but envy may reduce the satisfaction of their peers. Increasingly, workers in Britain seem driven by perceptions of relative income. If everyone's income rises people may feel no better off.

This is subtly different from a third explanation which is that people become used to new found wealth, and take for granted that they cannot live on less income. This is the habituation factor, where U.S. Gallup polls have found over many years that people say that the absolute minimum level of income necessary to live in society rises with actual incomes.

Finally there are rising aspirations. As Emerson said, 'Want is a growing giant that the coat of Have can never be large enough to cover'. Foreign travel becomes an aspiration for all through advertising, followed by increasingly exotic foreign travel.[16]

These four explanations can be summarized as: economic 'bads'; relative status; habituation; and rising aspiration. They mean that we must look elsewhere for an answer to what would produce a real increase in the true happiness or life satisfaction of our society as a whole. There are issues of social justice related to the distribution of income, and the need to reduce poverty (especially child poverty and poor health) is, of course, important. However there are other factors to be taken into account. It appears that happiness is increased by social cohesion. From many surveys it appears that factors other than individual income are important to perceptions of happiness. Layard lists six main factors. These are: the importance of promoting good mental health (for depression is a major unacknowledged contributor to unhappiness); satisfying and secure paid work; a secure and loving private life; a secure community; freedom; and moral values.

Social vision

Prosperity with a Purpose seeks to hold together four elements – employment, prosperity, life satisfaction and poverty – in a way that does justice to each of them but also provides a vision of how society as a whole might do this. Such a vision cannot be too general. It must encompass the particularity of each issue in a concrete and truthful way. It is common for the intractability of each of these areas to be discussed without seeing how changes in one area might impact on others. In employment there is the issue of the work/life/family balance, to take but one concern. In prosperity there is the great issue of inequality, while the debate about the role of the state remains lively (as was illustrated by the arguments about foundation hospitals or school vouchers). The reality of poverty has been altered by the sharp decline in the number of long-term unemployed in the years since ***Unemployment and the Future of Work*** was published in 1997, but much poverty remains.

A theological vision must contain the ability to tell the truth, with integrity. Integrity has two dimensions. First our report has to be recognisably Christian and not simply secular ideology with a top dressing of religious language. This is why we reflected, to take just two examples, on the relationship of the gifts of the Spirit to employment practice, and on the vision of trust offered us in worship in relationship to vandalism in deprived areas. Many more such connections need to be made, and it is at the heart of theological conversation to do just that. How these links are made will always be a matter of dispute, but that is the essence of the theological task.

The second issue to do with integrity is whether, granted that this is a Christian report, the Churches can be seen to embody its values in their own life. Do churches act in ways that are consonant with what they believe? This is no mere rhetorical point as the issue of racism, and the employment of minority ethnic staff within the churches, makes clear. Christians are very much part of society but can sometimes give the impression that they live by high moral standards for which there is little evidence in the way they operate in practice.

In all of this the relationship to the environment also looms large. Fear of destroying the whole world can produce no more than a prudential ethic. Christians have a far stronger imperative: they must care for the environment because the Spirit of God created it in Genesis and because of Noah's covenant with creation and all animals. Christians will disagree deeply about where the limits of bio-engineering should be, and what interpretation should be put on the charge to humanity to take responsibility for the earth. Nevertheless, in all of this we need to consider the triangular relationship between the Spirit of God, humanity and creation. It is not that there is a relationship between God and humanity which must also take account of creation. Rather the relationship of God and humanity is one in which creation is centrally woven into every fibre of our being.

In scientific terms the 21st century will be one in which the genetic code that encompasses all of life will be laid open for our inspection. How we respond, and with what degree of respect for creation, is a central issue for our world. Again the calling to new creation includes the whole creation in Romans 8, where the ultimate vision is one of the peaceable kingdom. This vision is the fruit of being conformed to the truth of God's life as the whole of creation is transformed by God's spirit (peace between humanity and creation as the fruit of righteousness in Isaiah 11:6-8).

The Churches' vision for society cannot stand on its own. The renewal of political discourse is a task which must be tackled by the whole of society. We hope that these essays will promote discussion and criticism which will contribute to that renewal of political conversation. The central task is that of enabling a pluralist, pragmatic society to reflect on itself and to recognize judgement as a meaningful concept. We want to argue against a crude fatalism which sees the way in which society will develop in future as inevitable and unable to be changed or challenged. It is also about whether politics is to become more and more commodified, as has been the tendency in recent years. Must politicians abandon vision and values in favour of simplistic soundbites as they bid for votes with packages offering bigger tax cuts, more security on the streets, and the like? Christians, by contrast, should be open to change and committed to help bring about change in themselves and the world they inhabit. Such a task will only be achieved in alliance with others, and that partnership is perhaps the greatest challenge for the churches in 21st century in Britain.

We can conclude by summarizing the values, which this essay has sought to express. One is the importance of work as service, and the way in which prosperity must be harnessed to allow people the chance to express themselves in a variety of ways, with vigour and dynamism. If prosperity becomes simply an opportunity for excessive expenditure then this value is lost. At the same time it is crucial that society preserves a sense of trust so that cynicism and corrosive ways of life do not increase. There is certainly evidence of this, but where work is done in a way that recognizes the inherent dignity of the person then the value of such work, whether in the public services or the private sector, is enhanced.

Secondly this essay shows how our society is still deeply divided by poverty and an absence of true community. In the language of today's politicians this may be termed social exclusion. The 1997 church report, ***Unemployment and the Future of Work***, spoke powerfully of the great social need caused by poverty and unemployment. Unemployment has indeed fallen substantially since then, especially among the long-term unemployed, but there remains much to be done.

The final and key point is that, once a certain level of national income is reached, happiness is not related to prosperity. What really matter are relationships. The stigma of mental health, the pain of divorce, the benefits of a cohesive community, a satisfying job, freedom and moral values can all be assisted or harmed by policy.

This is not a plea for a return to some imagined 1950s golden age of untroubled and cohesive communities. Rather, this essay has argued that the rising tide of prosperity has enabled many people to flourish in ways that are far from the often hierarchical and conformist world of 50 years ago. However there is much evidence to suggest that, as a society, we are not getting happier as we get richer.

Christians need to address this fact with some urgency, and our clear message should be not just to celebrate prosperity, but to consider what it is for. What matters is how we use prosperity. We should invest far more in mental health, we need to give far more thought as to how stable relationships can be nurtured, and how communities can be good places to live in. There are signs that political parties are increasingly aware of this. Much more energy needs to be invested in such dialogue both by politicians and by the Churches themselves.

4

Global justice: Ian Linden

Our opening essay claimed that great increases in human well-being had been made possible in Europe through the judicious combination of market innovation, public welfare expenditure, and the creation of a social order that encourages human flourishing – prosperity with a purpose. It remains to be seen if a similar expansion of social justice can be achieved in a worldwide setting. The aim of this essay is to explore those possibilities.

One succinct definition of globalization is 'the process and policy of developing a global economy such that its units are all interconnected in time and space'. Globalization is both old and radically new. The development of interconnected societies, foreshadowing this progressive worldwide integration of national economies, did not begin a few decades ago.

For example, by 1900, at the apogee of European imperial outreach, a major wave of economic expansion was in full swing. This was boosted by investment within territories politically controlled by the imperial centre, at the hub of wider linkages to other national economies. It created a modern, open and integrated system for trade in agricultural products and in the new industrial commodities. The dominant power of the nation-state had become the dynamo generating a complex international economy. From 1870 to 1914 trade expanded at an average rate of 3.4% per annum and the share of British wealth invested abroad rose from 17% to 33% – though more of this investment was outside the Empire than within it. Economic expansion was accompanied by a prodigious movement of labour out of Europe, some 36 million mainly economic migrants moving to the USA. The key commodities – cotton, sugar and coal – were now being carried around the world by steamship, the new industrialized means of transport. Trade increasingly depended on effective means of fast, real-time communication, the intercontinental telegraph and telephone.

The recent wave of globalization is distinguished from this and the first wave of proto-globalization in the late 18th century by the predominant role of the multinational corporations in global trade and by the importance of financial flows in dominating economic outcomes. For much of the 20th century globalization retreated as countries withdrew into isolationism or limited blocs in the face of economic adversity, while totalitarianism and two major world wars fragmented the global economy. However globalization re-established itself towards the end of the 20th century and the world economy today is a complex interaction of nation-states, the market and multinationals, fuelled by cheaper and faster transport and communications. But it needs to be emphasized that this global interconnectedness has not only an economic dimension but involves important impacts on diverse cultures, each of which is adapting to the new information age by integration, reaction or simply neglect.

The reaction of threatened cultures, which develop their own defences, sometimes gives rise to what is dubbed 'fundamentalism'. The clash of such world-views – for instance between the different fundamentalisms displayed in Saudi Arabia and middle-America – preoccupies international relations. Japanese, Korean, Indian and Overseas Chinese business cultures, far from fundamentalism, also have an important influence on the global economy. In the global market-place, numbers count. But so does war and terrorism.

The recent waves of globalization have relied on technological change in the communications revolution, and business re-organization designed to cut labour costs, with their attendant effects on productivity growth. This has been responsible for much of Britain's economic growth. Though innovation is central to the maintenance of competitiveness, if productivity gains exceed growth in output, unemployment results. There is clear hardship where production and therefore jobs have been exported, for example in textiles or in the service sector, as in the case of many corporate call centres moving outside UK. The challenge is to generate desirable new products and services at a competitive price while sustaining the skills and employment of a dwindling labour pool – easier said than done, and hardest on the poorest.

The consequence of this challenge not being met by nation-states is that the most striking feature of the global economy is a growing inequality. And, in the rich world, the nation-state is still the chief arbiter of its peoples' fates, despite the pressures of globalization. The rich nations trade overwhelmingly among themselves. This means in practice that many countries in sub-Saharan Africa are almost bereft of productive investment, the benefits of equitable trade and the advantages of insertion in the global economy such as the transfer of technology.

This is largely because civil conflict, bad governance and corruption, the economic consequences of HIV/AIDS, plus a limited range of primary commodities, make these countries unattractive to corporate and private investors, companies and entrepreneurs (save in high value extractive industries).

Such countries need the amount of aid that would be available if our national international development budget represented 0.7% of the UK GDP. But, more important, they need the support of the richer countries for initiatives such as NEPAD (New Partnership for Africa's Development) to improve governance and instil genuine democracy as a prerequisite for access to financial flows from the North. There are many reasons why such initiatives may fail and one is the North's tendency to write them off as failures before they can gain momentum. NEPAD cannot be allowed to fail.

Meanwhile, the processes of change that make all nations more productive, and thus materially richer, bring with them transitional pressures which can be so damaging to the precarious lives of the poor in traditional industries and in agriculture in both poor and rich countries. Schumpeter's 'creative destruction' preceded the present phase of growing global prosperity; nonetheless the destruction side of the equation is often more evident to the poorest than the creative. Worse deprivation may occur within a rich country than in a poor one. Amartya Sen's comparison of the life chances of a cohort of black American men compared with those of many poor people in China and Sri Lanka provided a striking example. For this reason the division of countries into 'low income' and 'middle income' can be thoroughly confusing. By aggregating income data, South Africa, for example, is taken as a middle income country, though the vast majority of its people are either poor or relatively rich, and few have 'middling' incomes.

For some, including some of the poorest, globalization carries in its train much more new hardship than the promise of future well-being. To use the old English phrase, it brings to some of the poorest more 'woe than weal', more poverty than wealth. Amartya Sen has a useful account of human development as the nurturing of human capabilities, being able to do more. But for some people, the changes resulting from globalization shut off avenues of opportunity and can leave them isolated or marginalized. In short globalization does not by itself create a commonweal or a common-wealth, nor the pervasive social well-being implied in the term the 'common good'. It produces aggregate economic growth which is another matter altogether. In the words of Monsignor Diarmuid Martin, speaking to the United Nations Economic and Social Council on behalf of the Delegation of the Holy See in 1998: 'the basic criterion for evaluating the process of economic globalization is how far it helps strengthen and reinforce the *primary global reality,* namely, that humanity consists of one global human family, of which all are members with equal rights of access to the goods of creation, for which all bear responsibilities of solidarity'. The Christian call to the architects of globalization must therefore echo that of Muslims, with whom we share the worship of the Creator God, for the muezzin daily calls them to prayer with the words, 'Come ye to well-being *(falah)'.*

The majority of the world's poor people, though, are not the poorest of the poor, and they have an intermediate experience of globalization. China, India, Indonesia and Brazil have all responded in similar ways to the needs of their new masses of urban poor. The formula 60% winners 40% losers, 10% big winners and 10% big losers, reflects this reality. The strategies of the developing countries which have achieved 'take-off' have been largely those of market-orientated, urban, commercial development. As a result the world is already more than 50% urban, and there are now many cities of more than 10 million people. Urbanisation is one of the central features of the new globalization as migrants are drawn into successful productive 'nodes' of the new network society. Some cities have become 'global centres' with a high concentration of affluence, skills, technology and productivity, alongside an expanding penumbra of poor migrants, with crime burgeoning at the interface.

This process would still be under way even if the pace of globalization had not been accelerating from the 1970s. Much of this urban development has been created in the wake of recent changes in the global economy. A majority of the poor in these new commercial societies have yet to see the benefits of this transformation, and many of them are at present its victims. But the ruling elites of these societies, and the larger constituencies of the successful which control them, have powerful interests in this process expanding. These interests are expressed internationally through the major inter-governmental bodies and led by the unparalleled power of the United States (and, to a lesser extent, the

European Union) in structuring the global economy in its interests. The sometimes ruthless projection of this power is itself often seen by its victims as the core component of globalization. It is deployed both as 'hard power' (military strength), and as 'soft power' in international bodies, getting people to want what the USA wants – most particularly in the realm of political economy.

Many other poor nation-states and their citizens have little to gain, and much to lose from these changes. For them, their nation-state has little power and they are trapped between the impotence of the local, and the apparent omnipotence of the global. The small proportion of global trade that includes the poor of the world is usually biased adversely against these nations. They have few urban generators of wealth, and produce only commodities whose revenue value is declining, largely as a result of rich country measures such as subsidies on agriculture and forms of protectionism despite an apparent commitment to liberal economics.

A striking contemporary example of this stark absence of a 'level playing field' is Africa's difficulty in marketing its cotton. Not only does cotton production employ 10 million Africans, but it has been one of the few means of stimulating 'linkage' to new industrial development open to African nations. Factory production of cooking oil, animal feeds and soap from cotton seed arose from an agricultural base in the desert-edge nations around the Sahara. But Africa has been and is facing intense competition from cotton producers around the world who, to a remarkable degree, are directly subsidized for the cotton that they produce.

Farmers producing cotton in the USA and Europe during 2001 received government subsidies of 1.21 Euros and 1.49 Euros respectively per kilo of cotton, based on a report in ***Le Monde*** of 22nd June 2002. The level of subsidy was 25% and 50% more than the sale price of a kilo of cotton which traded at around 0.95 Euros. So European and, in particular, US farmers have – and have had – a spectacular advantage in the market. Put in context, USDA statistics published in April 2004 showed that Africa produced about 10% of estimated global cotton production in 2002/03 (down from about 15% in the late 1990s) and contributed about 20% of total exports. In contrast, the US accounted for 20% of world production in 2002/03 and 39% of exports, while the corresponding shares for the EU were 2.4% of production and 4.5% of exports. Not surprisingly what Africa has been able to earn from the price of its cotton on the world market has dropped threefold in real terms over the last 30 years as the continent faced the additional problem of synthetic fibres flooding the market and reducing demand.

It might have been expected that after the advent of the World Trade Organisation (WTO), with its principle of the level playing field, subsidies for cotton would have begun dropping in line with decreases in direct subsidies to food crops. But not so: 50% of world production received direct subsidies in 1998; subsidies were given on 73% of production in 2001. Today some $360 billion is spent on <u>subsidies</u> to agricultural producers in the richer North compared to a grand total of $54 billion in <u>aid</u> given to the South, much of it tied to production in the North. At the G8 in Evian in 2003 the US refused to concede any ground on its payment of £1.8 billion equivalent per annum in hidden subsidies to its 25,000 cotton farmers. Despite this, African cotton as shown by its market share has struggled to remain competitive – at the expense of the producer.

So there is a strong element of hypocrisy in the avowed commitment of the USA and the EU to Africa's development. Their trade policies have blocked promising avenues for rural development amongst their weaker competitors. This damage must be rectified. But the planned rate of tariff removal on key Third World exports – agriculture, textiles and footwear – is much slower than that on the industrially produced goods of the OECD. Whether it is citrus fruits, aluminium or steel, when push comes to shove, neo-liberalism gives way to protective tariffs designed to consolidate votes in key sections of the electorates of the North. Here is a major injustice, and a practical problem for the North; the partly enforced poverty of the South excludes people from the opportunity to increase global prosperity by taking away their capability to engage in international trade. Further, by denying opportunities to the poorer South in this way, the North is stunting the growth of potentially large markets for its own exports and capital investment. To use economic language, protection is very inefficient and the North's manipulation of the market heightens the impact of poverty globally.

The most critical area of this protection is, of course, European and US agriculture. The Common Agricultural Policy (CAP) was designed to give Europe food security in the post-war years, but it dramatically distorted prices and production through subsidies on a range of crops. Its reform has been slow and gradualist owing to the entrenched opposition of the powerful farming lobbies which have been supported by the ruling political parties. But now agricultural protection is being gradually reduced and a more holistic approach involving concern for the environment and the wider rural economy is beginning to prevail. This, however, is too slow for the unsubsidized poor farmers around the world who have to compete with cheap subsidized agricultural products. The proclaimed liberalization of the global market remains a sham as far as agriculture is concerned and both small European farmers and unsubsidized Third World farmers are being driven off the land.

One major question for Europe raised by these disparities in wealth and productive capacity is that of inward migration. In fact surprisingly tiny proportions of the world's population move from poor to rich countries, often with the help of criminal gangs. Yet this movement generates a flow of xenophobia and racist sentiment, easily manipulated by unscrupulous politicians and the right-wing tabloid press. The free movement of people – labour – is a corollary to that of goods and capital in liberal economic theory. The process has, historically, been unregulated, and was once from rich to poor countries. But, however irrational, the rich now feel threatened by migration from poor countries . The just regulation of trans-border movement – even more now that the 'war on terrorism' heightens anxieties to an even greater degree – is a pressing issue for European governance and demands courageous rejection of chauvinist and populist sentiment. For the aging populations of Europe, which are not replacing themselves due to low birth rates, there are cogent arguments for encouraging immigration even if the current demand for unskilled labour is dropping.

The global economy operates according to an ideology of development: that the market is good at allocating scarce resources and thus good for poor people. But it has to be properly regulated. In the words of Pope John Paul II: 'Now that commerce and communications are no longer bound by borders, it is the universal common good which demands that control mechanisms should accompany the inherent logic of the market. This is essential to avoid reducing all social relationships to economic factors, and in order to protect those caught in new forms of exclusion and marginalization' (***Address to the Pontifical Academy of Social Sciences,*** 25 April 2001). This principle is not simply yet another fiat being handed down from North to South. Indeed many of the Asian countries have resisted pressures to conform to inappropriate prescriptions for growth and have instituted control mechanisms to insulate their economies to some extent from international market forces. Indonesia pursues the path of Malaysia; China follows that of Japan, Korea, Hong Kong and Singapore, and this has happened despite the prescriptions of the international financial institutions dominated by the USA. In some instances excessive insulation has permitted some of the resulting prosperity to be frittered away by poor corporate governance, leading to subsequent painful adjustment, but generally this approach has succeeded.

The attraction of the fruits of the Western political economy has led to the weakening of solidarity worldwide as individuals are encouraged to pursue their own material interests on the assumption that a rich, cosmopolitan lifestyle is available to all. As the Commission of the Bishops' Conferences of the European Community (COMECE) states:

> *'Solidarity is central to organising and strengthening the very fabric of the world economy, which is now "one" in a real sense. For industrialized countries, global solidarity does not simply mean sacrifice of the superfluous, it means dealing with vested interests and entrenched power structures, with life-styles and models of consumption.'*

This emphasis on the need for structural change, as well as personal change, and the removal of structures of injustice, goes back to Pope Paul VI's thinking on international development contained in the 1967 document ***Populorum Progressio***, which emphasized the importance of fair trade and adequate aid. Change is thus desirable in at least four areas.

Working for global justice: four areas for change

Firstly, the regulation of corporate power. The government and people of poor countries need internationally acknowledged legal rights in order to challenge the activities of subsidiaries of multinational corporations (MNCs) in their countries. MNCs sometimes behave in world markets in ways that would be illegal in their own nation-states. The arena for discussion of these issues is the World Trade Organisation (WTO). But the powers of the WTO need to serve the poor majority of its members rather than, as at present, the rich. Western consumer pressure is an important part of the Christian vocation to achieve this change. Pressures for stocking 'fair-trade' items in supermarkets have begun to take effect and are an important means of bringing this about.

Secondly, the regulation of global capital flows. The new world economy creates great instability through large unregulated and short-term capital flows. This has affected the newly industrialized economies of South Asia – Thailand, Malaysia and Indonesia; and elsewhere, for quite different reasons, Mexico, Argentina and Turkey. Contraction of the older South Asian economies caused by precipitate capital flight has affected employment prospects in vulnerable areas of the UK. However the mobility of international capital is an important discipline against poor or corrupt corporate and national governance, which can sometimes flourish in overprotected economies in all parts of the world. Global means have to be sought to anticipate these crises, and to ameliorate them when they occur. There has already been progress in improving national economic policy-making and corporate and financial regulation, as well as developing better co-ordination among regulators But good economic management will justifiably also entail national restrictions on short-term capital movements at times of crisis. Certainly, forms of regulation that restrict capital flows to the world's poorest defeat the object. Properly managed, productive forms of investment create a huge opportunity for the poor and are essential for the future of Africa, at present starved of capital and investment.

Thirdly, the reduction of rich country protectionism. Current US policy flagrantly breaches its proclaimed free trade principles in extending subsidies in the areas of steel and agriculture. Such measures simply follow the pattern institutionalized over half a century in Europe through its Common Agricultural Policy. The abolition of these malpractices will have very serious medium-term effects on many poor people, particularly small-scale farmers in the US and in Europe. Compensatory action in countries in which this occurs will be required that is not market-distorting and does not disguise subsidization in another form of payment.

The WTO is the body with the powers to regulate and penalize these breaches. The Churches should exert prudent judgement on what is an issue of the common good, and stand on the side of the poor world, even to the short-term detriment of their own faithful in the rich world.

Fourthly, the encouragement of good governance in poor countries. Integral human development is impossible in countries whose governments are not interested in implementing pro-poor policies. Many of the world's poor suffer within kleptocracies and failed states. It is impossible to develop societies based on commerce without fostering the commercial virtues and institutions without which their political economy becomes grossly inefficient, oppressive and inhuman. Both Hernando de Soto and Amartya Sen have shown that there are in addition more subtle and pervasive patterns of exclusion than the banditry of public office experienced in several states.

De Soto has described how difficult it is in many countries for a poor person to get title to property or to register a business in such a way as to use his or her few assets productively. The establishment of property rights, providing securities for poor people, will create an enormous new capacity for earned prosperity within poor communities. De Soto attributes the inability to realize this untapped wealth of the poor as a major cause of poverty and the refusal of states to do anything about it as a major breach of a fundamental right to private property. Sen describes the importance of democracy in famine-prevention and the way in which unjust structures reduce the capabilities of the poor. His contribution to understanding development, a careful analysis of the means, the bundles of assets and private and public goods required in different cultures and economies, and the ends of development, the ability to realize capabilities, provides an important framework for situating the role of economic growth, environmental protection and governance within the quest for wealth. The insights of these two thinkers need to inform public policy.

The measures described above would vastly increase the prosperity of the least-developed nations and increase demand in the world economy. The enrichment of the world's poor countries provides an opportunity for an improvement in the prospects of the rich world's poor. There is much to be gained in pursuing these reforms at a regional level in the poor world. But this does not follow automatically from increasing global prosperity. But, as Amartya Sen emphasizes, increased material prosperity is always a means to an end – the goal of human development. It must not become an end in itself. Moreover, the already rich must be extremely tactful in seeking to help the developing economies avoid the mistakes that they, the rich of the developed world, have made – and continue to make. A conversation between rich and poor about the disciplines of prosperity and the nature of wealth and well-being is urgent, necessary and difficult.

However, if the Churches are to bring the good news of solidarity to the poor that globalization does not have to bring more 'woe' than 'weal', that changes can and must be made, it has to be asked whether the life and structures of the Churches adequately reflect this commitment. For the primary question asked by the Churches today, or at least what occupies the energies of their leaderships, is not how must we be and how must we act if we are to be faithful to the task of bringing the Good News, but how can we maintain our parochial, denominational and national structures and personnel. In this way the Christian development agencies look like an appendage grafted on to the Body of Christ, and their advocacy becomes something of an alibi. Alongside the critique of government set out above must then come a question, as a matter of integrity to ourselves, to the Churches. What comes first: do we fit the task, the mission, into structures inherited from the past; or do we make the structures fit the new task and the mission? For it may be argued that the contemporary phase of globalization heralds an epoch-making change in how we live and interact in the world. This change is no less important than the advent of industrialisation, and the Churches would be grossly misled in believing they can respond to this reality with only minor adjustments.

That said, it is possible to suggest a coherent structure that would enable the world's peoples to enjoy an increasingly prosperous future.

The global common good: instruments of change

The regulatory agencies needed to deal with these issues are in an early stage of development. One approach to the possibilities is suggested in COMECE's document ***Global Governance***: our responsibility to make globalization an opportunity for all. This document was produced under the leadership of Michel Camdessus, former head of the IMF. It shows that global interdependence has grown in a generation, yet the needs of the world's poor have remain unsatisfied, and the damage inflicted upon the environment advances. A global institutional response is required, but one that is legitimated by the world's nation-states rather than usurping their sovereignty. That response must also address the inequality in power relations between rich and poor countries. This must include for the myriad firms and associations which create the material and spiritual wealth of any society the freedom to govern their own affairs.

A first step should be the revision of the mandates of existing international organisations. The WTO should be more responsive to the needs of the poor, as discussed above, especially in agriculture. The International Labour Organization (ILO) needs a stronger mandate to defend core labour standards. Environmental degradation requires a further element of institutional architecture. The United Nations Environment Programme (UNEP) should be reformed to create a new World Environment Organization to initiate and supervise action on international environmental issues. The need for such a world body is evident from the failure of key nation-states to sign up for the Kyoto Protocol reducing carbon emissions. The role of the USA as one of the most profligate consumers of non-renewable resources in opposing the protocol and its failure to propose alternatives commensurate to the gravity of the environmental crisis is a moral scandal. It needs stating clearly that a calculated disregard for the integrity of creation both by individual voters and by governments today is a sin crying out to heaven and a crime against future generations.

Even more controversially, the document proposes a Global Governance Group, to ensure a minimum of co-ordination and coherence in the system. This should comprize the heads of those 24 governments which appoint executive directors to the boards of the World Bank and the International Monetary Fund. Here too, membership of such an influential body should seek to redress the balance of power between rich and poor countries

The prospects for global paralysis threatened by these proposals are evident. But some such international ensemble has significant potential for good if we have the courage to pursue it.

5

The Environmental Challenge: Jennifer Potter

The global environmental crisis

Is it scaremongering or indulgence in apocalyptic overstatement to refer to the present state of our environment as being in crisis? Many people try to maintain so. But humankind has had an enormous impact on our planet especially in the last two hundred years; in pouring polluting gases into the air, pouring polluting substances into the rivers and seas, and in the last century, in moving enough rock and soil to rival natural movement for the first time in history. Humankind has been short-sighted, some may even say blind, to the fact that quality of life for humans is inextricably bound up with the health and well-being of the entire planet. Sustainable human thriving cannot be attained in isolation from the place where we live and how we treat it. It is not only religious people who have recognized that at the heart of our current crisis is a spiritual problem. Jonathan Porritt in ***Seeing Green*** says what many other have intimated: 'some kind of spiritual commitment or religion in its true meaning (namely the reconnection between each of us and the source of all life) is a fundamental part of the transformation ecologists are talking about when they speak of what needs to happen to our attitude to the planet on which we live.' The people of the world can cope with more than the dumbed-down soundbites of political campaigns. They/we want deeper questions to be faced and answered – questions about our future and where we are all headed; questions about the values and beliefs that underpin our living together on our planet.

As Christians we are not concerned only about the continued existence of poor people in our own well-off society but also about the impact of our lifestyle and our consumption patterns on people in other parts of the world and on us. Nor should we forget that our responsibilities are not only to our own generation but also for the generations yet to come, so that they will not have reduced possibilities for well-being. As the environmental impact of developing countries grows, the co-operation and collaboration between North and South in environmental policies and international agreements becomes more vital. Yet we live in a context where developing countries are encouraged by the world trading system and the policies of the World Bank/IMF to produce for export.

In Brazil this has meant devastation of the forest cover in the Amazon Basin, as land is turned over to the rearing of cattle or the production of cattle fodder crops. In 2004 we witnessed the great loss of human life in the Caribbean and in the Philippines when heavy rain washed away vast amounts of top-soil because the roots which used to bind the soil together have gone as areas have been denuded of vegetation. The local people are not environmental vandals but people trying to eke out an existence where possibilities are few. Global agreements on aspects of the environment will only be reached and implemented if they address social and economic development in the countries of the South more effectively.

We, in the rich, developed world have to recognize the level of exploitation that current economic practices have bred with regard to people in other parts of our world and with regard to the resources of the natural world. Our 'footprint' upon our world is far, far greater than it should be, far greater than it need be and is not sustainable globally as other regions aspire to the same standard of living as the affluent West. We have also to recognize that in our globalized world the effects of our way of life are not contained or containable within the nation-state. Greenhouse gases know no national boundaries and extreme weather events, made more frequent by global warming, are not under the control of any national authority, nor indeed of any 'authority'. Political leaders, nationally and internationally, know this and say it, especially at large international gatherings; yet years go by without any serious change of attitude.

Kofi Annan, speaking at the Millennium Assembly of the United Nations said, 'we now face an urgent need to secure the freedom of future generations to sustain their lives on this planet – and we are failing to do it. We have been plundering our children's heritage to pay for unsustainable practices ... our responses are too few, too little and too late'.

Over and above our concern with enlightened self-interest and a just world order, our Christian faith demands that we take up our responsibility towards creation and, in particular, towards our own home, planet earth. Our God is a God who spoke creation into existence and whose spirit continually infuses all that is and will be. God and creation are bound together in a creative inter-relationship, with humankind having a special responsibility for the stewardship of the created order. For good or ill, human beings are co-creators with God of our ever dynamic and evolving world. Although at times we may think of the environment as something we can manipulate and control, earthquakes and hurricanes, tidal flows and rampaging flood-water show us that we disregard the natural world at our peril. This is why environmental issues cannot be dismissed as an optional concern only for those who are interested. Ecological concern must become a significant element of the Christian calling and of Christian witness in the public sphere.

Climate change

Climate change – induced in part by human economic activity – is generally agreed to be the single most serious environmental problem confronting our world. Leaders of all the main political parties now talk about it. There has been considerable disagreement about how serious a problem this is; how far it is the result of human activity as opposed to the cyclical changes in the world climate; and how to plan ahead to cope with its effects. Over the past ten years much effort has been expended in getting an international agreement on limiting emissions of greenhouse gases. Significant countries, notably the USA, have not yet signed and ratified the Kyoto Protocol, though Russia took everyone by surprize by doing so. Even if the Protocol does come into force soon, its provisions are just too tame to make a significant change. Kyoto's threshold was deliberately kept low in the hope of inducing the USA to get on board, but the net result is that now, internationally, we have a set of targets that merely delay the rate at which matters get worse.

However, even the most sceptical observers, such as the Danish statistician, Bjørn Lomborg, concede that global warming is an unavoidable fact. One of the most noticeable consequences is the melting of the ice-caps and glaciers and a subsequent rise in sea-level. This affects some parts of the earth much more than others, and the small islands and low-lying coastlands are most at risk of disappearing under the water. Even here in Britain the increasing frequency with which the Thames Barrier has had to be closed in recent years is an indication of the impact of rising sea-level.

Mark Lynas ***(High Tide: News from a Warming World),*** has just spent 3 years travelling the world to witness the effects of global warming. Tuvalu, one of the world's smallest and most obscure nations with a population of 10,000, is already experiencing the effects of rising sea level and its dire consequences.

'I had been in Tuvalu for only two days when the first puddle of water appeared at the side of the small airstrip. More puddles soon joined it. ... Sea-level rise here is a crisis of national survival; very little of Tuvalu is much more than twenty inches above the Pacific and its coral bedrock is so porous that no amount of coastal protection can save it

...Tuvalans will have to move. Tuvalu has recently started legal action to try to win compensation from the countries emitting most greenhouse gases. But how do you put a price on a whole nation being relocated? How do you value a culture that is being wiped out?' Extracts from ***Hot News*** by Mark Lynas, published in *Granta 83:* **This Overheating World,** edited by Ian Jack, 2003

Much more disturbing is the melting of glaciers. Take, for example, the situation in the Andean region of Peru where glaciers are receding at a rapid pace. This spells disaster not for ten thousand but for ten million people in and around Lima who depend on the glacial run-off for their daily water supply. Already they have had to drive an aqueduct through a mountain range to a new watershed in their search for water supplies. They are living off their capital and, in all likelihood, on borrowed time.

Lynas travelled the world looking for evidence of global warming. More surprising is the fact that researchers at the Pentagon have recently undertaken a study entitled ***An Abrupt Climate Change Scenario and Its Implications for the United States National Security.*** They freely admit that they have taken an extreme scenario but that 'research suggests that once temperatures rise above some threshold, adverse weather conditions could develop rather abruptly'. The results would be colder conditions in some northern hemisphere areas because of the disruption of the course of the Gulf Stream and considerably warmer conditions in the southern hemisphere. The security implications of this are:

i) food shortages due to disruption and decline in agricultural production

ii) decreased availability of water in some areas due to changed patterns of precipitation but leading also to more frequent extreme weather phenomena such as floods and droughts

iii) disrupted access to energy supplies due to sea ice and storminess.

We know that at the core of many existing conflicts is the struggle for the control of vital resources, especially oil and natural gas and, of course, water itself. These can only grow more serious and widespread if nothing is done to avert massive climate change.

How surprising that with so much research and so great a consensus among scientists all around the world, it is still so difficult to bring about a change in mindset that will release people and their political leaders to tackle the current crisis creatively. A great gulf yawns between the urgent necessity of collective international action and the failure of a corresponding political response.

Globalization and the environment

The question which has exercised the minds of many economists and environmentalists and which has been at the heart of numerous international conferences is 'How do we move towards living and consuming in a way less damaging to our environment?' Or to put it another way, is it feasible to reduce the damage being done to the environment without decreasing social and economic welfare as currently experienced in the rich world and aspired to by all?

For the contemporary campaigner against the negative effects of globalization, corporations, especially in their multinational form, are the chief targets. They are accused of the profligate consumption of natural resources, of deliberately locating in areas where environmental standards are low and of exploiting labour in low-wage areas whilst making vast profits for their rich-world based shareholders. Yet these very same corporations are the chief engines of economic development and the main providers of employment in those parts of the world where people have become or are becoming more prosperous. The multinationals are a feature of our economic landscape, and are here to stay for the foreseeable future. They come in a variety of forms but are neither the devil incarnate nor the solution to the world's problems. Ironically, it is those international corporations which have a reputation to safeguard that usually have better social and environmental policies than many of the locally based companies. Of course, that does not mean that many multinationals could not do more, especially if the price signals encouraged them to do so.

Over the last 20 years especially, the multinationals and other companies have made production processes less damaging to the environment. Initially this has come about by governments setting minimum standards for pollution levels. More recently the impact of public pressure on industry to take corporate social responsibility more seriously and holistically has led to some companies adding the environment to their existing social and financial concerns. The growth of the ethical investment movement has added yet further pressure to companies not only to look at their own modes of consumption and production but also to pass a positive influence down their supply chains. It is often overlooked that 'consumption' is not just an activity of individuals but that industrial consumption and public procurement are huge areas that are amenable to much greater environmental scrutiny.

The more crude ideology of 'free markets' suggests that the invisible hand of market forces will yield optimal pricing mechanisms which will ensure that the market's superior wisdom will prevail for the good of the greatest number. Economists have, of course, always recognized that this conclusion is only valid under certain conditions, and that these are not necessarily met when we are dealing with, for example, the earth's atmosphere which is a 'public good'. Such goods cannot be parcelled up and sold in the market-place. No individual, family or community can opt out of climate change by buying their own patch of 'retro weather'. 'Quality air' cannot be sold without there being 'free riders'. The only way that 'selling' could be achievable would be through the taxing of all. There is also another aspect of market failure because the enormous changes in weather patterns will only produce a shift in the price signals when it is too late to reverse those patterns.

So we need to recognize that there will be a variety of ways in which to bring about reduced consumption of resources, more efficient ways of production and disposal of waste and indeed a changed attitude towards 'consumer durables' and their durability. Market forces will be used where they can be effective but with a recognition of their shortcomings, especially regarding those 'goods' which can not be parcelled out and sold to individuals. Nor must we lose sight of all those in our time who are too poor to express their choices through the market-place.

The way forward

All of these measures already mentioned have the potential merely to tinker at the edges of the problem. What is needed is for companies to move to a wholly different way of working with market-based incentives towards technical innovation aimed at cutting the amount of new resources consumed, of energy used and of waste generated. New technologies can deliver win-win situations – improved environmental performance and reduced costs. This has not happened to any large extent so far because 'soft barriers' deter companies from investing in new technologies. Such soft barriers are:

1 *the complexity of environmental issues* – no simple line can be drawn from one cause to one effect

2 *uncertainty* – scientists do not agree on the impact of, say, the release of chemicals into the atmosphere and the time-scale of their impact

3 *short-term company planning* – it is evident that environmental damage is cumulative over the long-term

Research into business attitudes (conducted as part of the Global Environmental Change Programme based at Sussex University 1991-2000) has pointed up the difficulties for business, the most crucial being hard economic fact. With rare exceptions there are inadequate economic incentives to allow firms investing in cleaner products and processes to gain commercial advantage over their competitors.

This is beginning to change with regard to low-pollution vehicles for public transport and the development of renewable forms of energy. Many businesses have not yet seen that being in the forefront of environmentally driven innovation has the potential for giving them the economic cutting edge. Business itself, as well as government, needs to promote learning and information exchange, together with technology transfer to its operations in the developing world.

One innovative way in which pressure is being brought to bear on companies is through the Carbon Disclosure Project. Organized by an influential group of institutional investors, the project asks companies to disclose the amount of carbon their operation produces as a first step to working on methods to reduce the amount. This project has succeeded in getting some FT500 companies to sign up and to begin to take on board the enormous costs of climate change and of their own carbon emissions as states impose tighter regulation and penalties on its production. In 2003 alone it has been estimated that the costs of weather-related natural disasters topped the $70 billion mark with a great impact on industry.

Although much remains to be done, it is encouraging that the mainstream investment community is engaging seriously with the implications of responding to climate change. It is this sort of initiative, combined with regulation and fiscal incentives from government, which can begin to move industry into modes of production which are not only greenhouse gas neutral but also have the potential to yield highly marketable innovations.

Transport and the production of electricity are the two largest contributors to greenhouse gas emissions and a closer look at energy and transport will reveal the challenges facing those who are committed to more environmentally sensitive production.

We consume a great deal of energy in our homes for lighting, heating and cooking and a great deal more energy is expended in producing the food, clothing and durables – the so-called 'white goods' – that we consume daily. Yet more energy is expended on the transport of goods across the world.

For example, as trucks bring French and German yoghurt to the supermarkets of Britain, so do other trucks criss-cross the continent with the same cargo in the other direction. 'Choice' is held up as a vital constituent of a modern lifestyle. Flowers and out-of-season vegetables are flown across the world. Parts for the assembly of cars or computers are brought in from a variety of places on a 'just-in-time' basis.

As some countries try to reduce the greenhouse gases that are poured into the air from power stations or vehicles, more recently industrializing countries continue to rely on fossil fuels with high levels of pollution. The most profligate users of energy are often the least efficient economies, especially those of Eastern Europe emerging from a command economy.

The emissions from the power plants, from vehicles and aircraft are the chief contributors of the gases which are affecting our atmosphere and leading to global warming. The Kyoto Protocol has sought to address the issue by a mixture of both regulatory measures and market-based incentives such as emissions trading between countries.

One of the problems with the Kyoto Protocol has been its perceived unfairness, locking into place for decades to come the advantages of the 'haves' and the disadvantages of the 'have-nots'. The Global Commons Institute has developed a scheme to deal with climate change on a global basis. It claims to be both comprehensive and fair. This global framework is referred to as 'contraction and convergence'. Briefly, this states that climate change is a global problem driven by over-consumption, and which results in the burden of its consequences being unequally borne. It is proposed that there should be a global contraction of carbon emissions. The fairest way to work towards this is to allocate the right to emissions on the basis of equal per capita shares. Participating states would fix a long-term target for total global greenhouse gas emission and the necessary cuts in emissions required to meet it (contraction). They would then adopt the principle of according every person in the world an equal entitlement to emit greenhouse gases by a certain date – perhaps between 2030-2050 – so that a country's emission limits would, by then, be determined by its population. In the transitional period a global market in emissions would transfer resources to poor countries that have surplus emission allowances and force rich countries to drive down their emissions by applying the technologies developed for a post-carbon age. Clearly, the reduction in emissions caused by the heaviest polluters will have to be very dramatic indeed. But this is precisely the kind of challenge that a prosperous society is equipped to meet; its capacity to innovate in the market-place is its greatest strength. Again, the somewhat sceptical Bjørn Lomborg has calculated that the costs of addressing the problem of global warming are not great; it is essentially imagination and political will that is lacking.

The scheme 'contract and converge' is bold and far reaching, and above all equitable. It does not polarize the world between rich and poor, North and South in the way that the Kyoto negotiations have done. Embraced fully and managed creatively this scheme could help towards new technology for a low carbon emission world. Some such global approach to the problem, more radical and effective than Kyoto, must be embraced. In the meantime, piecemeal approaches must suffice.

Transport, for example, is not free from governmental interference. Air transport is a particular case in point. Carbon emissions released above the cloud level has double the impact than that released below and bizarrely emissions from international air travel do not count in terms of the cuts required for the Kyoto targets. In the case of airline fuel, there is a hidden subsidy as the usual fuel taxes are not levied. Whether for passengers or for freight, air transport is more attractive than the more environmentally friendly rail because of that hidden fuel subsidy. Here government regulation can have a great impact in moving the situation toward a more level playing field, which would allow the more environmentally efficient forms of transport to compete for business and would be a catalyst to technological innovation. The shortest and most direct solution to the problem would be to increase oil prices sharply, and then use the accruing revenues to solve environmental problems. That seems, however, beyond the realm of political possibility. Governments are more likely to accept a degree of agreed external regulation, which requires it to make hard choices of the oil price increase sort. Despite its weaknesses, the Kyoto Protocol has indicated that this approach is viable.

Secondly, in the production of energy, the 'externalities' involved are not usually factored in to the costs. This is largely because the problems arising from global warming in the form of floods or droughts are borne not by those who contribute to the warming but by totally innocent 'third parties', not to mention future generations who clearly cannot express their desires through the market mechanism. Greenhouse gases pumped into the air in large quantities by power stations in the US and Europe, for example, contribute to rising temperatures which in turn melt the icecaps, raise the sea level and cause flooding in low-lying areas of the world – coastal Bangladesh and the islands of the Pacific (as noted above) to name but two.

It is generally recognized that Britain urgently needs a new energy policy and not only because of climate change considerations. As our oil and gas production reduces and we face the fact that we have become a net energy importer, we need to face issues of energy reliability and the updating of our energy infrastructure. Again these challenges are also opportunities to be seized, for they open up the possibility of developing leading-edge technologies for a low carbon economy with their export potential.

There is a clear need for the privatized energy companies and the energy regulator, OFGEM, to see the long-term future of British industry in terms of diverse sources of energy, for example many local small combined heat and power facilities (CHP), photovoltaics and a variety of renewable sources from which the surplus capacity may be sold to the grid. Most difficult of all is the need to decide whether nuclear energy has a future as an emissions-free source of power. The costs and risks involved make this energy source deeply problematic. It carries obvious environmental hazards, though these may be overstated. As a recent report on radioactive waste management from the House of Lords' Science and Technology Committee says: 'the small uncertainties associated with radioactive waste disposal that still exist must be balanced against the spectre of global warming.' It also needs to be said that the generation of nuclear power is not attractive to the high-tech entrepreneur seeking to make a profit, as the costs arise soon, and the benefits accrue late. Nuclear power is a political issue which is continually avoided, not least by environmentalists and by the Churches. It is very clear, however, that it will be extremely difficult to reduce our emissions level in Britain and in Europe in line with our Kyoto pledges, let alone to the level really needed, unless nuclear-generated power is part of the solution.

Central to the future market framework will be the existence of a carbon trading scheme. By setting caps on emissions the scheme will provide clear incentives for investment in energy efficiency and cleaner technologies at the lowest cost. These technologies will not just be for the energy industry itself but for the building industry as it seeks to raise the standard of energy efficiency in both new buildings and refurbishments thus contributing to the lowering of demand for energy – one of the most overlooked factors that can contribute to the reduction of our energy consumption and thus of emissions.

Even within British cities the true costs of vast numbers of cars and lorries and the congestion they cause are only now beginning to be realized, and then only in those places where the costs have become so unbearable that the encouragement of public transport over private has become (almost?) politically sustainable. Most people have no idea of the effect of vehicle emissions on their health nor of the cost to the economy and the health service. Governments fear to challenge motorists because of the short-term electoral cycle. The Church has no such constraints and is able to face people with the consequences of their own lifestyles and communal trends.

The issue of transport is a good place from which to shift focus from the way that firms operate to the lifestyle of individuals. In Britain we live in a society of conspicuous consumption driven not by basic needs but by the desire to cut a particular image. Advertising keeps us buying but is also driven by a need for companies to sustain production and therefore employment. Desirable as changes in our pattern of consumption are, they cannot be achieved overnight without considerable adjustment to the whole economic system.

Let us return to the issue of transport by way of illustration. Cars, par excellence, are the status markers in our society. Those people who drive huge 4x4 vehicles around our cities are often trying to make a statement about their affluence and standing in society. Cars are marketed on their qualities of speed and acceleration, versatility and elegance. But driving in London or any large city is another experience. Speeds are scarcely higher than they were in the early 20th century because of congestion, and the parking of vehicles is a nightmare and a costly one. Hundreds of individual decisions to buy and drive cars make the roads so congested that driving becomes an ordeal for all.

As prosperity has allowed people to consume so much more there is also the realization that well-being and quality of life are not improved by ever increasing individual consumption. As people seek for increased 'quality of life' there is a realization that it is fresh air and green parks, crime free streets and clean seas that really add quality; for most people, these things cannot be bought but are public goods.

As advertising is so good at persuading us to buy what we do not need, what possibilities there might be if the force of advertising could be harnessed to show people how they could contribute to the communal quality of life by the nature of their purchases, by the activities they pursue and the work they are willing to do. As the nature of employment changes there will be the need for society to value and pay for all those services which contribute to enhanced 'quality of life' – care of the very young and the very old, visiting in the community and work to improve the environment. All of this will demand a radical shift in society's priorities. But we are living at a time when those who are prosperous are beginning to realize the value of public goods and to appreciate that individual choice is no choice if the structure and cohesion of society is falling apart. The Church should be well placed to articulate a vision of shared values for communal living. Sustainable development is not just trying to ensure that our human lifestyles do not jeopardize the future of the planet and of future generations, but should embrace an ideal of fulfillment of human potential for people the world over.

Christians make their most significant contribution to environmental improvement by their engagement with the political process, in its broadest sense. We are involved as consumers, as workers, as strategic players in the economy, as civil servants and as politicians. But the Churches have a distinctive attachment to buildings, so as institutions and as congregations in their localities they need to consider their environmental impact and provide examples of good environmental practice in the communities where they are set. Many churches already house 'fair trade' shops or have recycling bins on their premises. Good environmental practice needs to be taken into the bloodstream of the churches – including the use and maintenance of the grounds, the efficient use of water and electricity and the responsible sourcing of supplies. Perhaps most importantly, we need to consume environmentally friendly energy wherever possible. The Christian environmental agency Eco-Congregation has been engaged in this area for some years now. The Churches campaign to encourage a switch to green energy supplies, Operation Noah, is a more recent example of this activity. In addition, Churches need to think about where they hold meetings and how they transport people to services and other events.

The Churches have a long and honourable history of engagement with the issues of social justice. Poverty remains a worldwide scourge, although many millions of people now enjoy a share in modern prosperity. The Churches have become much clearer about the kind of global governance which can combine an expanding market with the hope of social justice. We are much less familiar with the urgent environmental questions that confront the planet, and we must learn with others how to be more intelligent and persistent in our pursuit of environmental integrity.

Recommendations

1. That the British Government should embrace the concept of 'contract and converge' as currently the most effective and fair global solution to the addressing of the problem of climate change and that other policies for a low-carbon economy be set within this wider framework.

2. That the British Government should produce a new energy policy for the UK based not on short-term delivery of cheap energy to the consumer but on a long-term policy of diversity and security of energy sources and of low carbon emissions through a mix of renewables, nuclear energy, new clean plant and the integration of locally produced power into the national grid.

3. That the British Government – in collaboration with commerce, industry, the academic and voluntary sector – should set the regulatory framework for the limiting of carbon emissions, develop fiscal instruments to reward companies that reduce emissions and develop innovative, clean processes and continue to refine emissions trading possibilities.

6

The political economy of poverty and prosperity: Niall Cooper

A tale of two fêtes

At the primary school my children attend in inner Manchester, several parents worked hard to organize a traditional summer fayre, with games, stalls, raffle and home cooked cakes. After a hard, but enjoyable Saturday, all involved were pleased to have raised around £300. Later in the same week, I spoke to a close relative, who had just been to a fundraising auction at their eldest child's school – a private prep school in North London. Up under the hammer was a week at a couple's holiday home in France, a tour of the BBC newsroom, a month's worth of free flowers... The result of one evening's fundraising? £30,000.

Things have got better

The UK has had virtually ten years of continuous economic growth. As a nation we are more prosperous than ever before (measured in terms of GDP). There are record numbers of people in work, although working the longest hours in Europe. Unemployment is at the lowest level it has been for more than 25 years. The British situation, for good and ill, contrasts quite dramatically with the outlook in much of the rest of Europe. The prospects for growing prosperity, and increasingly shared prosperity, need to be looked at in a wider European context. The continental achievement in creating more widely spread public amenity stands in stark contrast to the more modest British levels of attainment. But the various continental systems of public provision are in serious crisis in many areas, and indicate the limits to improvement for which the British hope.

Prosperity, poverty and European Union public policy

The social policies of the European member states are many and various. A common policy exists mainly in important areas of employment. But in health, education and pensions, state sovereignty rules and enlargement makes it likely that this will continue. These areas are not greatly susceptible to the 'Community Method' which imagines common policies proposed by the Commission, then debated and agreed by the Commission and the Parliament.

Welfare systems are hugely different, and increasingly expensive. They account for the great bulk of public expenditure in the EU, which ranges from 30% of GDP in the Republic of Ireland to over 50% in Germany and Sweden (though we are warned by a recent OECD study to take great care in interpreting such figures). Gosta Esping-Andersen, among others, has categorized this bewildering variety of systems for welfare provision. But one factor is common to them all. They are underpinned by that dynamic, innovative economy, allowing for high tax yields and a commitment to sharing wealth as widely as possible.

The British have opted for a very cautious relationship with Europe, and a markedly different welfare model, sharing more with the Anglo-Saxon world than with its EU partners. Britain was the world's first large-scale commercial society, yet one which failed subsequently to reach European levels of economic growth, or to attain the level of social provision which many continental Europeans have done, as indicated above. It could be claimed that the UK fails to reach acceptable levels of health care, vocational training and pension provision.

Britain's levels of productivity are low, and hours worked are high. Low-paid jobs are plentiful, and there is a high level of employment, and of participation in employment.

Britain has the highest proportion of funded pensions in Europe, making the richest retired people the best off in Europe. But Britain suffers the worst public pensions system of the rich European countries. It now transpires that private pensions may perform much less well than has been the case since this kind of enterprise burgeoned 40 years ago. No system can escape the vulnerability that arises from increased longevity and a declining working-age population. But the British case is one in which state provision has become scandalous, and private provision has become problematic, squeezed by erratic investment performance and adverse tax changes.

The projected levels of cost in these areas are truly fearsome, whether British or Continental. Yet citizens of many member states are naturally unwilling to vote for the changes that would move the burden of provision from the state to the individual. The politics of France and of Germany have been racked by this issue for over a decade now.

The broad European picture is hugely diverse, with each state taking different routes to achieve prosperity, offering different levels of public provision in quite different social models. Each of these social models has a distinctive origin in a particular Christian context. As the global economy tests Europe's capacity for wealth-creation ever more sharply, each member state, old or new, is likely to pursue differing methods to sustain desired levels of social inclusion, while seeking to ensure that those aspirations are sustainable, both economically and politically.

UK public policy

In common with most other major developed economies, policies addressing the well-being of citizens in the UK are being framed with a greater recognition of the interdependence of both the social problems being dealt with and the policy solutions offered. Progress is being made towards addressing people's problems in a more integrated manner, rather than through a piecemeal approach, which at times in the past has turned out to be poorly co-ordinated. Some of the key areas are discussed further below.

Government has also shared with the churches a recognition of the positive role that work can play in the lives of its citizens and society as a whole. Work has the potential to draw individuals into constructive economic and social relationships. It is also a vehicle for individuals to make their contribution to the betterment of society and to be rewarded for doing so. Work is the means by which individual talents and aspirations come together to find their place in a common creative purpose. It is above all one of the most important ways in which people achieve meaning, as individuals, as families, and as members of a wider social enterprise.

Welfare to Work programme

The Government elected in 1997 has shown some recognition of these points. Its election saw a new and more positive approach being taken to tackling poverty and social exclusion. Since 1997, the Government has made a series of policy commitments in relation to tackling child poverty, social exclusion and promoting work as the best route out of poverty.

That Government embarked on a major 'Welfare to Work'

programme and established a new 'Social Exclusion Unit'. Most strikingly however, in March 1999 Tony Blair committed the Government to 'abolish child poverty within a generation'.

The Welfare to Work programme has, in many ways, been the central plank of the Government's anti-poverty strategy. In contrast to more traditional Labour welfare based approaches, its central tenet is that 'work is the best route out of poverty', and has therefore focussed resources on increasing the skills and employability of individuals, and creating financial and other incentives to work. This has included large scale employment and training programmes for under 25 year olds, lone parents, disabled people and the over 50s under the overall heading of the 'New Deal'. Government has also sought to increase work incentives by introducing a National Minimum Wage (£4.85 an hour from October 2004) and Tax Credits to boost the wages of low to middle income earners. In addition, the 'SureStart' programme has directed substantial resources at providing early interventions and support to families with children under five. These policies seek to address some of the problems highlighted in ***Unemployment and the Future of Work.***

Responses to social exclusion

The establishment of the Social Exclusion Unit was a significant sign of the Government's commitment to address a number of deep-seated social issues, foremost of which has been the situation facing people living in many of Britain's deprived urban neighbourhoods. On most of the more disadvantaged estates in Britain community resources are very poor. Many shops have withdrawn from poor areas and banks do not exist. Levels of crime and violence are very high and public spaces are often run-down and degraded.

The Government has sought to address these issues through a ten year 'National Strategy for Neighbourhood Renewal'. Although co-ordinated by a national 'Neighbourhood Renewal Unit' and in part funded centrally, the programme is intended to be delivered by 88 'Local Strategic Partnerships' that seek to co-ordinate the efforts of central and local government, private, voluntary, faith and community sector organisations. Alongside the commitment to partnership, there is also a growing interest in the ideas of 'social capital' and 'community empowerment':

Investing in the human and social capital of marginalized individuals and groups enables them to develop the capacities needed to thrive, and to play an autonomous role in developing and renewing their communities.[17]

But there is still much to do

In spite of the Government's efforts, there has been only limited success in reducing child poverty. The number of children living in poor households was 3.6 million in 2002/03, which represents a drop of 700,000 since 1997. In 2001, a child had a one in three chance of being in a household living on less than 60 percent of average (median) income, compared with a one in seven chance in 1979.[18]

In 2002/03, 12.5 million people were living on incomes of less than 60% of median household income. In spite of record levels of employment, 70% of poor people continue to rely only on state benefits for their income.[19] Women are 14% more likely than males to live in households with incomes below 60% of the median. But the real number of women living in poverty is likely to be far higher. Government figures reveal that almost half of all women have total individual incomes of less than £100 per week, compared with less than a fifth of men.[20] Poverty also disproportionately affects members of black and ethnic minority communities, disabled people, older people and those living in London and other major urban centres.[21]

Stubbornly unequal: wages and incomes

The last twenty years has also seen a massive shift in the structure of the labour market in the UK. Both the nature of work and the types of jobs have changed as the importance of the male dominated manufacturing sector and heavy industry declines and the numbers in the female dominant service sector increase. The number of full-time permanent jobs has decreased while the number of part-time and short-term contracts grow as the labour market moves towards ever greater flexibility. Women's increasing involvement in the labour market has not raised household income as much as might be expected, because women tend to work in lower paid jobs and to work for fewer hours than men. 3.5

million poor people live in working households. There are more working poor than there are unemployed people, or poor pensioners. People work hard for long hours, and in the absence of a living wage, still fall below the poverty line.[22]

Wages for the lowest paid workers have barely increased at all in twenty years, whereas for those near the top of the earnings distribution, they rose sixty percent in real terms.[23]

At the same time, wealth inequality has increased substantially. Between 1988 and 1999 the top one per cent of the population has increased their share of personal wealth from 17 to 23 per cent. The top 2.4 million households own wealth to the tune of £1,300bn, while the bottom 12 million households own only £150m.[24]

Income equality has grown substantially since the 1970s. During the period 1994/5 to 2001/02 the incomes of the richest fifth of the population continued to increase relative to those at the bottom. Whilst wage and income inequality has now stopped rising, it stubbornly refuses to decline, in spite of the Government's commitment to tackle poverty.

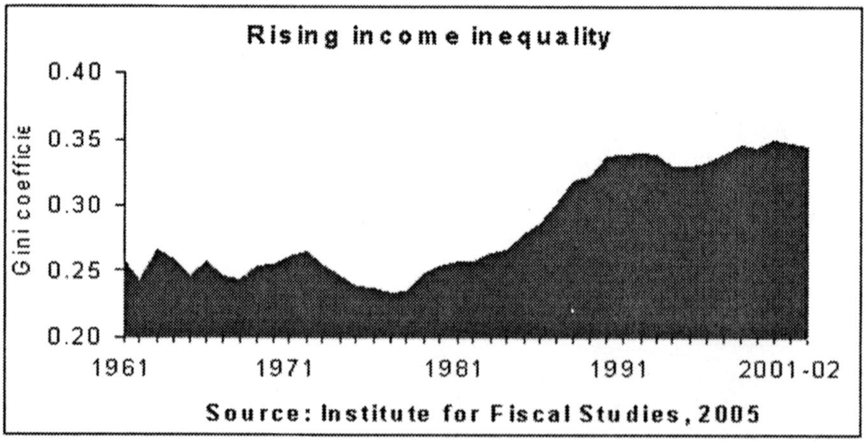

The minimum wage (£4.85 per hour from October 2004) has improved the living standards of lower-paid families with children – but many still remain in poverty. Even with the assistance of the Working Families Tax Credit, families still fall short of a 'low-cost but acceptable budget' (See Policy Issues, below). Even for a full-time job, this equates to less than the European decency threshold of 60% of average earnings (roughly £10,000 a year).

'I work as a cleaner/porter in a hospital. I worked 36½ hours last week, and after tax etc., my take-home pay was £131.' Belfast.

In spite of the strength of the economy significant levels of unemployment persist in many areas of the country. The Government's existing employment programmes, which focus on increasing the 'employability' of the long-term unemployed are of limited value in areas where there are simply not enough jobs to go round.

A survey by the United Reformed Church[25] in 2002 found that the number of job vacancies reportedly available is significantly over-estimated, and that the Government's claim that there were a million job vacancies available cannot be supported. In 40 local authority areas across the UK, unemployment persists at more than twice the national average.

The persistence of economic inactivity and regional inequalities

Worklessness – or economic inactivity – continues to be a major cause of poverty. The number of people of working age who are economically inactive but would like work has remained stable at around 2.5 million people and the proportion of households none of whose members work has fallen only from 18% to 16% since 1997. The energy and drive that went into the original New Deal programmes for young people and lone parents have not been followed by similar successes in encouraging the growing numbers on long-term sickness and disability benefits to take work, in spite of surveys which repeatedly show large numbers of them wish to work.[26]

There are also huge and growing regional disparities in economic activity, income and wealth. Upwards of 25/% of men and 40% of women are 'economically inactive' in the areas worst hit by long-term economic decline – Knowsley in Merseyside, Merthyr Tydfil in South Wales. The regional imbalance in terms of GDP is greater in the UK than in other EU countries and getting wider.

Progress on regenerating poorer neighbourhoods has been slow – partly because community involvement takes time, partly because of uneven delivery capacity, and partly because of polarisation in terms of neighbourliness, civic engagement and trust.

The emergence of debt and financial exclusion

A further emerging issue of concern in relation to poverty in Britain is the growth in household debt amongst low-income families. This is especially problematic for families with children, with limited or no access to credit at reasonable rates. These people have very few, or no savings and are vulnerable to any kind of crisis or shock.

Local markets have a tendency to opt for the rich. The National Consumer Council has documented how people in poverty pay more to access a range of goods and services within the market. It found that in relation to the utilities (energy, water and telephones) in particular, affordability problems are created by the poor having to pay more. They do so because they prefer or are stuck with payment methods and supplies which are expensive; they need to use more of the utilities than most; and market-driven supply is insufficient as a means of ensuring affordable access since providers have insufficient incentives to design services that benefit low-income consumers.[27]

Citizens Advice Bureaux reported a 47% growth in debt problems over a five year period to May 2003, whilst almost 8 million people are systematically refused access to mainstream credit. This has led to a growth in legal, but largely unregulated, money-lending businesses. Over 3 million people regularly borrow money from doorstep lenders, frequently at rates of interest in excess of 170% apr.[28] In the words of one woman who attended a Church Action on Poverty Policy Forum on debt in 2001:

> *'I have a fifteen year old daughter and she needs clothes so I have to get a Provi loan or vouchers. It's hard. At the end of my benefit I've nothing left to pay back the loan and vouchers. I can't spend money on shopping and bills.'*[29]

These challenges are discussed further in 'Policy Issues' below.

The impact of poverty

These levels of poverty put untold pressures on family life. Poorer parents have frequently been shown to try to protect their child from poverty – often by going without themselves. Nila is an articulate Asian woman, married with three young children, who spoke at Church Action on Poverty's National Poverty Hearing in 1996. For her – and thousands of families like hers – the consequences have been devastating: redundancy; poverty; debt; mortgage arrears; homelessness:

> *'Eventually the building society repossessed the house, and we found ourselves at the mercy of the housing department. On the morning we were due to move I sent my son to school as normal. He asked me where we would be sleeping that night and I had no answer to give. We had been through rough times before. I had always had an answer, and explanation. I had never lied to him. The look in his eyes as he refused to look into mine haunts me still.'* [30]

Constraints on future policy

There are clear grounds for optimism in the achievements that have been made in recent years, and in the increasing degree of consensus across the political spectrum on the need to tackle poverty and disadvantage.[31] However, the challenges and constraints on future policy making should not be underestimated.

Economic constraints

A more active role for in tackling poverty does of course require there to be additional resources for the Government to deploy. But in order to generate the wealth needed to address the issue of poverty, an economy is needed which provides sufficient incentive for the entrepreneur to thrive. The temptation is to identify additional public expenditure without identifying the extra cost in taxation; even if the proposals are costed, there is the risk of assuming additional taxation can be levied without any adverse change in the behaviour of the taxed.

Increases in both direct taxes on income and indirect taxes on expenditure can affect economic decisions at the margin and create incentives for individuals and businesses to organize their affairs to reduce the impact of those taxes. This manifests itself in several ways, especially in a globalized society: the growth of the cash economy and cross-border journeys to purchase goods subject to high indirect taxation, such as alcohol and tobacco,; the relocation of successful businesspeople and corporate head offices in response to income tax differentials; and the organization of corporate affairs to book profits where the impact of corporate taxation is least. Beyond a certain point, these consequences can potentially threaten to subdue the growth in prosperity that enables effective action against poverty.

This is not to say that increases in taxation are out of the question, nor to suggest that the tax regime cannot be improved; indeed later in this essay we identify examples of both. However, in any overall policy strategy it is important to have regard to the impact of the way any policy options are funded. Equally, it is not acceptable to allow the market freedom to exacerbate trends in inequality.

The English and Welsh Catholic Bishops' Conference statement, ***The Common Good***, was clear on the deficiencies of the market in relation to tackling poverty. Although the market is clearly strong on wealth-creation, its appeal to self-interest had to be set against wider social goals represented by the notion of the 'Common Good'. The same Conference offered further analysis and guidance in 2004 in ***Taxation for the Common Good***, in which it highlighted the essential contribution of a range of tax-financed services to the effective functioning of a complex modern economy. It concluded:

Taxation is neither a burden nor a necessary evil; but as a positive contribution to the common good, it is a responsibility of citizenship.[32]

Maintaining or improving the UK's global competitiveness to ensure continued high levels of investment and employment, is a significant driver of economic and social policy. The need to ensure labour market flexibility constantly has to be balanced against the demand for stronger labour rights. In a different context, it might be argued that the Government's welfare to work policies are as much driven by the need to ensure a continuing flow of new workers into the labour market as with meeting the needs of the workers themselves. UK productivity remains lower than in many other countries, though the labour productivity growth rate has been steadily increasing.

The Government's No. 10 Policy Unit has fairly made the point that there is no settled view of the keys to national performance. A lot depends on history, the effectiveness of institutions, demography and geography,

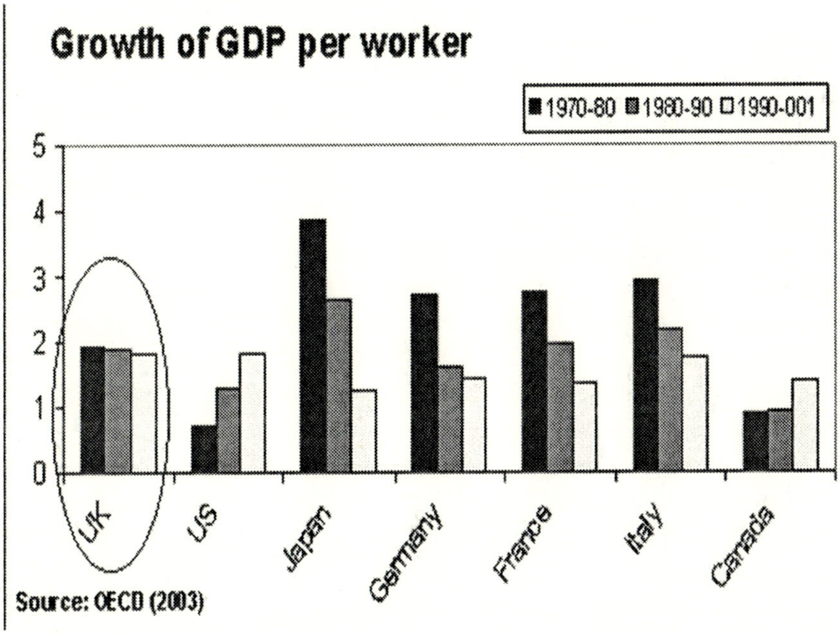

leadership and luck. However, much of the recent theory on growth and well-being focusses on a relatively limited number of factors which can all be seen in today's best performers across the world. First, open competitive markets and open competitive democracies – systems which tend to reward continuous innovation and continuous improvements in performance. The front-runners all have low external barriers, competitive markets, internationally oriented businesses and deeply entrenched democratic cultures. Second, high levels of human and social capital – which together ensure that new knowledge is learned, shared, and applied efficiently in business and public services. The front-runners tend to have high investment in public services; high social trust; high social mobility; high investment in science.[33]

Political constraints

The political constraints on the Government's ability to tackle poverty and inequality are possibly even greater than the economic constraints. The political importance of 'Worcester Woman' and 'Mondeo Man' have been well articulated in recent years. Such archetypes represent the political and electoral power of 'Middle England': the vested interests of the articulate and comfortable majority.

JK Galbraith has identified this as the 'culture of contentment'.[34] He suggests that Western society has reached a point where the social and political wish to retain short-term contentment overrides any wish to accept and act upon the deeper problems within our society. Anything that threatens contentment is undesirable to the political majority. It is a political disaster to be really honest about the deeper social, economic and environmental problems that seriously threaten contentment, because people won't vote for the truth if it threatens their contentment – they would rather live in a world of blissful ignorance. So we see an all too obvious process of social and political denial and avoidance.

Set against this is the increasing geographical and social invisibility of the poor. In the work that Church Action on Poverty (CAP) has done with people in poverty over recent years, one theme that consistently crops up is the way in which poor people in today's society feel 'invisible'. Peoples' own direct experiences of poverty, and their own attitudes and ideas about what can be done to tackle it are held to be of no value whatsoever. In the words of Wayne Green, another speaker at CAP's National Poverty Hearing in 1996:

> *What is poverty? Poverty is a battle of invisibility, a lack of resources, exclusion, powerlessness ... being blamed for society's problems.*[35]

In consequence, Nicholas Timmins, writing for the Joseph Rowntree Foundation has argued that:

> '*Recent history suggests public spending in the UK remains fixed by an iron electoral law which rules that it will not rise much above 40 to 42% of GDP... This heavily limits the room for straightforward redistribution.*'[36]

While this may be true for the average politician, the Churches do not need to feel similarly constrained. This essay goes on to identify some challenges that may not be popular elsewhere, or may even be thought politically difficult.

Policy issues

In the 60 years since the Second World War we have become a much more prosperous society than ever before. The benefits of the successful development of both the economy and our way of life are being spread more and more widely through society. The majority of us are moving further and further away from subsistence; we now enjoy ever-broadening discretion over how we spend our money and live our lives.

This increasing prosperity presents us with both an opportunity and a responsibility to share its benefits more fairly among all members of society. With continuing prosperity, our capacity to do this can only increase further in the years ahead. Promoting growth with fairness and sharing our future economic and social prosperity more equitably should be a key goal of economic policy. In part, this springs directly from our moral responsibility as members of society. But a moment's reflection on the costs of deprivation and disengagement – reactions to exclusion, vandalism, crime, conflict – indicates that a fairer and more inclusive society also offers the potential to improve further our prosperity in its widest sense, through reducing these costs and increasing the potential of society as a whole.

Against this background the remainder of this essay identifies five specific policy issues, which offer the potential to promote greater fairness, in terms of wealth, income and opportunity, as part of a broader strategy for tackling poverty and social exclusion in the years ahead. The summaries of the policy issues offered here are based on the work of a range of faith and non-faith based think-tanks, researchers and indeed, people who themselves have first-hand experience of poverty and exclusion. A strong economy and equity are not inconsistent. The Joseph Rowntree Foundation has shown that in principle it is possible to tackle relative poverty over 20 years by diverting a relatively small percentage of economic growth to poorer groups.

Our objectives in putting forward these five policy areas constitute a demand for social justice. They are as follows. First, an increase in the National Minimum Wage, and promoting wage restraint among higher income earners. Second, more equal access to markets, and market intervention and regulation which favour the poor. Third, a more even sharing of risks through state action on pension provision. Fourth, a more positive attitude to the virtues of taxation and the public sector. Fifth, the empowerment of people as members of communities rather than merely as consumers. Underlying all these is a broad concern to ensure a balance between fairness, sustainability (environmental and social) and growth, rather than seeking growth at all costs. The constraints on future policy discussed earlier in this essay are also relevant in designing policy actions.

This is not an exhaustive list of policy issues, but they illustrate the nature of a society that could be both more just and more efficient. Some, for example, might wish to advance policies to promote the well-being of children. Nor do we offer proposals sufficiently precisely defined to justify detailed costing. This is deliberate. However, it is acknowledged that in each case action to address these issues will involve costs and might therefore lead to some increases in taxation. It is left to the political parties to make judgements about the combination of new policies, tax adjustments and cost-savings elsewhere that will best serve society's interests. Our policy issues are:

- Minimum income standards
- Poverty and low pay
- Debt and financial exclusion
- Ending Pensioner poverty
- Taxation and the common good

Issue one: the establishment of transparent minimum income standards to inform benefit policies

Income is an essential measure of poverty. An objectively-determined set of minimum income standards allows benefit levels (and tax band thresholds) to be debated and decided in the light of the levels of income necessary to meet reasonable basic needs.

Background

'Budget standards' are set by costing a defined basket of goods and services, which are regarded as the minimum necessary for a representative household to maintain a basic standard of living. This approach allows the goods and services comprising the basket to be listed, described, understood, quantified, priced and adapted to fit different sets of circumstances. The standards represent living standards across the life cycle that are transparent. They have been available for many decades.

Budget standards are valuable because the judgements involved in setting the levels are less arbitrary than other existing or proposed ways of fixing thresholds. Such work can also deliver a range of other information about quantities needed and prices to be paid by low-income households crucial to the monitoring of progress and to sound policy formation. For example, the cost of some items is higher for the poor – their housing costs often exceed housing benefit and they have to pay more for utilities, phones and loans – and living costs, especially housing costs, vary regionally.

Modern budget standards methodologies involve empirical and scientific effort to justify what items are included, their quantities, durability and retail prices. They use official standards for both nutrition and heating. They use consumer surveys on patterns of consumption. They use focus groups and other methods to validate the judgements made. They can be triangulated with other relevant research to validate judgements and set minimum incomes standards. Hunger and poor diet, poverty-related ill-health and stress, and the growing burden of debt are not properly addressed by policies based on current or proposed measures of poverty.

Minimum income standards are set in a number of countries – for example Norway, Sweden, Germany and Canada – and have been influential in policy in a number of others – for example the Netherlands, Australia, and the US.

There are some particular considerations that arise in using budget standards in practice and a few of these are outlined in the following paragraphs.

Setting budgets

It is readily apparent that households in different circumstances might have very different basic requirements. Particularly important in the policy framework is the need to ensure that *children* are adequately provided for and have the opportunity to grow up as fully participating members of society. Aside from the crucial question of whether children are present in the household or not, however, there are a number of other ***household-specific*** factors that should be taken into account in setting the budget standard to be used. These include:

- Whether the beneficiary is a long-term recipient of benefit (e.g. pension; sickness benefit) or a short-term recipient (e.g. unemployment benefit)
- The composition of the household concerned (e.g. number of adults and number of children)
- The stage of the life cycle the household has reached

Setting benefits

The aim of minimum income standards is to inform benefits policies, rather than to remove policy discretion over benefit levels, by determining objectively a 'decency threshold' that allows households to meet a basic standard. They should not remove from the policy debate considerations about *entitlement* for support, nor about *conditionality* of benefits. However minimum income standards serve to make clear the implications of setting benefits below the budget standard relevant to the household concerned.

In this context, it is interesting to note that the international covenant on Economic, Social and Cultural Rights, to which the UK is a signatory, includes 'The right of everyone to be free from hunger'. Nevertheless laws have been introduced that deliberately make certain UK citizens and asylum-seekers totally destitute, with state support for both at destitution level.

Adjusting standards over time

The budget standards – and the baskets of goods and services underlying them – can be re-based from time to time to keep pace with changes in social needs, technology and tastes. In between times it is now arguable that benefit levels should be upgraded by earnings indexes rather than price indexes. This would be an appropriate way of sharing increasing prosperity more widely.

Potential action

Official transparent, published minimum income standards could help focus policies targeting poverty. If their basis of calculation and their levels are clearly specified, then they will add constructively to the public debate about how best to help the least well off in our society. It is arguable that they could be most useful if they were compiled and maintained by a body independent of government. The success of the Low Pay Commission in its field points to one potential role model.

Issue two: low pay and poverty

Government and employers should recognize that at its current level, the national minimum wage is not sufficient to lift many households out of poverty. Our society should be working towards paying the overwhelming majority of employees a socially responsible living wage.

Background

Low pay and increasing inequalities in income and wealth remain central obstacles to the achievement of the Government's commitment to end child poverty. The TUC's 2003 submission to the Treasury Review on Child Poverty points out that there have been marked changes in the proportion of various types of household living in poverty.[37] In 1968 24% of households with just one person working in a low paid job were poor. In 1996 that proportion had risen to 53%. By contrast poverty among the workless and pensioners, although high, had hardly increased over the period.

The 1998 Acheson Report (***An Independent Inquiry into Inequalities and Health***), noted:

> *'Average incomes grew in real terms by about 40% between 1979 and 1994/5, but this growth was far greater (60-68%) amongst the richest 10% of the population. For the poorest 10% average income increased by only 10% (before housing costs) or fell by 8% (after them)'*

The growing dispersion of wages is a major factor underlying the increasing relative poverty of those in work. For every year since at least 1987 the earnings of the top decile of full-time workers have been increasing faster than those of the bottom decile (***Social Trends***, 2003, Figure 5.6). This has had a very marked and cumulative effect on income dispersion. It also translates into growing differentials in wealth. Between 1981 and 2000 the share of marketable wealth (disregarding dwellings) held by the richest 10% increased from 56% to 72% (***Social Trends***, 2003,Table 5.26).

Work on budget standards (see Issue One for an explanation) has estimated Low Cost but Acceptable (LCA) standards in certain locations. A comparison of the LCA studies carried out so far [38] and the latest figures from the New Earnings Survey illustrate the shortfall between the income of substantial proportions of the population nationally and the income necessary to live at LCA level in the various areas studied:

	LCA level updated to early 2004 (hourly) (2 adult household, 1 working FT, 1 PT)*	Approximate % of FT adult workers below this (NES)
York	£5.80	12%
East London	£6.83	25%
Swansea	£5.78	12%
Brighton and Hove	£6.51	22%

** assumes a 37½ hour full-time (FT) working week*

LCA is a stringent level. The adverse health and other consequences of living below this level, and the costs this must impose on various public budgets, were spelled out in the Brighton and Hove study.[39] In this case, and in other high cost areas, particularly around London, the national minimum wage affords virtually no protection. On this evidence a very significant proportion of the working population are living at earnings levels that pose a threat to health and social inclusion and produce heavy cost consequences for the national economy. Various types of job are characterized by low pay:

Job type	Typical range of hourly pay rates
Care Assistant	£4.31 to £6.33
Catering Assistant	£4.20 to £7.15 (night shift)
Cleaner	£4.31 to £5.80
Nursery Nurse	£4.15 to £5.60
Restaurant Worker	£4.20 to £6.01 (supervisor)
Sales Assistant	£4.20 to £7.63

Source: www.idspaybenchmark.co.uk/payjobs/prod/jobslistresults

Most of these jobs are done predominantly by women.[40] In some of these cases the entire range of hourly rates shown falls below the LCA levels identified in the studies and in others it is necessary to work anti-social hours to reach this level.

There is a cost to the Treasury of supplementing the low pay of employers. Nationally the proportion of working families in receipt of in-work benefits and credits has risen from about 3% in 1994 to nearly 8% in 2002.[41] To escape the poverty trap altogether and avoid very high marginal tax rates for the household, a weekly income of £435 is required for a two adult plus two children household (data from the Department of Work and Pensions, April 2003). The best evidence available for the Brighton and Hove area indicates that between 20% and 25% of local households are living below this income level and are thus caught in the poverty trap.

A recent initiative by TELCO, a community-based organization in east London, has achieved some striking results.[42] The organization draws attention to the huge local disparity in incomes and living standards between many working in the finance sector itself and most of those providing essential support services to that sector in the cleaning, catering, maintenance and security sectors. Some banks are offering new graduates starting salaries of up to £35,000, while their cleaning staff and other support workers typically earn between £4.50 and £6.00 per hour. TELCO also draws attention to the marked ethnically based differentiation in incomes, the difficulty of finding low rent housing and the problems faced by local schools.

TELCO have had marked success in persuading some employers to pay their support staff at rates which enable them to meet basic living costs without means tested benefits. In practice a 'socially responsible' contract for support workers in 2003 would have needed to specify a 'living wage' of £6.70 per hour (the figure derived from the East London LCA study in 2001, updated to 2003 for inflation), plus other additional benefits (e.g. an employer pension contribution). TELCO's work raises the question whether public funds, in the form of tax credits, should be subsidizing low pay for profitable companies.

Against this background, it is recognized that a minimum wage is a 'blunt instrument' at the margin against poverty and that to set it to support adequately the least skilled single parent with children will lead to too high a benchmark, with attendant risks of job losses and undue compression of skill differentials. Some element of benefit support is always likely to be necessary for a minority of working adults in greatest need. However this does not undermine the argument for a meaningful real increase in the national minimum wage from its current levels.

Potential action

There is a genuine opportunity for further real increases in the national minimum wage to achieve positive social and economic benefits in current circumstances.

The compelling background set out above, coupled with:

- the benign success of the introduction of the minimum wage with no material adverse consequences; and
- the potential benefits of increasing the Minimum Wage at a time when the UK is approaching full employment, so as to encourage structural adjustment towards the 'high skill/high wage' economy, to which policy aspires;

makes a strong case for further progress towards a real living wage for the overwhelming majority of employees.

Issue three: debt on our doorstep

A two-pronged programme to reduce the burden of low income consumer debt through (1) the introduction of a reasonable ceiling on interest rates and charges and (2) facilitation of the expansion of Credit Unions and other forms of community development finance institutions.

Background

There are 13 million people in Britain struggling to exist on low incomes: as little as £107 a week for a single person and £188 a week for a lone parent with two children. The National Consumer Council and others have shown people on low incomes frequently pay more than the rest of us for the 'privilege' of access to many of the essentials of life – gas, electricity, water, phone bills, and even food.[43]

Disadvantaged consumers are frequently offered less attractive deals. They may be required to pay up front, or face premium prices for their preferred (or required) payment methods. In many cases they are also prevented from switching to a better deal because of debts incurred. More vulnerable consumers are not protected from being targeted by unfair marketing practices which can result in them switching to a worse deal.

But nowhere is the 'excess cost' of being poor greater than in relation to money itself. Over 1.5 million households lack even the most basic of financial products. Over 3 million are unbanked. Almost 8 million people are judged by the institutions that make these decisions, to be uncreditworthy and would be refused access to mainstream credit.[44] This is not to say that such people do not need credit. Indeed on a 'tight' budget credit is essential to cope with the 'uneven' nature of household expenditure – birthdays, school uniforms, Christmas – let alone the 'unforeseen' events – a broken cooker, or a funeral to attend at the other end of the country.

Since the deregulation of the consumer credit sector in 1974 and the abolition of the ceiling on interest rates, there has been a mushrooming in the 'alternative' credit market. Chief amongst these is 'home credit', lending relatively small amounts of money (typically £150-500), and collecting repayments on a weekly basis. It is a perfectly 'tailored' product, designed to cater for people living on a tight weekly budget, managed in cash and accounted for down to the last penny. The only problem is the cost: anything from 170% to 800% APR (and in a few cases even more).

Home credit is big business: the sector as a whole is valued at over £3 billion, and serves more than 3 million customers each year. The market leader is Provident Financial plc, a FTSE250 company, with profits of over £150 million from its home credit business alone in 2003, averaging over £90 from each of its 1.61 million customers in that business. It is argued that the high APRs in this sector reflect the high costs of weekly collections; that lending is at the most 'risky' end of the market; and that other forms of credit available to low income households are equally expensive.[45] All of these things are relevant, but independent analysis still suggests that rates could be reduced.[46]

The effect of borrowing money at 170% APR is to reduce the purchasing power of every £1 borrowed to just 70 pence. Not only do people on low incomes have less to start with, but the pound in their pocket is worth less as well. The impact of all of this on individuals, families and whole communities is incalculable.

There is a clear case for tightening regulation of extortionate lending, and for some form of legal ceiling on the levels of interest and other charges that can be charged. Interest rate ceilings apply in various forms in Germany, France, many US states, Canada, Australia, and indeed in most developed western economies. But greater regulation alone will not achieve the desired outcome.

> *Without action across government, tighter regulation alone could make matters worse. To be effective, tougher legislation needs to be combined with support for initiatives that widen access to affordable credit and money advice.*[47]

A survey of residents in a poor neighbourhood of Bristol in 2001 found that people aspired to save but frequently needed to borrow. They were attracted to schemes that link saving and borrowing, giving them access to low-cost loans. But they often needed to break the cycle of borrowing from high-cost lenders to be able to start saving. There was a widespread mistrust of banks, insurance and credit companies and a high level of disengagement from financial services. Asian residents faced problems as most financial services do not comply with the teaching of Islam.[48] The researchers conclude that needs for financial products and services in deprived communities are best met by a combination of national provision with a local presence and city-wide 'one-stop shop' services run in partnership between national providers and local organisations.

Credit Unions, as mutual savings and loan co-operatives, provide a very effective vehicle for mobilising the savings and assets of the whole community in an equitable and inclusive way. Less than 1% of the UK population are currently members of Credit Unions. Yet almost half of the Irish adult population are.

Clonmel Credit Union, serving a small town in South West Ireland, has over 16,000 members. It provides loans at 0.875% per month (around 10% APR), and also offers a wide range of financial services to its members including savings protection and an annual dividend on savings, life savings, loan protection, death benefit insurance, house contents and car insurance, mortgages and even bureau de change facilities, rail tickets and hotel discounts. The Irish Government also funds a national Money Advice and Budgeting Service, with over 60 centres across the Republic, providing access to high quality money advice, financial literacy training and a special budgeting account (set up *via* the local credit union) to enable weekly payments into an account, from which outstanding debts and regular bills can be paid by direct debit and standing order.

Whilst there are a number of Government and other initiatives in this area, they are currently piecemeal and unco-ordinated: The 'Savings Gateway' to promote savings by low income households excludes the involvement of Credit Unions. Money advice services are offered on only a patchy basis, and frequently in isolation from any other services; a number of national 'financial literacy' schemes have been established, which may promote increased 'literacy' but do not address the lack of choices available to people on low incomes (especially in relation to sources of credit). And crucially, no department or statutory agency has any direct responsibility for promoting access to affordable credit, in spite of this being a central element of financial exclusion.[49]

At the local level, a significant number of schemes to promote access to savings and credit have emerged in recent years: Credit Unions provide over 500,000 members with access to affordable savings and credit. Whilst some are struggling with the new regulatory regime introduced by the Financial Services Authority in 2002, others are now growing rapidly and developing as robust social businesses. Over 70 Housing Associations are involved in promoting financial inclusion in some form or another, and some have established specific (mostly arm's length) savings and loan initiatives. A number of 'community development finance institutions', most notably in Portsmouth and Salford, have established schemes to provide access to affordable credit to those on low incomes.

However, to date, most of these schemes are relatively small scale, and have been developed by local social entrepreneurs, with only mixed levels of support from the statutory sector. Only a handful offer services to more than 1,000 individuals. The situation is crying out for some 'joined up' thinking: a bold strategy to mobilize the strengths and assets of the public, private and community sector – and indeed, people in poverty themselves – in order to end poor people's reliance on extortionate lending, and to put easy and affordable credit within the reach of those who need it most.

Potential action

Carefully designed ceilings on the interest rates and charges applying to consumer credit can protect the poor and vulnerable from the most extortionate lending practices. However these need to be set at realistic levels to avoid choking off the supply of credit from the more responsible lenders in this sector. An appropriate balance needs to be struck between the availability of credit to the poor and the fairness of its cost.

There is also scope to expand the supply of low cost credit to the poor through encouraging and facilitating the establishment of more community based credit providers, such as credit unions and other forms of community development finance institutions. Financial literacy is of limited use if there is no real choice available.

Issue four: addressing pensioner poverty

The most urgent need is to improve the benefits paid to pensioners currently aged over 75. Longer-term strategies are also needed to enhance basic pensions in real terms and to permit pensioners to share in rising real incomes through having their payments linked to earnings rather than prices.

Background

The inequalities of working life get even grimmer in retirement. The top fifth of pensioner couples now have a retirement income averaging £45,000 a year, yet one in five pensioners – over 2 million older people – still live below the level of income support. What is worse – and unlike children in poverty – a large group of pensioners (17%) live in permanent poverty. 4 million live in the country's 88 most deprived local authorities; 44% live in accommodation that is not in decent repair or thermally efficient. As Help the Aged has noted, this is a major contributing factor towards the excess number of winter deaths of older people; Britain has the highest proportion in the EU with between 20,000 and 45,000 a year.

Millions more pensioners are struggling to meet the rising costs of living that include increased council tax and utility bills, and many are unable to afford even the basics of a civilized lifestyle such as buying new clothes, taking a holiday or decorating their homes.

With longer life expectancy, rising real incomes and the advantages that today's working age population enjoys as a result of the efforts of the older generation during their working lives, there is a strong case for sharing the fruits of our resulting prosperity with the retired on a basis that is more generous than current policy.

So far, the government has relied on means-testing – firstly through the Minimum Income Guarantee (MIG) and now with the Pension Credit – to target extra money at those with low incomes. However, means-testing is demeaning for older people who have to parade their poverty in order to receive a few extra pounds and ineffective at getting help to those who need it most because of the disappointing take-up level.

Those hardest hit tend to be the over 75s, the vast majority of whom are women who spent years bringing up families or working in badly paid or part-time jobs. As a result, they do not have an occupational pension or enough National Insurance contributions to qualify for a full state pension. They, together with many ethnic elders who also suffered similar problems during their working lives, are forced to rely on means-tested benefits.

The quickest first step to help this particularly vulnerable group is to pay Pension Credit automatically to the over-75s, where the vast majority of the poor are. There are 4 million pensioners in this group, of whom approximately 1 million are eligible and not claiming the Credit worth up to £33 a week for couples. The changes that came with the Pension Credit scheme in October 2003 (writing to all to encourage uptake and not penalizing modest levels of savings) are steps in the right direction, but still seem to be missing out some of the most vulnerable.

Even these changes will not help many older women and ethnic elders who have paid insufficient National Insurance contributions to qualify for a level of benefit even close to the basic state pension. For many of these people it is arguable that a contribution-based insurance scheme does not appropriately reflect their contribution to society and their deserving to be treated decently in retirement.

In a similar vein, approximately 40% of those estimated to be eligible are not claiming their Council Tax Benefit, worth an average of around £425 per pensioner household per year. Automatic payments or opt-out rather than opt-in systems would largely address the problems of inertia or ignorance that currently appear to plague such well-meant and well-deserved initiatives.

More widely, since the index linking of the basic state pension to average earnings was abolished in 1980, its value relative to what it would otherwise have been has fallen by more than £30 a week for an individual and £50 a week for a couple. As a result, millions of pensioners now feel that their contribution to the nation is being ignored. This points to policy action in two complementary areas.

First, there is a case for an upgrading of pension levels to compensate for the erosion suffered under the indexation policy prevailing since 1980 and to bring pensions to a level that bears a sensible relationship to a budget standard (see issue one above) appropriate to pensioners. This is complicated by the demographic changes happening in our society, with an increasing proportion of older members, but that does not absolve society from its responsibility to provide adequately for them. However it is likely that such changes will need to be made gradually over a period of years.

Second, the basic state pension should be uprated annually in line with average earnings or inflation (Retail Price Index), whichever is the greater, to enable pensioners to share in the growing prosperity of the nation. The earlier this change is introduced, the less is the cumulative underperformance that will present a challenge to future pensions policies.

This discussion has focussed on a few of the key considerations affecting policy towards basic state pension provision. However it is noted here that there are also challenges arising in the area of private pension provision, which might potentially increase the call on the state to support retirees in the future. In particular, the combined effect of the elimination of the payment of dividend tax credits to pension funds and the decline in share prices in 2001 and 2002 has caused many private pension schemes to be fundamentally recast. Final salary schemes are largely being closed and replaced by money purchase schemes, shifting risk to the individual and away from the pension provider, while at the same time the opportunity is being taken to reduce the percentage of current salary being provided by employers as private pension contributions. Persistent underprovision in occupational schemes will store up future problems of pensioner poverty and potentially increase the call on the public sector for means-tested benefits.

Potential action

The most urgent case for action on pensions is to improve the lot of those currently aged over 75. Universal payment of Pension Credit (or upgrading the basic pension to include also the maximum Pension Credit) in this age group would help some. Others, short of national insurance contributions as a result of their life circumstances, will need other kinds of assistance to be able to enjoy their old age with some dignity.

Indexing pensions to the greater of average earnings and retail prices will permit pensioners to share more fairly in the increases in prosperity benefiting society at large.

Beyond these two measures, society owes its current and future older members a long-term strategy to enhance pensions to levels commensurate with appropriate budget standards.

Issue five: taxation and the common good

After years of under-indexation and patchwork reforms the burden of personal taxation now falls unduly heavily on the low paid. Revised tax and national insurance scales can share these tax obligations more fairly with those more able to contribute from their increased wealth and income. Direct taxation continues to need to be supported by a broad range of other taxes.

The Catholic Bishops' Conference of England and Wales have recently reported on the relationship between taxation and the common good. This asserts the importance of placing debates about the role of taxation within a clear moral context:

> *What is often missing from debates about taxation is a realisation of what taxation represents in terms of a shared commitment as citizens to building up a society that serves the common good.'* (Archbishop Peter Smith).

Over the last 50 years the growth of the public sector, coupled with frequent ad hoc changes to tax scales, have led to profound changes in the way that tax obligations are shared within our society. Paul Johnson,[50] Professor of Economic History at the London School of Economics, has calculated the proportion of earnings actually paid by workers in income tax and national insurance contributions since 1948. This research shows that the more or less continuous fall in the headline rate of income tax, from 48% in 1951 to 22% today, is of almost no relevance to individual taxpayers, who have experienced a very different pattern of change over time.

A single person on a middle-class income of one and a half times average earnings (£37,128 at the time of the study in 2003), in spite of the 'headline' higher tax rate of 40% plus 1% national insurance, is actually only paying 28% of total earnings in tax and national insurance. This is about as low as it has been at any point in the last 30 years.

It is a different story for the low paid. A full-time worker on the minimum wage of £4.50 an hour earns about £9,500 a year, which is around 40% of average earnings. This sort of low-paid worker was almost exempt from income tax until the early 1970s, and paid only social security contributions. A major reform of personal taxation in 1973, combined with a failure to increase tax allowances in line with inflation, saw the average direct tax burden of a low-paid worker shoot up to 22% by 1983, since when there has been a gradual drift downwards, helped by the introduction of a lower starting rate of income tax in 1992. Compared to the 1980s, therefore, the total direct tax burden on a low-paid worker has declined, but it is still much higher than in the 1950s and 1960s.

In contrast, 'fat cats' have never enjoyed so much fiscal cream. According to the LSE figures, someone earning 10 times average earnings (£247,520) is likely to be paying around 38% of their total earnings in tax and national insurance. This compares with around 47% in the 1950s; 70% in the 1970s and over 50% for the most of the 1980s. Even if a 50% tax rate was introduced, someone on an annual income of almost £250,000 would still pay no more than 45% of their total income in direct taxation – a lower rate than at any point between 1950 and 1987.

It is recognized that there is no place in our society for punitive higher rates of direct taxation. They are both unfair and ineffectual insofar as higher income earners who regard themselves as unfairly heavily taxed are able to organize their affairs to pay tax in lower rate jurisdictions. Equally, an examination of the 2004-05 income tax and national insurance (NI) scales suggests some obvious areas for beneficial reform.

Income band	Income tax rate	NI rate	Combined rate
£0 - £4,732	0%	0%	0%
£4,733 - £4,745	0%	11%	11%
£4,746 - £6,765	10%	11%	21%
£6,766 - £31,720	22%	11%	33%
£31,721 - £36,145	22%	1%	23%
Above £36,145	40%	1%	41%

Source: Inland Revenue website for rate information. (Assumes personal allowance for taxpayers under 65 (£4,745) with no special allowances and multiplies NI weekly income thresholds by 52 for annual figures.)

For example:

- Tax and NI starting rates are confusingly intertwined (in 2003-04 the tax personal allowance is below the lower NI threshold; in 2004-05 it is above it) and when the effect of benefits means tests are included, many households face steep and confusing marginal rates of income loss. Further, tax and NI burdens commence at what are now very low levels of income.
- Equally the step-down in the combined marginal rate from 33% to 23% at income of £31,721 has academic logic but no common-sense appeal at all.
- There is room to introduce one or two additional higher rate bands (e.g. up to a maximum of 50% combined) commencing at a higher level of income in order to share tax obligations more fairly among the more prosperous – a prudently more progressive tax structure.
- In the longer run it would be healthy to debate the appropriate structure of national insurance. Should old age benefits be linked solely to years in paid employment? Should they continue to be financed by a regressive scale of employee contributions when employer contributions have no ceiling? Should unearned income remain exempt from national insurance contributions?

One of the important benefits of the rising prosperity noted at the start of this paper is the opportunity, and indeed responsibility, to seek to share the benefits (and obligations) of our progress more fairly, so as to enhance social cohesion and inclusion and to improve the productive capacity of society overall. There is room for thoughtful reforms, carefully implemented, to produce lasting and real benefits to our society as a whole.

Potential action

There are clear arguments in favour of redistributive justice, reducing the burden of taxation upon the poorest in society, while at the same time asking for a more equitable sharing of the inevitable tax obligations of a modern market economy with the more prosperous. The pace and scale of changes in this area will depend on the tax revenues required as a result of other policy changes, together with the need to maintain a broad consensus about the fairness of the tax system overall. Whilst it may be difficult to put a brake on inequality in a growing market economy, at present the state is part of the problem, not part of the solution; poor people are taxed too much.

There is therefore a clear and cogent case for reducing the tax burden on the poorest, by significantly increasing the starting point at which tax is paid, and at the same time introducing a higher tax band (50%) for the top one percent of the population, who earn more than £107,000 per annum.[51]

Beyond these measures, there are strong grounds for a wider review and rationalization of the tax and national insurance system, both to iron out some of the current anomalies and to increase work incentives for those currently working in marginal and insecure employment.

7

Scotland: David Sinclair

Abdula Keder and Ahmed Kader arrived in Scotland destitute, with no money, no home and unable to speak the language... They work at McPhie's Craft Bakers in Glasgow's Shettleston, rising at 4am, arriving on time and working hard all day – basic skills which McPhie's have found appear to be beyond most Scots they have employed... Despite having run his own business and possessing business skills, Mr Keder was unemployed for a year when he first arrived. He said, 'The biggest problem was the language barrier, but I am getting there. The people of Glasgow have been very friendly and helped us settle in to our new home and have found me a job which I enjoy.

Now Jack McConnell [Scotland's First Minister] wants to attract more workers like these. He is keenly aware that Scotland has a serious problem of population decline... However, one of the biggest problems has been that the Home Office in London has not approached the issue with the same enthusiasm... Mr McConnell has had to try to confront this and for the past few months the First Minister has been in detailed negotiations with the Home Office to try to find a way of encouraging the number of migrants Scotland needs to survive at the same time as appeasing the fears of middle England... He wants to stop Scots leaving after university, attract more people from England to come north, encourage foreign students to stay on after graduating and attract skilled migrants to live and work in Scotland... At the moment, overseas students from outside the EU have to leave Scotland on the 31 October after their university course finishes... McConnell will announce a change to this rule and will offer foreign students the right to a further two-year visa once their studies are over. The aim is to help them secure employment which then would give them the leverage necessary to succeed in getting a proper work permit after the two-year period is up...

For Jim McPhie and his son Craig, who own McPhie's bakers in Shettleston, their experiences with Iraqi asylum-seekers has been nothing but positive. They have struggled over the years to find workers, despite being in an area with huge unemployment: 'So-

called "soft skills" like turning up for work on time are practically non-existent. Abdula and Ahmed have been working here for about six months and have been like nectar from heaven. Their hard work has turned the business around and has restored my faith in humanity.' *(The Scotsman, 25.02.04)*

Scotland's economy

In the 80 years between the 1750s and the 1830s, Scotland's population virtually doubled. In the 80 years from then, it doubled again, so that in 1911 the population of Scotland stood at 4,761 million.[52] It has hardly risen since. Tom Devine argues that the employment released by the industrial economy of Scotland was what permitted the population to rise; it might, therefore, be reasonably presumed that economic factors were also responsible for the fact that population growth was not sustained. The Scottish economy grew during that time through its involvement in the British imperial adventure, allowing it to thrive on tobacco from America, on sugar from the West Indies, on jute from India, and on slaves from Africa. By the end of the 19th century it was Scotland's heavy engineering which put Scotland, and particularly Glasgow, in the limelight. Devine recounts the opening of Glasgow City Chambers by Queen Victoria in 1888; and also the International Exhibition in 1901 in Kelvingrove Park which attracted 11.5 million visitors, including the Tsar of Russia.[53]

Nearly 100 years later the picture is very different. In 1999[54] Botham and Downes argued that, with growth in electronics, the service industries, oil and gas, much had been achieved, but warned that much of this had been driven by inward investment, much of it was assembly and manufacturing work, with little research, design or product development. Electronics, they said, was virtually the only sector in which there had been growth in manufacturing output. They spoke also of the threats of globalization for those industries which were insufficiently competitive, and of the inability of Scotland to compete on the basis of relatively low wage costs against the incoming accession countries of the European Union.

In 2002 Jim Cuthbert and Margaret Cuthbert[55] compared Scotland's economy to the UK as a whole. The average annual rate of growth in the Scottish economy in the 25 years from 1973 was 1.6%, while in the UK it was 1.9%; unemployment in Scotland over a similar period was anything from 1% to 3% above the rate for the UK; population growth in Scotland for the century from 1901 totalled 14%, while in England the comparable figure was nearly 80%. 'This chronic economic underperformance,' they said, 'has occurred despite substantial government action to improve Scotland's economic position.'[56] This action has included regional selective assistance, the creation of enterprise bodies, and significantly higher public expenditure than was available to the UK as a whole. For example, education spending per head in Scotland is higher than the UK as a whole by no less than 25% and, when the Cuthberts' article was written, Scottish participation in higher education was already at the 50% level which is still only a target for government policy in the UK.

The Scottish Economic Report, laid before the Scottish Parliament in September 2003, identified, as the strength of the Scottish economy, the service sector (continuing to outperform the UK as a whole), and particularly financial services (with increasing employment levels). The strengths of electrical and instrument engineering, whisky, tourism and the North Sea sector were also positive. However, manufacturing fell by 10% in Scotland in the year to the first quarter of 2003, and had experienced a continuous fall in output for eleven quarters, most marked in electrical and instrument engineering. Construction was also underperforming and, although job losses recently might have indicated a reserve of labour, those who had been recruiting reported difficulties in doing so. North Sea oil and gas production had fallen considerably – with unexploited reserves now in difficult and challenging locations. In agriculture, forestry and fishing labour productivity had risen, but these sectors were declining in their share of total Scottish output.

Although exports from manufacturing fell by a quarter in one year to the first quarter of 2003 (though the report puts this in the context of a global slowdown) exports generally are regarded as strong. Investment is virtually stagnant, but consumer confidence seems to be recovering. Employment has risen slightly and seasonally adjusted unemployment stood in the summer of 2003 at 5.5%; but there is a continuing trend from male to female employment and from full-time to part-time work. House prices, in spite of all this, continue to rise – though more slowly than the UK average, making housing in Scotland 'relatively affordable'. In all independent economic forecasts, Scotland is expected to continue to lag behind the UK as a whole. Scotland still suffers from a greater concentration of poverty, with long-term unemployment more prevalent, and levels of long-term sick and disabled a third higher than the rest of the UK.

Poverty and social inclusion: the Scottish Executive response

The Scottish Parliament has legislative powers in all areas which are not specifically reserved to Westminster (in the Scotland Act 1998). This gives the Parliament competence in health, education, local government, social work, housing, planning, economic development, financial assistance to industry, tourism, aspects of transport, most aspects of criminal and civil law, criminal justice and the courts, police and fire services, environment, heritage, agriculture, food standards, forestry, fisheries, sport, and the arts. Strong committees are at the heart of the new parliamentary process Their remits are meant to avoid departmental territorialism and promote joined-up thinking, they combine the functions of Westminster standing and select Committees, and they can initiate legislation. They are seen as a key factor in the accessibility of the Parliament. Key also in that effort is the system of public petitions, by which anyone may petition the Parliament on any subject; a petitions committee exists to channel the petition in the appropriate direction and to ensure that it is suitably dealt with. The Scottish Parliament is uni-cameral, having no upper or revising chamber. The Ministers making up the Cabinet are referred to as the 'Scottish Executive' – though, because the Scottish Executive is also the term used to describe the Civil Service in Scotland, many now refer to the 'Scottish Government'.

Since devolution there has been a renewed focus on poverty, and on a social inclusion agenda, which has included a programme seeking to ensure adequate statistical evidence for future policy development. No single indicator gives a clear picture of the overall levels of poverty and this is why the Scottish Executive uses both absolute and relative measures, and poverty groups choose a variety of indicators. It isn't simply that the measure used to define poverty can be misleading, but also that national average figures on poverty often obscure local problems (see the discussion of Edinburgh below). Of the 29 social justice milestones set by the Scottish Executive, some measure inequality, some measure ‘absolute’ poverty and others deal more with opportunities. They range through the stages of life and across areas like health and education, from reducing the proportion of children living in low-income households to ending the need for rough sleeping, from increasing internet access to reducing the fear of crime amongst older people.

There is also a commitment to producing an annual report on progress towards the milestones. There have now been four of these. The report in 2002, for example, claimed that progress was being made on 16 of the milestones, seven were broadly constant, two were moving in the wrong direction and for the remaining four there was insufficient data. The publication, on December 17th 2003, of ***Social Justice, Indicators of Progress*** reported that progress had been made in taking children, families, working age people and pensioners out of poverty, that there were increasing levels of employment among lone parents and ethnic minorities, and that there were now more people living in temporary accommodation. It also confirmed a move away from target-led government policy.

The powers held in Scotland with which an impact can be made on these issues range from childcare provision to university tuition fees, from homelessness strategy to reducing health inequalities and community regeneration – without getting into the possible use of the power to vary income tax. Executive strategy is that, rather than having specific social justice policies, the commitment runs across all their policy-making. They claim (with some justification) that improving public services is central (since the poorest depend most on these services), and that crime impacts most heavily on deprived communities. In 2002 they published ***Closing the Opportunity Gap***, in which the total Scottish budget is presented in terms of plans to ‘tackle poverty, build strong, safe communities and create a fair, equal Scotland’. There have, however, also been specific initiatives in a number of key areas, including debt and financial exclusion, child poverty, fuel poverty, homelessness, community regeneration, active communities, and rural poverty. The effectiveness of many of these initiatives (and the adequacy, or otherwise, of resources devoted to them) remain key party political issues, yet there is a fair degree of agreement on broad directions. And there are signs of commitment across the apparatus of government to tackling these problems as central.

Legislation in the first term of the Scottish Parliament included the

Abolition of Feudal Tenure Act 2000 that symbolically ended the archaic feudal system of land ownership in Scotland, where 'feudal superiors' were able to exercise control over property they had sold. It paved the way for later reform, including the ***Land Reform and the Agricultural Holdings Acts.***

The ***Land Reform Act 2003***, another powerfully symbolic, but controversial piece of legislation, gave, for the first time, the 'right of responsible access' to Scotland's countryside. Rural communities were given a right to buy land in which they have registered an interest, but only if the land comes on the market, and crofting communities were given an absolute right to buy the land they work and live on. Though likened by some landowners to a 'Mugabe-style land grab', the Executive argued that the Act would redress one of the most concentrated patterns of land ownership in Europe, by empowering rural communities to promote their own sustainable development; the reality has so far been much more modest than either predicted.

The ***Housing Act 2001*** aimed at 'fostering successful balanced communities with high quality affordable houses to rent and to purchase'. Paving the way for transfer of local authority housing stock to housing associations, it introduced the Scottish Secure Tenancy to standardize the tenancy agreements of council and housing association tenants, with enhanced rights against eviction and to information and consultation from their landlord, and a 'modernized right to buy'. The Act required local authorities to assess homelessness in their area and develop a strategy to tackle it. ***Communities Scotland*** was established as a new agency to assist in the regeneration of communities and improve housing standards. The Act also made statutory the Executive commitment to end fuel poverty by 2016, 'so far as reasonably practicable'.

As mentioned above, the creation of a social justice strategy with 29 milestones focussed attention on some of the poorest and most marginalized sections of Scottish society. The life-cycle approach used targeted vulnerable groups such as children and young people, low-income families, the homeless and older people. The Warm Deal programme has seen 8,500 central heating systems installed and 137,000 homes made warmer and more energy efficient through improved insulation. 21,000 new or improved homes have been made available for people on low incomes, including over 4,000 new or improved homes for people with disabilities.

The 'Breakfast Services Fund', announced in November 2001, is now funded to the tune of £300,000 in an attempt to improve the health of Scotland's children, particularly those from the most deprived areas. Although, the ***School Meals Bill*** – which would have provided free nutritious lunches for all school children (removing the stigma of free school meals being conditional on being from a low income family) – was defeated on the Executive's argument that money would be better spent being targeted to poorer families, the Executive established an expert panel on school meals. On the basis of their report, £63 million of investment was promised to ensure free fruit for pupils in primary 1 and 2, new nutrient standards for school meals, larger portions of more nutritious food at no further cost to parents, and steps towards raising awareness of the entitlement to free school meals. Glasgow City Council are about to introduce free meals in all their primary schools.

In its first term (in 2001) the Scottish Executive launched its theme of 'A Smart Successful Scotland' as the aim of its Enterprise Networks. The Ministerial foreword to the initial document spoke of the need to create the conditions for this smart and successful country to be born. It drew attention to the need to boost the birth of new businesses and to see a strong economy and strong communities as 'two sides of the same coin'. In particular the launch document identified productivity, in which Scotland (like the rest of the UK) lagged behind its competitors, as the key to economic success, to prosperity and to reducing poverty.

The Parliament is now well into its second term. In his foreword to the Executive's Draft Budget for 2004-05, the Minister for Finance and Public Services, Andy Kerr, set out the budget's goal, 'to create conditions in which improved economic growth can provide people with more opportunities in life.' He argued that the Executive's spending plans and policy commitments will, 'deliver better public services, greater economic prosperity, and an improved standard of living for the people of Scotland'. The policy watchwords to guide these plans are opportunity, equality and sustainability. ('Equality' should not be confused with any ideas of economic equality; the reference here is to tackling discrimination.)

'Closing the opportunity gap' is where to look for policies to tackle poverty and to increase prosperity. This is viewed as a 'cross-cutting' issue and involves health policy to increase life expectancy, closing the educational achievement divide between 'the most disadvantaged … and the average', reducing crime, improving public transport, and closing 'the opportunity gap on employment and learning'.

The Ministers charged particularly to close the opportunity gap are those for Communities and also Enterprise and Lifelong Learning. The Draft Budget gives five objectives for this:

- Delivering good quality, sustainable and affordable housing for everyone
- Regenerating our communities
- Building safer communities by tackling anti-social behaviour
- Tackling poverty and helping vulnerable people
- Promoting equal opportunities and active citizenship

Within the regeneration of communities is to be found the target of closing the opportunity gap in education, health, justice, transport, housing and jobs. The targets under the heading of 'tackling poverty' concentrate on homelessness, central heating for the elderly, fuel poverty, debt advice and childcare.

Scottish Enterprise and Highlands and Islands Enterprise seek to 'grow business', but to do so with particular activities and particular sections of the population in mind, listing some of these as women, residents from disadvantaged areas, environmental activities, farm businesses, social economy organizations, young people. Highlands and Islands Enterprise has a stated role (which is not shared by Scottish Enterprise) in social, as well as economic, development. This gives it targets in the provision of community facilities and, importantly, in community land acquisitions. Job creation and economic assistance are also to be provided by Regional Selective Assistance and by the implementation of the European Structural Funds. Regional Selective Assistance is demand-led and follows the setting up of businesses. It has as its objective, 'to contribute to competitiveness, increase prosperity and help close the gap in unemployment rates between the worst 10% of areas and the Scottish average'. The Draft Budget acknowledges the fall in inward investment – and assumes that the level will not rise again.

In his report to the Scottish Manufacturing Steering Group, in November 2003, the Minister for Enterprise drew particular attention to Regional Selective Assistance in areas such as broadband and transport, but also emphasized transport investment generally. Other remarks were concerned with image, marketing and promotion. He was responding to the Steering Group's report of May 2003, ***Nurturing Wealth-Creation.*** This report had brought forward 33 recommendations, ranging from direct financial support and tax reduction and review, to the reduction of regulation and bureaucracy and the improvement of literacy and numeracy skills.

Assessments

A Rowntree report in 2002 found that, of 34 indicators, 7 were improving, 6 worsening, 15 steady and 6 had insufficient data. Key trends included these:

- At 30% (equivalent to some 310,000 children in 2000/1), the proportion of children living in relative low-income households barely altered over the period 1997/8 to 2000/1.
- Over the same period, the proportion of people in Scotland with relative low incomes rose slightly, to around 1.2million people in 2000/1. Taking a longer view back to 1994/5, the overall sense is one of no change in this number. (This proportion, over the UK, increased from 13% in 1979 – 7 million people – to 24% in 1990 – 13.5 million people; it has remained fairly steady since then.)
- In spring 2002, nearly 210,000 working-age households had been without work for three years or more, the highest number for at least a decade.
- Fewer of those on relative low income are now unemployed, while more are working.

The authors concluded: 'Up to 2000/01, there was no sign of a fall in the number of people on relative low income, but beneath the surface there is change, with unemployment falling and low income in work becoming more prevalent ... and with benefits, though rising in real terms, still leaving people solely reliant on them far short of the relative low income threshold; and there remain some deep-seated and long-standing problems where progress is slow or non-existent. There are signs of progress within the education system but the gap in attainment remains considerable, with only slight improvements at the bottom ... Scotland is making progress in cutting its high rates of premature death, but the (health) inequalities within Scotland remain substantial ... The halving in just four years of the number of homes without central heating is very positive, but homelessness remains a persistent and growing problem. Finally, particular groups face disproportionate problems, including some that are long-standing, well-known and the subject of official attention (for example, people without access to basic banking facilities).'

The CPAG concluded their '***Poverty in Scotland 2002***' report by saying that 'important steps towards the eradication of poverty have been taken but a great deal more needs to be done'. Church Action on Poverty's work with community groups across Scotland found a similar recognition of real advances but also gaps still evident:

- Housing and homelessness are still a major issue in many parts of Scotland.
- The complexities and inadequacies of the benefits system still make the system a nightmare to navigate, and one in which people feel considerably disempowered.
- In spite of government policy it's very clear that getting people into work isn't necessarily going to get them out of poverty.
- Indebtedness is both a major consequence and a major cause of poverty.
- There are ongoing concerns about funding local groups in ways that enable them rather than force them into a straitjacket.

The most recent Rowntree 'Findings' report, Monitoring Poverty and Social Exclusion 2003, shows that only one of their measured indicators in Scotland is improving (that on school exclusions). The report highlights Scotland for its particularly poor record on health, with premature deaths being much worse than in the rest of Britain. Interestingly, however, the report describes Scotland as being, 'more typical of Britain as a whole than any of the English regions'. Part of this 'typical' picture is of more people in work with no decrease in the number of low-income, working households.

Researchers draw two important general conclusions from their analysis. The first is the stubborn refusal of so many of the key measures of poverty and exclusion in Scotland to show any signs of movement. The second is that a strategy to reduce poverty, built on getting people into work, faces a serious challenge when 40% of the working-age poor are actually already in work. That 'stubborn refusal' represents a major challenge to the policies that attempt to translate targets into reality.

Difficulties, limitations and alternatives

The most obvious difficulty for any Scottish Executive in tackling these issues, however, is that most of the key economic levers, such as the tax and benefit system and macro-economic policy, remain with Westminster. Even there, it is suggested, there are limitations to what can be expected: in the ***September Scottish Economic Report***, Scottish Ministers say: 'the downturn in global demand over 2001 and 2002 and the associated restructuring in the electronics sector hit the Scottish economy harder than the UK as a whole... The fortunes of the Scottish economy are more linked to the global economic position rather than domestic spending... The global recovery that would sustain growth in the Scottish economy is not yet definite.' To suggest, however, that there is nothing that can be done and that the global position is the only factor might be a little dangerous. Stubborn refusals generally indicate that alternative approaches ought to be considered. There is no shortage of thinking being done – at many levels and on different scales.

Prosperity and sustainable development

The first strand of thinking here is sustainable development, concentrating on the cities of Edinburgh and Glasgow, and with work emanating from their city councils. In Glasgow, David Webster[57] argues that social inclusion policy places insufficient emphasis on 'promoting jobs that are accessible to the unemployed in terms of both skills and location'. He says that Scotland has not followed the English, Welsh and Northern Irish examples of investment in derelict land reclamation and urban transport infrastructure development. Glasgow has both large areas of derelict land and also half of the measured 'social exclusion' of Scotland. Webster argues directly with the supply-side economics of Richard Layard and the Labour government, with the resulting policies of the New Deals and welfare reform. He contrasts the huge expenditure involved in these Westminster programmes with the 'comparatively minor and inexpensive' policies of the Scottish Executive. His emphasis is on the connections of unemployment to poverty, out-migration and relationship breakdown, with the consequent effects of ill-health, low educational attainment, crime, bad housing, neighbourhood abandonment, homelessness, dereliction and demolition. All this affects cities disproportionately. An exclusive emphasis on education, he says, will not automatically lead to a higher rate of employment since the aim seems to be 'to shift substantial numbers of blue collar workers into the managerial and professional category – a tall order'.

At the time the article was written, Glasgow had 4000 acres of derelict land (almost 10% of its land area) and twice the proportion of any other Scottish local authority area. To reverse the out-migration, the housing dereliction and demolition and all the other ills that come with unemployment, Webster argues that this is where economic thinking should start. Since he wrote this, the Scottish Executive and Parliament have given their backing to perhaps the most controversial of his recommendations – the M74 extension. Webster argues against the critics of this piece of road building that, 'the environmentally sustainable refocussing of development within existing built-up areas can only be achieved if access is improved where necessary'. Indeed, his main argument is that, contrary to what has been imagined before and suggested above, the main levers for economic recovery do not lie with the fiscal and social inclusion powers of Westminster, but rather with the physical and economic development powers of the Scottish Parliament and Executive.

In Edinburgh, and before devolution came into being, a Lord Provost Commission was set up to examine the subject of sustainable development for the city. Much of the concern was (and still is) that Edinburgh was developing in a way and at a rate that was unsustainable. Indeed Edinburgh can be held up as a model of how an overall picture of economic growth can mask an extremely varied reality. Daniel Mittler[58] gives an account of the Commission's work and report. He describes the house-price inflation (which has since accelerated), the growth in tourist numbers, the booming economy, and the international attention achieved by Edinburgh – and points out that air pollution was getting worse (killing 100 citizens a year), that there were 20,000 damp properties in the city, that long-term unemployment was rising – with rates in some areas of the city at as much as 16%. His description of the Commission's work also demonstrates that what people see depends crucially on where they stand. Edinburgh was viewed as a city where great wealth and dreadful poverty lived side by side, where (for example) the rate of death before the age of 65 was three times higher in Granton than in the wealthy suburb of Balerno. Economic development in one place (for example, the new Gyle shopping centre) can create both environmental and economic damage (in this case, an extra 200,000 car kilometres in Edinburgh every day, and the loss to shopkeepers in nearby Corstorphine of 80% of their business).

These issues are neither straightforward nor self-evident; it is not the case that a simple explanation of 'facts' will be enough to create a common analysis and set of recommendations. From general issues of economic development to issues of particular policy, everything was contested. They were contested because, 'Edinburgh is a booming and prosperous city. But it is also a socially divided and polluted one'. To be sustainable, they discovered, economic development and prosperity must address division and pollution.

Prosperity and culture

The second alternative takes us from the urban life of Scotland to the most rural, and asks if prosperity is simply to do with economics or if there might be a relationship with culture and with language. Wilson McLeod[59] examines the effect of support for the Gaelic economy in the Highlands and Hebrides. The Gaelic economy, he says, provides well in excess of 1,000 jobs – a significant number in a sparsely populated part of Scotland. It challenges the perception, he argues, that Gaelic has no economic value. The rather less positive news is that, 'the overwhelming majority of jobs created in this sector are entirely dependent on public funding'. This economy is not in a position to be a net contributor to economic performance. There is also little evidence to show that there is a linguistic payoff by way of increased use of Gaelic, which remains largely excluded from economic life. He argues, in effect, that to concentrate on providing money as a way of sustaining the language is not enough; the language must be integrated much more fully into economic life.

McLeod discusses the problems of tokenism and performance in Gaelic policies, particularly when related to tourism, the media and the arts. He also discusses the circumstances in which economic development can actually damage the language by encouraging the immigration of monoglot English speakers with no incentive or intention to learn Gaelic. He argues that the industrialization of the Irish Gaeltacht in the 1970s encouraged the move from Irish to English as the language of normal daily intercourse. In other words, he says, 'economic development may come at a linguistic price'. His thesis is that to make Gaelic the language of the work-place a much more concentrated effort needs to be madework-place. He thinks that steps should be taken by those such as local authorities, as in Wales, to designate jobs as requiring the ability to speak in Gaelic, aware of the inevitable outcry from those who up until now have known no linguistic barrier to their employment. In addition, he advocates the measuring of the use of the Gaelic language in the work-place – with targets set and progress measured.

The effect of this kind of discussion, echoed in other current discussions in Scotland of language policies not only in Wales and Ireland but also in Quebec and Catalonia, is to ask if the price of prosperity is homogeneity. Is a nation's search after economic goods to be bought at the price of giving up its cultural goods? It is, on the global stage, the same kind of question that fuels the French antipathy to American cultural and economic hegemony. It forces on all of us the question of what we mean by prosperity, and if we might have been giving that word too narrowly economic a definition. In many industries Scotland has decided to aim at 'niche' markets, usually at the luxury end, where quality can demand a premium price. This can be seen in textiles and in beef production, for example. In these fields difference is promoted, even in a globalized economy, as something worth paying for; difference and diversity are therefore worth preserving. What small countries need to decide is how their prosperity is to be measured, what it is they have to offer that is distinctively their own, and how best to make that available.

Prosperity and population

At this point we return exactly to where we started in this essay – to patterns of migration, to population growth or decline, and to the connection between these and economic performance and well-being. It has been argued cogently by many that Scotland's greatest export over the years has been its people – and current estimates of the expatriate Scottish population (that is, those of Scottish descent) put it at around 40 million. The exodus that tends to be remembered is that occasioned by the Highland clearances, but numerically other departures have been more significant. Over the years Scots have left to find work, to find hope, to find a new life; there have been thousands of individual stories and at least as many individual reasons for leaving, but the economic truth is that they went. Scotland, Ireland and Norway top the league tables of emigrants as a proportion of total population between 1821 and 1915 [60] – and, if emigration to England is included, Scotland leaps well into the lead. The early development of the Scottish education system made Scots desirable in-comers in many places, but the inevitable concomitant of this is that those people were no longer available to develop the economy of Scotland.

Jack McConnell has argued that immigration is vital to the economic health of the nation. It is not simply about having enough people of working age to pay the taxes to pay the pensions for the ever-increasing number of pensioners who are living longer and longer – though it is partly that. It is also about the general level of economic activity and the effects which that activity, or its absence, have on the lives particularly of those who live on the margins. Without immigration the Scottish economy, and any possibility of a prosperous nation (however defined), will disappear. This brings all the discussions about 'economic migrants' and asylum-seekers and immigration – controlled or otherwise – directly into any discussion of prosperity.

Malcolm Anderson[61] argues that a rigid immigration policy is bad news for the world, and this for many reasons. He argues that, while social exclusion is an evil in rich countries, on a world scale it is a much greater evil; it shuts people out forever from any chance of closing the gap between rich and poor societies. He goes on: 'the main economic argument against control of immigration is that by severely limiting the mobility, on a global scale, of one factor of production, labour, the allocation of resources is sub-optimal and economic welfare held at a lower level that would otherwise be the case.' He calls for 'a great utopian imagining' of a world where there was free movement of people – but he acknowledges that he expects to be disappointed.

While Anderson argues for an economic case which increases world prosperity, the case is also made for a much more self-interested opening of boundaries. The Home Secretary says that he is granting more work permits to people from outside the EU than ever before. Scotland, with its stagnant population levels and ageing population, needs to take active steps to bring economically active people to take the place of generations of emigrants.

Fiscal autonomy

No sooner had devolution been put in place and the Scottish Parliament elected, than the calls for more powers began to be heard. Lindsay Paterson,[62] one year in to the Parliament's first term, said, 'given the indisputable limitations on the parliament's powers in relation to social inclusion, the first point to note is that there has to be a debate about acquiring extra powers'. This debate has, effectively, being going on ever since, both within the Parliament and outwith it. Support for fiscal autonomy comes from different sources and for varying reasons. For example, the business community and the Conservative Party support it because it would bring enhanced accountability.

Fiscal autonomy could also mean a variety of things.[63] Scotland could, at one end of the spectrum, raise whatever taxes it liked and spend them in any way it saw fit. A modification of this would mean that Scotland would raise its own taxes and pay to Westminster an agreed amount for reserved services. At the other end, the UK Government would make all decisions on types and rates of taxation, with Scotland receiving as its share that part of the tax raised in Scotland. In the middle might be a scheme involving UK-wide equalisation, which takes into account taxable capacity or differential needs. Heald and McLeod, in their introduction to a symposium on the subject, argue that any scheme of fiscal autonomy would have to encompass borrowing powers.

Jim and Margaret Cuthbert[64] present a discussion offered in the context of the chronic underperformance of the Scottish economy (comments noted above); and they do so in the light of arguments concerning the euro. The UK Government, they note, has been remarkably reluctant to give up fiscal autonomy within the EU; it argues that tax harmonization would leave the UK within a very clumsy and unresponsive system which could not react in any subtle way to answer particular economic conditions in particular countries. They then contrast that with the attitude to the monetary union within the UK itself. The argument they then wish to advance is that the chronic underperformance of the Scottish economy is in part due to the operation of the UK monetary union.

To answer this, they believe, the Scottish economy would need to be able to achieve a significant devaluation relative to sterling; this would have to be achieved by large tax reductions. The taxes under consideration would need to be those with most direct influence on these matters – income tax and corporation tax. Transitional arrangements would need to be introduced, because otherwise the juxtaposition of such measures with Scotland's fiscal deficit would unleash an even steeper economic decline. The aim is to increase competitiveness, not to make matters worse! Because of these considerations and the obvious drawbacks they present, they go on to look at alternatives to fiscal autonomy itself. They argue that the UK Government could retain control of tax, while abandoning the idea that taxes must be uniform throughout the country.

'The problems,' they say, 'of achieving balance between the constituent parts of the UK monetary union are unlikely to be materially different from the problems of achieving balance between the constituent countries of the [European Monetary Union]. We therefore suggest that the UK Government should seek to achieve greater consistency in its policies at these two different levels'. They suggest that Scotland's discussion of fiscal autonomy might be a stimulus to addressing the economic issues of other parts of the UK, all of whom must deal with the dominance of the south-east of England in setting fiscal policy.

Strength and weakness

The Scottish Executive summarizes the strengths and weaknesses of the Scottish economy by looking not only at economic factors but also at social factors. Scottish society is strong because its size makes cohesiveness, coherence and co-operation easier to achieve. One of its weaknesses, they say, is that there is a cultural aversion to risk-taking. There is a sense in which these ought not both to be able to co-exist. If Scotland really had a cohesive society in which we looked after one another that ought to make risk-taking easier because the risk would be shared. This appears not to be so. Perhaps the reason it is not so is that the rewards are not shared either. The Executive argues that the Scottish quality of life and the quality of Scotland's natural environment are high; but also acknowledges that problems of inequality, social exclusion and poverty persist.

One of the strengths of Scotland, it is argued, is its high production of graduates – but one of its weaknesses is that an overly large percentage of the young and well-qualified leave for greener grass elsewhere. This accentuates another recognized weakness, namely that among non-graduates in Scotland work-force training continues to be at a poor level. It may be that young Scots are indeed willing to take risks, but that they prefer to take them in other places, places where the calculations produce more hope that the risk will be worth taking. The Scottish business birth rate, therefore, remains low, leading in turn to a dependence on inward investment.

Indeed, Scotland's strengths in general are also its weaknesses. The strength of our natural environment is that it is unlikely, because of its geography and topography, to be industrialized or heavily commercialized; but this, of course, is an economic weakness. The trick, generally, is to play to your strengths. We have seen in the discussion of the Gaelic economy that the weakness of small numbers and geographical marginality could become a strength if we could develop new definitions for what we mean by prosperity, definitions that invest in variety and diversity. The discussion of migration also needs to take place in this context, because future prosperity may well hinge on our ability as a nation to celebrate diversity. In Edinburgh, the discussion of sustainability made it clear that prosperity fails to reach its potential if it only benefits a section of the population. And in Glasgow we heard a call for a way of working which builds from where the people are, rather than from where someone decides they ought to be. In essence, that is also what lies behind the discussion of fiscal autonomy – the recognition that equal treatment will not necessarily produce equal results, something long recognized in the field of equality legislation.

Before you can play to your strengths, of course, you have to decide what they are. What these discussions have shown is that, while many Scottish strengths can also be seen as weaknesses, the reverse is also true. Perceived weaknesses may be strengths. Glasgow, Edinburgh and the Gaeltacht all in their own way called on economic discussion to see weakness as strength – as the place to value, to build, and to include. The economic 'yardstick' of Scotland has long been that of Norway. It has recently been pointed out that Scotland's economic statistics are already quite comparable to Norway – all you have to do is to exclude Glasgow from the picture. Glasgow, however, or large parts of that city, has felt excluded from the picture for many years. It is in changing how we look at the picture, in recognising that the biggest difference can be made in the places where that difference is most needed, that economic weakness can be seen as developmental strength, as the locus of greatest potential.

The Scottish Churches Social Inclusion Network[65] believed that the place to look for strength was in weakness when it supported Church Action on Poverty in its project to allow the impoverished to be the experts on poverty. The questions they raised ought still to be prominent in forming the agenda. Among them was the need for a focus on communities rather than on individuals:

- Does there need to be a more fundamental devolution of power, to local communities, along with the resources to enable them to shape their own futures?
- Does policy focus too much on helping individuals to escape from poverty rather than tackling the multiple problems of deprived communities?
- Should social justice move from the model of 'service delivery' to one of 'creating public value' (from 'committees to communities', and from the managerial debate that characterized the 2003 election to one about values)?

Churches are traditionally well-placed to talk on the subjects of community and public value; and they are so because of their location and their work 'on the ground'. A study by the University of Glasgow[66] looked at churches and social capital, focussing particularly on the Church of Scotland. It produced many recommendations for churches and also for policy makers, but significantly it called on policy makers to recognize and to encourage the impact on social exclusion and on neighbourhood renewal that churches have.

The Church Action on Poverty project also evinced a desire for a greater focus on the seemingly unfashionable subject of redistribution:

- Is there still a reluctance (or lack of political nerve) to face the need for significant redistribution of wealth resources?
- Is the increasing emphasis on the 'opportunity gap' an adequate way forward, or should there be more emphasis on directly redressing present inequalities?

These questions too are still the focus of much thinking within

Scottish churches. For example, the report of the Church of Scotland's Church and Nation Committee to their 2004 General Assembly says: 'what, for the wealthy, is often perceived as a problem of poverty, is for many living in poverty a problem of wealth. For the creation of wealth to add value to society it requires to be more adequately distributed.'[67]

8

Wales: Mervyn Phillips and Robin Morrison

A personal story

I was born and brought up on Gellideg, known locally as Swansea Road Estate, which is a council housing estate North of Merthyr Tydfil Town Centre which, like many other Local Authority owned estates throughout the valleys, has always been perceived as a run down area where people are low skilled with high unemployment levels and benefit dependency, mostly through sickness and ill-health.

When growing up, educational achievement was never valued – the norm was to finish school and work in a local factory, irrelevant of low salary or working conditions or go for the other option – the benefit system just like a large proportion of our parents did at that time. I was raised in a culture where claiming benefits was seen as a more secure option than work as you could depend on having your giro at the end of the week! This culture resulted in my leaving school at 16 years of age with no formal qualifications and joining a YTS scheme the following week earning £25 per week which gave me a minimum amount of disposable income. My father at the time was claiming incapacity benefit and had been for a number of years and my mother was working long hours for little pay to make ends meets and therefore mostly all the money I was earning I was giving as a contribution to household bills etc.

I was also in a relationship and engaged at this age to a boy who also lived on our estate, went to school with and had known most of my life, much to my parents insistence that I was too young and needed to 'live a bit!'

Then came the biggest turning point in my life – at the age of eighteen I lost both my parents within a short time of each other, both suffering from cancer. Being the youngest in a family of four and the only one living at home with my parents I felt that I had lost my support mechanism, my stability in life and the two most important people to me.

After this I made a conscious decision that I would not have children late in life like my mother, who was 42 when she gave birth to me.

I became more independent and determined to take control of my life and never to be left in a vulnerable position, ensuring that I regained my security, support and stability.
My partner moved into my family home and we made a conscious decision to start a family, marriage never being an option as I felt I was giving a piece of my independence away. I had my first child at the age of 24, returning to work part-time whilst my husband worked in a factory for 50 hours per week for minimum wages, which meant we had to 'work the system' to ensure we had enough money to survive, which was the normal way of life for me and countless others where I lived, never being judged by anyone as I was not the minority but part of the majority.
However, as my own child grew, went to school and I had another child, I wasn't comfortable in raising them in the culture that I had been brought up in. Like any parent, I wanted them to have the opportunities that I didn't and wanted to embed in them the importance of education, because no matter what happens in your life no one can take your education from you, a fact that became evident to me as I reflected on my own upbringing.
Through wanting to make a better quality life for my children in Gellideg, I worked with other mothers on the estate to form Gellideg Foundation Group which is a grass roots community organisation run by the residents of our estate, where I am now Project Manager, which today has a budget of £2 million, employs 22 members of staff running a variety of community projects from youth provision, after-school clubs, education programmes and health initiatives. Through this work my personal development, confidence and determination has grown massively, as have my educational qualifications. I still live in the same house where I was born, which has now become my family home, finally getting married at 34 years of age with first hand experience of how complex peoples lives are – life choices are never just black or white.
The thing which to drove me to do this was a passion for making things better in my local community. I believed I could make a difference and set out to do so.

Collette Watkins

Introduction

To describe the status of Wales is to enter contested ground, but one reasonably safe way may be to see it as both nation and region. An historic nation within the UK, Wales is linked to its past by its religious and political history and by its culture, which includes a distinct Celtic language spoken by 20% of its current population of 2.9 million. The Government of Wales Act, 1988, gave recognition to this special position with the creation of the Welsh Assembly and, although the powers devolved to it are limited, government policy in Wales is now distinctive and accountable to the Welsh electorate. The devolved government institutions have provided a political identity, which, as Archbishop Rowan Williams said in an interview in 2000, was 'already having an effect on the way people regard Wales as a nation'. More recently the Richard Commission has recommended that there should be a plan for more extensive powers, including primary legislative powers similar to those in Scotland.

But Wales is also a region. The policy making of the Welsh Assembly is largely related to the Welsh position as a region within the UK and European Union and from this perspective, Wales remains at the lower end of the UK economic scale of prosperity – 83% of UK average. Although Welsh GDP per head rose by 55% in the period 1970-1996, the region still has unacceptably high multiple deprivation levels and low average incomes. There are continuing problems of unequal wealth distribution and economic inactivity. In view of the challenge from the low cost economies in Eastern Europe and the developing third world, Welsh devolved government and the community it represents face a major task in the attempt to move from the present low base towards the average economic prosperity of the UK.

Prosperity cannot be judged by economic measurements alone and, like many other disadvantaged regions, Wales has a traditional quality of life and a sense of community identity that is important in considering the nature and purpose of prosperity. Concern for community and other quality issues like the environment at home and relations with others outside Wales are essential to the consideration of any targets for prosperity. Churches and chapels in Wales have experienced decline in attendance, but their continued presence in many communities is a rich potential resource available for personal and community support in a country where many still believe without belonging to any particular denomination. The churches also have a prophetic role that could help Wales respond to its new structures of government – presenting, as Noel Davies, former Secretary of Wales Cytûn, has said in an interview in 2000, 'a faith perspective and theological insight in relation to public life in Wales'. The challenge is to continue to translate theological insight and church ministry into new and practical forms of engagement.

Welsh identity arises from a historic cultural grouping that until the 20th Century was based upon the use of a living Celtic language and a religion that was, during the 19th century and at least until disestablishment after World War 1, mainly nonconformist. Alongside this strong tradition lies another culture whose roots are more recent. It is based upon heavy industry and mining, socialist politics, solid support for rugby and football and the majority language of English with a Welsh accent. The two traditions were sometimes in conflict but often overlapped and to some extent have merged in a country politically committed to bilingualism. Many people, however, have lost interest in both politics and religion and the old identity with the work-place has largely disappeared with the destruction of the old industries: the neighbourhood and family represent for many the remnant of shared community.

The challenge of prosperity in Wales should be driven by an active concern for the peoples and communities of Wales. Whatever moral and social caveats there might be about the nature and implications of prosperity, few would argue that it isn't a legitimate human goal in all its many dimensions. The local and human side of this is important, in Wales as elsewhere. Wherever there is the risk of further degradation of human settlements and social and economic disadvantage for local communities, we have to listen hard to the human stories involved and seek solutions which make their future sustainable. Many church members and clergy are involved in specific local projects which seek to address different kinds of social need. There are many stories to tell of the human face of this crucial work. The Church in Wales, for example, through its social responsibility officers in each Diocese, has about 130 project-based paid staff and over 1,500 volunteers. Each of them has a story to tell. Prosperity matters because individuals, families and communities matter. Every decision taken at a national or local level that reduces the opportunities for prosperity and economic development affects these individuals and communities, sometimes for generations to come.

Dimensions of prosperity and poverty

> *A prosperous Welsh economy that is dynamic, inclusive and sustainable, based on world class competitive business and skilled motivated people ...*

So begins the Welsh Assembly Government's ***National Economic Development Strategy (2001)***, later revised as ***A Winning Wales***. This strategic document should drive Wales's search for better economic performance for the sake of greater prosperity in Wales. It is an inclusive vision with global scope. It rests on the three strategic pillars of all Welsh Assembly Government's policy making – economic development, social inclusion and environmental sustainability. There is a policy commitment not just to make these pillars the political foundations for the future of a post-devolved Wales, nor even to seek balance between them, but to integrate them. This is a remarkable and impressive commitment with significance for a theological statement about prosperity and its reach.

The search for greater prosperity should be driven by a concern for the improvement of the quality of life in the communities of Wales and the well-being of those who live in these communities, as well as for the sustainability of the environment. To achieve this there is a commitment to achieve new levels of integration between the aims and remit of the key public agencies and organizations charged with developing and delivering these policy pillars, notably the Welsh Development Agency (WDA), Education and Learning Wales (ELWa) – the equivalent of the Learning Skills Council in England and the Welsh Tourist Board (WTB). The First Minister announced, in August of 2004, that these Assembly Sponsored Public Bodies (ASPBs) will be discontinued and brought into the political process, to be controlled and run directly by the relevant ministers and civil servants, as from 2006. It is argued by Ministers that this will bring closer co-ordination at a strategic level and more effective performance in the delivery of economic development, education, skill development and training.

To deliver the ***Winning Wales*** vision, both more effective differentiation and more partnership working will be needed. The

Confederation of British Industry, the Institute of Directors, the Trades Union Council, the Federation of Small Businesses, the Chamber of Commerce, the Institute of Welsh Affairs, the Welsh Council of Voluntary Agencies and other brokering organisations have an important role in encouraging and facilitating more co-ordination in addition to delivering services to their own customers and constituents. In Wales, it is particularly important for economic policy making to embrace the key organizations of civil society as real partners, not least to broaden the knowledge and experience base of civil servants. It is equally important for civil society to recognize the significance of wealth-creation for the development and sustainability of communities.

Prosperity as a rich quality of life should be the norm for human aspiration, rather than the preserve of a few. It is made up of overlapping and related elements of which economic or material prosperity is only one; good employment and education may be taken as examples of what makes for material prosperity but which have other dimensions as well. The non-economic dimensions have been described as social, personal and spiritual; and without putting any narrow religious limit to it, it is the spiritual element which pervades all the others. It adds value to daily life and can avoid us 'knowing the price of everything and the value of nothing'. Prosperity is part of a sense of well-being and is not just dependent upon the size of income; being rich in material possessions can have the opposite effect of limiting the quality of life.

It is possible for people and communities to fall well down the scale of social and economic deprivation and yet not consider themselves poor. The self-respect, which is not based upon material wealth, is important and should be recognized, but should not be an excuse for holding back on the personal and community provision of improved opportunities. In a different way, self-regard can sometimes arise from the experience of living with material poverty alongside others within the same town or county who have a better level of material prosperity. Here a low value economy, nurtured by a grey market where good jobs are seen as being elsewhere, can be an obstacle to the search for wider opportunities. Its existence can, moreover, be taken as an excuse by the more prosperous for what Galbraith called the 'culture of contentment', where the prosperity of the majority depends on and benefits from the existence of the poor as an underclass of underprivileged people.

Most of these issues arise elsewhere in the UK, but they are highly important in Wales because of the width of the poverty gap. Prosperity is predicated on the capacity of individuals, communities and organizations to prosper – to take advantage of new opportunities and to create those opportunities. In other words, spirituality is also at the heart of the prosperity agenda in Wales, as it embraces the profound questions of personal and community aspiration, ambition, attitude and motivation. Without a sense of esteem, the innovation and creativity so essential to economic growth will be undermined.

Wales has a community and political history that has met challenges of adversity in the past, and the new political endeavour of the Welsh Assembly to overcome poverty in Wales should find a good response and be encouraged as an attitude for the whole of the community. The opportunity still exists to seek a distinctive pattern based upon a prosperity supporting life in all its fullness.

Economic transformation

The Welsh Assembly Government believes that, because of its size, Wales has a special opportunity to plan comprehensively and bring economic transformation. This opportunity for change, of course, will by shaped by the resources available, by global and UK trade and industry policies and the changing position within the EU. The present system makes the policies of the UK parliament and government a critical part of the future of wealth-creation in Wales.

The task of achieving greater and more sustainable prosperity in Wales is widely recognized as a major challenge. How this challenge is understood and addressed is affected by underlying cultural values and the cultural narrative of Wales. For example, a Church in Wales' response to ***Winning Wales*** noted that its 'world class vision' was reduced to GDP comparisons with England, despite the increasing involvement of the Welsh Assembly Government in the enlarged EU, the commitment of the First Minister to raise the profile of Wales internationally in trade and cultural missions and the recognition of global competition, particularly in and by the business community.

A post-devolution Wales is having to deal with the consequences of its economic inheritance, seeking responsibility for its own new learning in order to branch out in new directions. The past in Wales is the key to understanding present economic and spiritual culture, but should not be allowed to limit the future. The Wales that partly fuelled and engineered the industrial revolution, the spread of the British Empire and later the two World Wars of the 20th century is largely gone. It must reinvent itself in order to create a new economic confidence. Lines must be drawn over the past in order to do this, and, as ever in Wales, education and cultural identity are crucial aspects of this.

Manufacturing is still important, accounting in 1998 for 24.6% of GDP in Wales, compared with 18% in the UK, and directly providing 16.85% of employment total and a similar percentage in dependant industries (CBI evidence to Welsh Affairs Committee). Wales still performs well against the UK average for inward investment and, with the active support of Welsh Assembly Government, UK policy has brought a number of success stories like Airbus, Toyota and Ford. It is not clear how far at present separate Welsh policies can influence new industrial development, but, as experience in successful regions elsewhere shows, there is a need for a strategy based upon rigorous economic analysis. While the Welsh economic strategy should recognize the need to support the manufacturing industry, manufacturing is not likely to regain the position that it and mining held in the past. The challenge will be to maintain the present share in the face of uncertain markets and increasing competition. Policies now seek to emphasize the importance of high value-added manufacturing, including the knowledge driven sectors and the link between business and the universities.

Entrepreneurship is seen as a crucial part of economic achievement in Wales. There are many notable Welsh entrepreneurs in Wales as well as in other counties. For many, there is a concern about increasing bureaucracy and regulations which stifle the development of enterprise attitudes. While the measurement of entrepreneurship is difficult, a comparative, university-based study of 39 different countries by the Global Entrepreneurship Monitor (GEM) used by the WDA, indicates that Wales still lags behind many other countries in entrepreneurship activity. There are 63,000 registered companies in Wales but only 21 floated companies. According to the Wales Management Council (funded by the Welsh Assembly Government to do this work) 99% of all businesses are employing under 250 staff, 98% under 20 staff. SMEs make up 66%

of the work-force, 57% of total turnover and 90% of managers (Wales Management Council). In strategic terms, start-ups and SMEs are crucial for the prosperity of Wales and also for the local communities where they are located, as well as their possible global reach. These kinds of businesses are often highly embedded in local communities and bring both direct and indirect benefits. This link is of significance for the local church as it shares in the concerns of these communities and their spiritual development. The growth of SMEs is crucial for the social as well as the economic sustainability of many small settlements of Wales and the church is well placed to see the consequences of failure and to make its own contribution with others to avoid this.

The Wales Management Council, working closely with the CBI, the IOD, the Chambers of Commerce and other brokering organisations, recognizes the importance of raising the levels of training and business support provided to small companies and removing the barriers to achieving this (p 58ff. 'Management and leadership development and training in Wales. Agenda for Action' published by the Wales Management Council 2003). Cardiff Business School's research in the Small Firms Research Unit ('The Competitive Disadvantage of Firms in South Wales' – an analysis of business growth constraints among SMEs 2001) claimed a lack of human resource development within the majority of SMEs in South Wales and its effect on innovative performance and subsequent competitive advantage. The average training investment by SMEs in South Wales per employee per annum is said to be £570 which is less than the average net cost to employers of training an employee to only NVQ level 2 (£1,000). Negative attitudes and low capabilities were seen as major constraints on management development. Small businesses are not taking up assistance with business start up, Investors in People and similar programmes unless they are heavily subsidized or free. The Wales Management Council's research shows low take up of funded opportunities particularly under Objective 3 with its clear focus on management and leadership development (see p 60 ff 'Management and leadership development and training in Wales. Agenda for Action' published by the Wales Management Council 2003).

The public sector is also seen as essential to regeneration in Wales, partly because it is such a major employer (no less than 29% in public service type work compared with 18% in UK) and good public services are essential. An effective public sector is needed to lead and deliver the policies for renewal and enterprise and public sector decision-making needs to be freed from unnecessary restraints and the burden of maintaining a process rather than delivery of a programme.

Education is one public sector based service that is fundamental to both individual and community growth. Good primary and secondary education must not be limited to teaching literacy and numeracy, although such skills are vital to an effectively working Wales. Education is essential to the well-being of individuals and is sensibly given priority by government, but there are cases where government programmes seem geared to the standard processes and teachers are constrained by limitations of resources. The higher education sector is providing opportunities for innovation in industry and services; working with the skills that are present needs to be positively resourced and encouraged.

Health is another part of the public sector which is vital to the regeneration process. An effective and equitably distributed system of health care delivery is essential for prosperity. The health service, often in conjunction with higher education, is also providing radical economic opportunities in the knowledge-based industries and this research should be given an important place in the system.

A successful economy is dependent upon the quality of its public service – its education, health and transport system are vital in attracting and sustaining new investment, and in contributing to the quality of life.

The Welsh Assembly approach to economic development by reference to skills and opportunities that already exist in different parts of Wales is realistic and starts to break down barriers caused by administrative boundaries. 'People, Places, Futures', the Wales Spatial Plan, transcends questions of land use and encourages new creativity across boundaries. Partnerships with industry and the voluntary sector are being developed. The public sector is also an area that should lead in dealing with low pay, and Church leaders in Wales, with Church Action on Poverty, Unison and TCC are campaigning for the Welsh Assembly Government to introduce a 'living wage clause' into contracts. This approach has to take into account competition from other parts of the world. If successful, it would help a large group of low paid workers in Wales and set a pattern for a better base level for Wales as a whole. Another cross-over point would be the encouragement of public sector procurement policies which support local business and, while best value practices must be maintained, experience elsewhere has shown that such mutual support contributes to economic growth.

Economic transformation is obviously important but improving the GDP figures and increasing personal wealth on its own will not be enough. Economic transformation policies must involve those at present in the poverty and low wage trap and the commitment must be to make sure, as Rhodri Morgan, Wales' First Minister, has said, 'all communities can share in the increased wealth and prosperity of Wales. The less well-off communities should be in the front of the queue to share in this prosperity'.

The GEM report indicates that it is also important to address attitudinal and 'spiritual' issues beyond skill-based competencies. Changing attitudes to work and performance isn't just an issue within particular companies, but is part of the larger regeneration agenda in Wales. Increasing confidence and ambition for greater creativity, flexibility, market access and competitiveness, particularly in a global context, is recognized to be a longer-term project. Training solutions with their hard target focus need to be embedded in longer-term cultural growth, where the invisible culture of communities and organisations is as important as the visible culture. Again, the former presents the churches of Wales and Cytûn with some formidable challenges and opportunities for ministry. Engagement with such opportunities will require a new sense of interest in the connection between spirituality and the economy and a commitment to work with economic providers as well as consumers.

Community and social transformation

The extent of poverty in Wales is illustrated by a gross weekly household income in 2001 of 17% below the UK average, with 21% of the income being derived from social security payments – the highest of any region in UK. Some figures produced by Oxfam Cymru and the Anti-Poverty Network Cymru state that 33% of children in Wales live in poverty, the highest rate in UK, the youth unemployment rate in Wales is 26.8% and 33% of the population have no qualifications at all. The Basic Skills Agency reports that 28% of adults in Wales have literacy abilities below functional levels and 32% have numeracy levels below functionality. The Welsh Assembly Government (WAG) recognizes the serious need for action and has recently created a cabinet post with specific responsibility for Social Justice and Regeneration. The First Minister pointed to the need 'to make sure communities are empowered to regenerate themselves and tackle the social problems inherited by neglect and economic starvation'. 'Empowerment' is important but so is the need for a general transformation of attitudes to see that prosperity should be shared by all parts of the community. More resources for initiatives in early childhood and schooling are crucial.

In Wales, as elsewhere, the targets for community and social transformation are sought through partnerships supported by public intervention. These partnerships are intended to create greater co-operation between statutory, voluntary and community sectors – this co-operation needs positive support to recognize the equal validity of the contributions that can be made. The WAG has initiated an £83 million Communities First Programme to reduce social exclusion. It is too early to know whether outputs from this programme will be generally successful. The programme is, however, only part of the answer – it covers particular areas but leaves other estates with similar problems. It is essential to bring forward other programmes which relate to the needs of deprived areas – lack of employment, poor health, lack of education and consequent low expectations: and a programme of empowerment needs new techniques of mentoring.

In the Valleys of South Wales and other important former industrial areas, in the outer estates of many towns, in parts of the inner city, in isolated rural areas, the extent of the regeneration challenge is obvious. The multiple barriers of the 'hard to reach' exist alongside the physical condition of some housing and infrastructure. Disadvantage and disaffection are reproduced by generational patterns of despair and sometimes of disorder. In other words, hard and soft regeneration must go together. Increasing economic capacity in these communities cannot be achieved without addressing social capacity. But, without the experience and responsibilities of work, how will young people rediscover a fulfilling economic role, developing their social and work potential? As Local Authorities try to find new ways of partnership working with the police, the churches, the health and the voluntary sector to address the mental health and substance misuse problems associated with anti-social behaviours, there is a great need to find appropriate interventions and to learn from the robust survival skills of such communities. They have their own stories to tell, of not only how to survive but to role model positive examples of community initiative and change. In each of the Dioceses of the Church in Wales, Social Responsibility projects are working with parenting skills and families to impact on the generational reach of these problems and to work with local communities as they find their own solutions.

The Social Economy is a diffuse but substantial part of local economies and communities. Partnership between the public authorities, communities, industry and voluntary organisations, including the faith communities, is still being worked out institutionally, but may provide a route to renewal. While attendance at churches may have fallen, many churches in Wales are responding positively in a wider contemporary role of community engagement. Encouraged by government policy to involve them and other faith communities in a social role, some churches and their leaders are sharing directly in social programmes as a key part of Christian witness. Spirituality is seen as including an outreach to communities in building self-esteem and confidence and the work place needs to be taken more seriously as an opportunity for personal and social development as well as a place for wealth-creation. A Church in Wales study on Rural Communities and Social Change called upon churches, in terms that apply equally to many urban communities, to take a lead in transformation processes and to ensure that 'church buildings and presence within local communities should become the hub of regeneration activity'. Archbishop Rowan Williams spoke in his interview in 2000 of the challenge to local church communities to play their part in civil society. He said, 'This is more than the encouragement of Christian involvement in political parties but is a challenge on attitudes towards society. Some particular issues are churches' response towards community development and the attitudes towards "debt on the doorstep" and the readiness to participate in practical efforts like credit unions'.

While the churches, the voluntary, not-for-profit and community sectors provide different kinds of social project support, Wales is slowly developing new styles of social economy and community enterprise. This third sector is supported by both the Minister for Economic Development and the Minister for Regeneration as being a crucial part of the regeneration industry, but more needs to be done to connect agencies and to develop new models of economic participation and activity. Regeneration is still a comparatively young industry in Wales and there is a need for more innovative solutions and joined up thinking. Less reliance on European structural funds will be important as EU enlargement develops.

As elsewhere, the problem is not simply a case of unemployment. It includes low wage and poverty traps in areas largely bereft of any substantial commercial activity. So the challenge is to find the routes out of poverty into prosperity via different kinds of local family support, quality of life improvement, skill development, training, behavioural change, business support and economic and physical infrastructure. The prosperity hologram in Wales has to recognize the spiritual basis of the problem.

Economic transformation and the environment

The environment in Wales needs to be protected partly because about One in six jobs and 10% of Welsh GDP depend upon its good management, use and enjoyment. In the farming/agriculture industry the policy in Wales is to move to high added value but linked to a more sustainable form of farming. The Welsh Assembly Government backed this with a target of 10% of Welsh agriculture to be under organic management by 2005. If successful the programme should lead to reduced dependence upon artificial stimulation of the growth of plants and animals with chemicals and pesticides. Another employment activity directly linked to the quality and maintenance of the environment is tourism, employing about 10% of the work-force and contributing about 12% of Welsh GDP.

While there are these good economic reasons to cherish the environment in Wales, there is a growing recognition that the richness and diversity of the environment is, in itself, an important part of a valid definition of prosperity. The Welsh Assembly Government's National Economic Development Strategy envisages a large increase in the number of new jobs to be created by 2010 but as required by its foundation statute – S.121 of the Government of Wales Act – it is also committed to promote sustainable development. This must mean that growth in the economy must avoid prejudicing the ability of future generations to meet their needs and the demand for local jobs has to be put in a wider context of environmental biodiversity. This requires both the political will to prepare and maintain a consistent strategy and a programme of public understanding that 'green issues' are a matter of common concern.

The value of the environment cannot be easily quantified, but attempts have been made. The Index of Sustainable Economic Welfare warns that the growth in Welsh GDP in the period 1970-1996 has taken place alongside a decline in the environmental quality. Much has already been achieved by the Welsh Development Agency in removing the industrial pollution of earlier years with its land reclamation programmes but the pressures to intrude into the quality of the environment are strong. Economic development should be balanced against the overall issues of quality of life in determining what is a prosperous Wales and investment needs to take on a more inclusive approach. Welsh Assembly Government has also supported 'ecological foot-printing' as a measure on a global basis of the relative resource consumption per resident. Like other first world countries, Wales is shown to have more than its 'fair earth share' – about three times as much! (Stuart Bond, Institute of Welsh Affairs Agenda 2001). Apart from providing a challenge to review our priorities for fair living, the measure should show whether we are becoming more or less just in our dealing with the natural resources. In a prosperous Wales we should hand on the environment in at least as good a condition as we have received it and should be ready to account globally for our use of it.

Globalization and transformation

The increased ability to communicate and share experiences globally is to be welcomed and the growth in reciprocal care for each other is a potential for good to be included in our definition of prosperity. Globalization has presented a fundamental change in the ability to create wealth but its effect on weaker communities makes it a mixed blessing. The concern for people elsewhere, besides those in our own nation, has created an awareness of the injustice of some of the global rules of trade. Prosperity needs a purpose and, as Geoff Williams says in the Welsh Independents' paper ***Globalization – Challenge for the Churches, 2000***, it is vital to recognize that efficient global markets have increased wealth but have resulted in a widening income gap between the world's richest people and the poorest. Christian Aid and other organizations in Wales and elsewhere raise their concerns and campaign for fair trade rules in an issue affecting the sense of prosperity of everyone. How can we think of progress to prosperity unless it encompasses all the nations on the globe?

Looked at from the perspective of the Welsh economy, the global market also presents a major challenge. Manufacturing in Wales may have outperformed the rest of the UK but most of it is dependent upon the world market and there is need to encourage the adaptability of skills, to attract more research and development work and to encourage a local back-up of small and medium enterprises. Inward investment from abroad has been very successful in Wales but some local examples have shown how these industries are particularly dependent upon decisions in the global markets beyond local influence. Diversity is important in a response to the global markets.

Minority cultures generally do not fare well under globalization and yet, as the church has come to realize, every culture and language is part of a God-given diversity in the world and all people have theological value as being made in the image of God. Applied to Wales it is argued that the quality of life in Wales will be measured by its ability to sustain its traditions as a small nation in a globalized culture. The historic language and culture of Wales has been supported by churches in Wales. For example, Gareth Edwards, the former Secretary of the Presbyterian Church of Wales, saw support for Welsh language and culture as one of two priorities for action by the Assembly Government in a 2000 interview. (His other priority was action in support of the disadvantaged). Community participation and identification are part of the programme for personal enrichment for people here and elsewhere and diversity is one element in it.

The theme of this paper has been to support the theologically based engagement of the churches with civil society and people in community. It is based upon the recognition of the democratic process and decision-making by public authorities. But, by their presence and concern, churches can contribute as partners to a holistic understanding of prosperity and respond positively with people and premises. The concept of partnership between the churches and other faith communities and voluntary organisations, as well as with the public sector, provides 'a potential for hope and transformation' (from the Manchester ***Faith in Partnership*** series).

The old idea of the Welsh nonconformist conscience was based upon an evangelical ethical theology which found in the Bible the knowledge that social practice for Christians arises from the personal outworking of Christ's revelation. It supported the creation of wealth in the community and by individuals, but called for care for people as seen in need. Social responsibility continued to be part of the Christian contribution to society throughout the 20th century and was developed in the last decade in Wales by Cytûn (Churches Together) in ***Wales, a Moral Society?*** 1996. There the attempt was made to set primary Christian concerns revealed in the Bible alongside evidence drawn from social practice and such a methodology should in contemporary society provide a view requiring both community involvement and global concern. In consequent action, churches should not be deterred from making the Christian view on values known, even if for some outside the church this perspective is only one of many.

All humans are made in the image of God and all God's people belong to the single extended family which is the human race. It is a matter of human right and dignity for all to share both in community and world prosperity and to accept the responsibilities of such participation. Theology, no less than social policy, calls for action based on a code of human rights, envisaging personal, material, social and spiritual rights and responsibilities for all individuals and societies.

9

England's North-West Region: John Devine

The Emerging Role of Faith Communities in Regional Development

There is a growing acknowledgement from central government that faith communities should put their knowledge of and involvement in local communities at the service of neighbourhood renewal. Local faith groups are increasingly invited to get more directly involved in political and economic partnerships with other stakeholders, a move which may feel like a departure from traditional spiritual and social roles. Several factors contribute to this change in attitude from central government (from both ends of the political spectrum) hitherto fastidious in keeping religion at arms length. There has been a reappraisal of the value of civil society in western democracies – specifically the part played by community and voluntary sectors and, latterly, faith communities. Civil society, sometimes referred to as the 'third sector', is that part of society not covered by government or private enterprise. It includes the voluntary sector, culture and, of course, faith communities.

Failure of attempts to narrow the gap between richest and poorest by generations of government grants have caused policy makers to look again at the role of other stakeholders in achieving sustainable development. The Local Government Association document ***Faith & Community: a Good Practice Guide for Local Authorities (February 2002)*** states: 'Faith groups may be the best means of reaching those in need within their faith community and sometimes those in the wider community also.' (3.2)

The message of the document is that faith communities should be taken seriously. They do not come to the table empty handed but contribute across a spectrum of priorities: 'good health, as providers of pastoral care, promoters of citizenship, and community development, voices for social justice, and as the locus for gatherings of people in varying economic and social positions, of differing political views, from a range of ethnic backgrounds with shared concerns.' (3.1) They bring leadership, resources and above all, volunteers. 'Guidance makes clear that faith communities have a part to play in the relevant processes and structures, such as local strategic partnerships and Neighbourhood Management' (4.7). Government's enthusiasm for faith communities extends even to funding. 'Both central government and many local authorities now accept the validity and value of funding services and activities run by faith groups. Some will argue that this is justified only if the services and activities are open to all, regardless of their faith. Others will argue that a service or activity, even if targeted at those within a faith community, can nevertheless be assessed in terms of its public or community benefit and a case for public funding can therefore be made.' (5.1) This realization is reinforced by a growing appreciation of the role of faith groups in social cohesion, given further urgency by civil unrest in northern towns and the consequences of September 11th 2001.

Opportunites for partnership working exist at all levels of government: national regional, local and neighbourhood. The document ***Working Together: Co-operation between Government and Faith Communities, Home Office Faith Communities Unit, February 2004*** extends the challenge made by the Local Government Association report ***Faith and Community*** to public agencies at national level. The Churches have also been working at regional level. Although no single pattern of engagement has emerged in each of the eight English regions (nine including London) officers appointed ecumenically in each of these regions to promote the partnership agenda have formed the Churches' Regional Network in order to share good practice. The decisive result of the recent referendum on an elected regional assembly for the North East of England does not appear to mark the end of the English regional project. In the majority of regions where elected bodies were never a realistic possibility, partnership working has proceeded without the distraction of a potential referendum. At the same time Regional Development Agencies and Regional Government Offices continue to have major responsibility for regional strategy and funding.

Since the Enlightenment, Christianity has been challenged by rational, scientific and secular values. This has been accompanied by a progressive decline in church attendance, accelerating rapidly in the last 40 years. In the second half of the 20th century the Churches became accustomed to being dismissed as irrelevant, retrograde, amateur and unprofessional. Religion was perceived as a personal matter best kept to oneself. Refusal to support anything with a religious dimension was seen as the politically correct approach to adopt by public bodies and even by personally committed Christians working within them. So adapted have Churches become to their perceived irrelevance that many still find it easier to relate to statutory bodies with their religious affiliation disguised. So successful has this strategy been that organisations such as the Children's Society (Church of England) and NCH (Methodist) and the Nugent Care Society (Roman Catholic) are perceived by many as purely secular institutions. New opportunities for partnership working, on the other hand, recognize the faith dimension as adding value.

There is some theological justification as to why churches should get involved in public life in a pluralist, post-modern society. A 'Theology of Partnership' must acknowledge a common ethical commitment, non-violence, respect for life, just economic and political order, tolerance and truthfulness, equal rights and partnership between men and women. It should also build on the rootedness of faith groups in local communities coupled with openness to learn from others' experience and traditions as well as tolerance of difference. Fundamentally it should recognize that the resources of individual faith communities are a resource for all rather than for an exclusive elite. Inevitably there might be some within every faith tradition who would find difficulty in embracing such open-ended engagement, perceiving it to be a threat to their core beliefs. The challenge for all faith communities, Christian and non-Christian alike, is a willingness to engage in a shared, negotiated agenda with other partners in pursuit of the common good. It is of necessity an organic process that cannot be accelerated to accommodate targets and budget deadlines. Confidence building can only proceed at its own pace.

Obviously the Churches and other faith communities do not limit their understanding of who they are and the role they have in society to that suggested to them by government. They are distinctive for other reasons. The Kingdom of God cannot be reduced to material outcomes and outputs. The Churches' contribution to civil society even on the government's own terms, however, is underestimated. Regeneration professionals have not in the past recognized the Churches as serious players. The message of ***Faith and Community*** has hardly penetrated. Britain's churches and other faith communities in turn are beginning to realize that they need to establish their credibility in a climate that is evidence based. It is only 'what gets counted that counts'. This was the motivation behind a recent report ***Faith in England's North-West: the contribution made by faith communities to civil society in the region*** (North-West Development Agency, November,

2003). The project was undertaken by the Churches' Officer for the North-West and the North-West Regional Intelligence Unit. Questionnaires were sent to every individual place of worship in the region.

Key findings

There was a high level of response with 54% of the survey's 4,400 questionnaires being returned. The response was particularly good for minority faith communities, including a response rate of 68.9% for the Sikhs, 53% for Jews, 50% of Baha'is, 43% for Moslems, and 39 per cent for Hindus. Christian responses account for 93% of the total with a response rate ranging from 63% for Anglicans to 22.4% for the Evangelical, Pentecostal, and Charismatic churches. This high response rate in itself illustrates the willingness of faith communities to seriously engage.

The distribution of faith communities who responded to the survey matches population density, with 45% of those who responded describing themselves as urban, 27% as rural, and 28% as suburban. Mapped against the Index of Multiple Deprivation, responses returned demonstrate that faith communities, whilst represented in the most affluent areas, are concentrated in areas of highest social need. Faith communities also assist some of the most vulnerable social groups, including older people and children.

Faith communities are custodians of built heritage. From the total of 2,325 faith communities who responded, 34% stated that their building was listed. Many of their buildings are a significant resource for the wider community. Almost all of those surveyed (2,282 respondents) indicated they have rooms used by other local community groups.

Faith communities respond rapidly and flexibly to local crises. At the time of the foot and mouth epidemic, 45% of rural Christian Churches who responded to the survey indicated an involvement in support initiatives.

One in ten faith communities who responded stated that they were managing or organising projects addressing a wide range of issues including housing, homelessness, anti-racism, crime prevention, drug and alcohol abuse, employment and training, social enterprise and personal finance. 14% of all faith communities also indicate that they organize environmental projects. A total of 5,140 non-worship projects were identified by the survey. Furthermore, faith communities are also engaged in 'official' government regeneration projects. The survey revealed that of those who responded 248 are involved in Single Regeneration Budget (SRB) schemes, 224 in SureStart, 62 in Learn Direct, and 95 in other programmes.

Virtually all activity undertaken by faith communities is dependent on volunteers and based on the estimates of those who responded, the survey demonstrates that there are 45,667 volunteers in England's North-West who are involved in activities in the community other than worship.

While government has indicated a desire to involve faith communities in Local Strategic Partnerships (LSPs), findings indicate that only 40% of all Christians who responded are aware of LSPs. Of these 53% have been approached by Local Authorities to participate. There remains a significant number who are unaware of such opportunities, or are being excluded.

Most significantly, the contribution of faith communities detailed in the report is largely self-funded. 27% of those responding to the survey indicate they have received public funding while 73% have not.

> *The picture that has emerged is one of faith communities often playing a multi-dimensional role in their neighbourhoods that touches people far beyond their own members. To use the current jargon, they are part of the important stock of social capital. They contribute towards community cohesion in its widest sense. The survey findings underline the social and economic role played by faith communities. They appear to reinforce the claim that the faith communities are close to groups that other agencies find 'hard to reach'. But the survey has also indicated that there are new opportunities for faith communities to work alongside others at both neighbourhood and local authority levels. Many faith communities have already successfully demonstrated that this is part of their mission. Others still have some way to go.* ***(Faith in England's North-West: the contribution made by faith communities to civil society in the region,*** North-West Development Agency, November 2003)

This study is to be followed by a further report ***Faith in England's North-West: An Economic Impact Assessment***, North-West Development Agency, February 2005, which will assign a cash value to the contributions identified in the first publication

Faith in partnership

There follow two examples of churches and other faith communities working in partnership with other agencies in England's North-West.

St Augustine's new Avenham Centre, Preston

Inaugurated in January 2004, this project involves creative development of a crumbling listed church building as a catalyst for the regeneration of Avenham, a deprived area of Preston, Lancashire. It requires partial demolition of St Augustine's Roman Catholic Grade 2* listed church building and its redevelopment as a multi-purpose centre costing over £5 million. Its prominent neo classical towers and portico are retained as a landmark in the neighbourhood and a symbol of the churches' continuing commitment to the area.

Designed as a multi-purpose sports, family learning, education, and enterprise centre, St Augustine's is to become the focal point for the delivery of a wide range of community services providing fitness and leisure activities, business start-up units, a crèche and childcare facilities, and will be a base for local community and voluntary sector organisations.

Due to open in late Spring 2005, the Centre has attracted some £1.5 million from the Single Regeneration Budget (SRB6), as well as over £0.75 million of European Regional Development Funds (ERDF) via Preston's Objective 2 Priority 2 Action for Communities Programme. Other funders include Sports England Lottery (£1.85 million), Lancashire County Council (£250,000), Preston City Council (£150,000), Preston Central SureStart (£125,000), and the RC Diocese of Lancaster, who will have spent almost £1 million in total to realize the Centre.

Closed in 1989 because of structural problems, the church was originally built in 1836 and extended in the 1890s to accommodate a growing congregation in Avenham – which numbered 5,000 at the turn of the 19th Century. Today 29.77% of people in the ward are from ethnic minority backgrounds, and the number of people from those communities in the 16-24 age group is 60% above the Preston average.

A significant feature of the project is a close inter-faith relationship with the local Islamic community. Recognising the diversity that exists within communities within inner Preston, the Roman Catholic Diocese of Lancaster has invested substantial resources and effort into ensuring their needs are met by the Project.

Speaking at the its launch in January 2004 Patrick O'Donoghue, R.C. Bishop of Lancaster stated 'This Project demonstrates what can be achieved by faith and community groups working alongside government to provide much-needed support to areas in need. It has shown us how to turn decline and adversity into opportunity.'

Operation Eden

Whilst the Avenham Centre concentrates on a church ***building***, Operation Eden brings the church's other primary resource into partnership: its ***people***, especially its impressive cohort of volunteers. EDEN is a unique community environmental initiative in Liverpool that has received substantial government funding.

Launched in April 2004, Operation EDEN is a £500k three-year project sponsored by the Church of England Diocese of Liverpool with funding principally from the North-West Development Agency together with the Environment Agency and Merseyside Waste Disposal Authority. Two key voluntary sector partners are also involved – Groundwork and Sefton Council for Voluntary Service. EDEN employs a Co-ordinator, Project Officer and Office Administrator who are working to expand the existing network of over 120 parish environmental representatives into an ecumenical and inter-faith network committed to the regeneration of local communities and the transformation of the local environment through micro-economic regeneration projects and training initiatives. This includes improving the way that communities understand and appreciate their environment. Local Groups will be helped to improve buildings that serve the community, develop local recycling schemes and reclaim and refurbish open space, in urban as well as rural areas.

The Bishop of Liverpool, the Rt Revd James Jones, has said:

'Project EDEN is one small contribution, bringing together local agencies, faith partners and volunteers to help make local communities better places to live. Christians must work together with others for the holistic transformation of the local environment, spiritually and physically'.

Steven Broomhead, Chief Executive of the North-West Development Agency (NWDA), has also stated: 'This unique scheme provides the perfect opportunity to engage and empower the region's faith communities in local environmental regeneration projects and initiatives. It will encourage different faith communities to work together on local projects, providing a strong and coherent approach to environmental regeneration and resource efficiency issues. I am pleased to support this innovative new scheme, which will create an improved environment for all Merseyside residents.'

Prosperity, policy and public policy

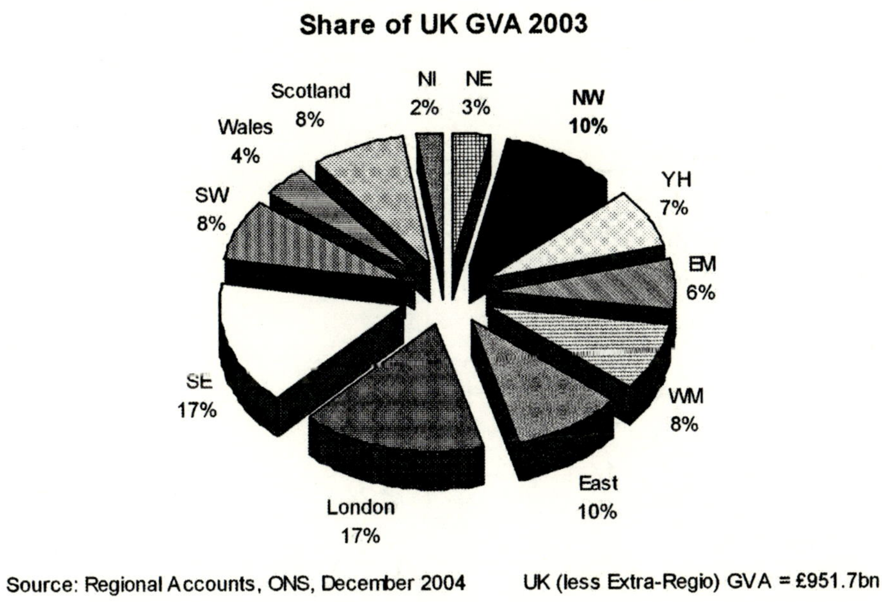

(National Statistics Regional Accounts 2004)

So the faith communities are closely engaged with issues of

prosperity and poverty in this Region. But they know that they work against a background of almost intractable disparities between rich and poor. For example, ***Reducing Regional Disparities in Prosperity,*** (a report of the ODPM Housing, Planning Local Government and the Regions 2002-2003), states that the gap between the North-West (population 7 million) and other UK regions is increasing. From almost equalling the national average in 1973 it has fallen to 10% below the 1996 national average. No other region has experienced greater decline. The health of the region is poor. The North-West has one of the lowest rates of life expectancy in the UK. In 2001 the North-West's GVA was £87.6 billion, 10% of the UK's total GVA making it the 3rd largest of the twelve UK regional economies after London and the South East. At the same time, however, with a GVA per head of £13,011 or 89.9% of the UK average, the North-West is ranked 7th out of the 12 UK regions.

UK GVA per head by Region	
London	134.9%
South East	119.9%
East of England	109.9%
Scotland	94.4%
East Midlands	91.7%
West Midlands	90.3%
North-West	89.99%
South West	89%
Yorkshire & the Humber	86.2%
Wales	78.8%
Northern Ireland	78.2%
North East	76.1%

GVA (Gross Value Added)[68] is the preferred indicator of economic performance rather than GDP (Gross Domestic Product) since direct comparisons can be made with European regions where different taxing regimes apply. Neither can GDP rates be calculated at regional level since VAT and alcohol duties are not available for individual regions.

GVA is one component in the calculation of standard GDP: GVA + taxes on products – subsidies = GDP. GVA is calculated on the basis of total of incomes and profits earned (plus taxes less subsidies on production). GVA ***per head*** represents the regional total divided by each member of the population. As is the case with any comparative measure of wealth or deprivation GVA can disguise pockets of prosperity or poverty within regions themselves. Well-paid jobs located within the city of Manchester, for example, raise the GVA per head for the city even though many of the higher paid work-force commute from outside the city boundaries. Pockets of extreme deprivation among those actually living within the city of Manchester are masked. However, although, deprived housing estates also exist within otherwise affluent southern regions, we do believe that statistics give some indication of where concentrations of inequality lie.

GVA growth in the North-West has always been lower than the UK average. Key contributors to UK GVA growth since 1990 have been real estate and business services. One reason for the gap between the ranking of the size of the North-West economy and its ranking on GVA per head has been its continuing dependence on manufacturing as well as less favourable demographics. *(North-West Development Agency,* 2004*)*

According to the Index of Multiple Deprivation 2000 (IMD 2000), six of the ten most deprived wards in the country are in the North-West of England. IMD 2000 shows overall levels of deprivation at both local authority and ward levels. It uses information from 33 indicators to describe ward level deprivation in terms of six 'domains' or dimensions: income, employment, health and disability, education, skills and training, housing and geographical access to services. There are 354 local authority districts in England. Forty three are in the North-West. When the IMD-based ranking of each ward level is averaged out to local authority district level, 22 of the 88 most deprived districts in England are found to be in the North-West. Inevitably, isolated deprived wards fail to be recognized in the statistics when they are located in otherwise prosperous local authority districts.

What interventions can be made to address inequalities within the UK and at what level? The real levers of control remain in the hands of central government. What influence can local authorities bring to bear when the standard spending assessment is controlled by Whitehall? Council tax rises in the affluent South in order to subsidize the more deprived North are political suicide for any government.

The Department for Trade and Industry controls the tasks given to Regional Development Agencies and they are the same for each of the nine English regions. The possibility of elected regional assemblies in the three northern English regions will bring the performance of RDAs under direct regional scrutiny. It will be interesting to see if a positive outcome in these referenda has an effect on reducing regional disparities.

One response to social exclusion is the provision of safety nets for the permanently disadvantaged. But real progress in tackling social exclusion has to be economic inclusion with employment recognized as the only realistic route to sustainable development. The Regional Economic Strategy for the North-West Development Agency promotes a skills strategy to go hand in hand with attracting the inward investment that will provide 'real' jobs.

North/South competition within the UK was illustrated in the year 2000 by the award of the Synchrotron project to the Rutherford laboratories at Harwell in Oxfordshire rather than to the Daresbury laboratories in Cheshire. There was only ever to be one Synchrotron in the UK. Its award to the already well-resourced southern half of the country was seen as a serious undermining of the North-West's science base with an inevitable negative knock-on effect for industry and jobs in the region. The subsequent political furore resulted in the award of two other projects by the DTI to Daresbury, interpreted by many as consolation prizes.

Efforts to narrow the gap between richest and poorest within England have centred on initiatives such as the Neighbourhood Renewal Fund. The NRF is directed towards the 88 deprived districts. Described as a 'top up' for local authorities, the fund is an attempt to improve core public services. It amounted to £100 million in 2001-2, £300 million in 2002-03 and £400 million in 2004. Community involvement in area-based regeneration initiatives has been developing for some time. In 2001 these principles were embodied in the concept of LSPs (Local Strategic Partnerships). LSPs bring together different parts of the public and private sectors along with voluntary and community sectors. Corresponding to local authority boundaries, they allow strategic decisions to be made whilst still being close enough to local communities for them to play a full part. (DETR ***Local Strategic Partnerships – Government Guidance***, March 2001, p.16).

The intention is for all areas to have an LSP irrespective of their socio-economic position. However, LSPs are also seen as an important means of achieving neighbourhood renewal. The LSP is the vehicle through which the Neighbourhood Renewal Fund is being distributed to the poorest 88 areas. Each partnership area is required to draw up a community plan to determine how the extra funding should be spent. This extra cash, however skilfully targeted, is only a very small percentage of any local authority's overall budget. Perhaps the real test for LSPs exists in non-Neighbourhood Renewal areas where they can only attempt to 'bend' mainstream budgets to address local priorities. Indeed this is the situation that will prevail even in the most disadvantaged areas when the special grants climate comes to an end.

Competition and dependency

One feature that characterizes the allocation of extra resources at regional, local and community levels is competition. To attract one type of funding, a city such as Liverpool has to demonstrate its cultural strengths, while at the same time it has to 'talk up' its failures if it is to address other funding criteria. The issue is further complicated when we examine the future of European structural funding post European enlargement. Hitherto the North-West region is currently the largest UK recipient of European Structural Funds. Only Cornwall within the UK will be eligible for new Objective 1 funding post enlargement. Current proposals suggest that Merseyside might be eligible for transitional funding as a 'statistical effect' region if its GVA ranking (according to figures to be published in 2005) suggest that it would fall below 75% of EU GVA. This support, beginning at 85% of current Objective 1 levels would taper to 60% by 2013.

The UK is a net contributor to the EU budget. So it should be. However, UK government proposals to 'renationalize' part of wealthier member states' contributions to European central funds in order to reduce them to a level sufficient only to support new member states would further disadvantage more deprived areas in the UK. It believes that current budget proposals are 'unrealistic and unaffordable'. There is a feeling among some UK beneficiaries of the current funding regime that Brussels is more effective in addressing national regional disparities than Westminster might be. In addition, the compulsory 'match' funding from the UK government that currently complements European grants, would be lost. All this, however, must be balanced against the view that quasi-permanent subsidies create dependency.

Competition exists at the heart of all attempts to iron out disparities between rich and poor both in the UK and in Europe. League tables designed to identify areas of greatest need and monitor their progress encourage competitiveness. There are winners and losers.

10

Ireland: Margaret Burns

Introduction

The Churches in Ireland, generally speaking, predate the partition of the island in 1922, and so they tend to be organized on an all-Ireland basis. They consult with one another very regularly. On public issues, one forum for such consultation is the Department of Social Issues of the Irish Inter-Church Meeting, a rather more informal instrument of consultation than its title suggests.

As noted elsewhere, the ***Prosperity with a Purpose*** project takes its cue, and its title, from a discussion initiated by the Irish Catholic Bishops' Conference in a pastoral letter of that name published in 1999. When the discussion on prosperity and its implications began to involve the churches throughout these islands, the DSI organized two expert seminars around the theme. One was arranged in Dublin, and treated the issues as they arise in the Republic. The other took place in Belfast, and looked at the questions as they present in Northern Ireland. What follows is mainly a distillation of the papers presented at those seminars.

The Republic of Ireland

Economic growth and employment

Following the economic stagnation of much of the 1980s – a period characterized by low and at times even negative growth, along with extremely high levels of unemployment and emigration – Ireland experienced in the late 1980s the beginnings of a recovery which has led to the most sustained period of economic growth ever seen in the history of the state.

Ireland now finds itself in the unexpected position of being considered a model economy, one that '[it] has become fashionable for economists to cogitate on'[69] and which is seen as 'providing useful lessons for other countries'.[70] The factors that have led to its economic transformation have been much debated but most commentators highlight the success of state policies aimed at attracting foreign direct investment. These are: the availability of a well-educated work-force and the ability to draw on previously untapped labour sources once growth began to translate into a high demand for labour (notably the entry into the work-force of significant numbers of married women); infrastructural development, which was substantially funded by European Union social funding; and the Social Partnership process which assisted in the moderation of wage demands, the creation of industrial relations stability and the generation of a common sense of purpose among key actors in the economy – Government, employers and trade unions. All of these internal factors were favoured by the general upturn in the international economy during the 1990s.

From 1993 to 2000, average annual GDP growth in Ireland was 9.3%; growth in GNP averaged 8.3%. (It is argued by many that GNP offers a more accurate measure of national income accruing to Irish residents given the high share of foreign companies who remit their profits abroad.) With the downturn in the world economy after 2000, Ireland's growth slowed substantially: in 2002, growth was 3% measured in GDP but less than 1% measured in GNP. However, there has now been a resumption of significant growth, with the increase for 2004 expected to be around 5% in GDP and 4.8% in GNP. Continued growth of around 5% is predicted for the next few years.

By 2001 Ireland was exactly twice as rich, measured in real terms, as it had been in 1990. Having long been one of Europe's poor relations, its status, for almost a decade, of being the fastest growing economy in the EU meant that it not only caught up with but surpassed the average income per head for the Union.

According to the National Economic and Social Council: 'The most remarkable feature of the boom of the 1990s was not the attainment of sustained high economic growth but the extent of the employment expansion associated with it.'[71] The character of Ireland's economic growth from the 1960s to 1993 was one of 'higher productivity on the part of a slowly growing number of people in employment'. The numbers at work remained around 1 million for decades; indeed, until the early 1990s there were fewer people in work in the Republic than there had been at the time of the foundation of the state. Economic growth since 1993 has had a very different outcome. Every year from 1994 to 1999, 60,000 net new jobs were created; in all, 450,000 net new jobs were created during the 1990s. From 1993 to 2000, the rate of employment growth (average

4.7% per year) was significantly higher than the averages of the EU, OECD and the US. Ireland's employment rate is now above the average for the EU whereas previously it was well below.

The rate of participation of women in employment has increased significantly, growing by 40% in the period 1994 to 2003 as against an increase in the participation rate for men of 15%. For women under 35, employment participation rates are now around the EU average; for older women they are still significantly lower. The participation rate for women with skills and qualifications is markedly higher than that for unskilled groups.

Ireland's economic boom and growth in employment took considerable time to impact significantly on unemployment figures. As recently as 1997, 10.3% of the labour force was unemployed. However, by early 2001 unemployment had dropped to a record low of 3.7%. It subsequently rose again but then began to decline once more and in November 2004 stood at around 4%. A notable feature of the fall in unemployment has been the marked drop in the number of households in which no person of working age is in employment. Whereas the proportion of working-age households that were 'workless' stood at 22% in 1994, by 1997 this had fallen to 18% and by 2000 it had dropped still further to 14%. Increased employment has therefore impacted positively on those families and communities where unemployment was most concentrated. Nevertheless, it is clear that several household types remain vulnerable to being jobless: lone-parent households; households where people of working age have low levels of educational attainment or have a disability; single person households.[72]

Whereas the 1980s in Ireland were scarred by mass out-migration, the past decade has witnessed substantial in-migration. As the boom got underway, significant numbers of workers, the majority of them skilled, arrived in the country. Half of the in-migration at this point was accounted for by the return of Irish people who had out-migrated during the 1980s. Since 2000, there has been a significant level of in-migration of unskilled labour. An estimated 40,000 work permits were issued in 2002, a figure not much below the annual outflow from the education system (46,000). In addition, Ireland since the mid-1990s has become the destination for the first time for a significant number of asylum-seekers. The number of applications exceeded 1,000 for the first time in 1995, rose sharply to a peak of 11,000 in 2002 but has now dropped again to an estimated 4,000 for 2004.

Despite the success of economic development and the multiple benefits this has brought to the country, there are several key areas where questions about the equitable distribution of the increased resources come sharply into focus.

Income inequality and poverty

It has become commonplace to say that 'the gap between the rich and the poor' has widened in Ireland since the boom. One analysis of changes in income distribution shows that by 2000 the three lowest income deciles had indeed experienced some decline in their share of income. However, the same analysis showed that although the four top deciles had experienced an increase they had not, in fact, drawn sharply away from the rest. Overall, the shape of income distribution had not altered dramatically. What was of key importance was that the initial distribution was highly unequal, with Ireland having greater income inequality than many other industrialized countries; the boom had not significantly altered the distribution but the huge increase in incomes generally had highlighted more starkly the gap between the top and the bottom.[73]

On one measure, Ireland has experienced a marked drop in poverty since the late 1990s. This, unsurprisingly, is the measure which the Government likes to refer to as evidence of its success in addressing poverty. This measure, based on the concept of 'consistent deprivation', was adopted in the National Anti-Poverty Strategy, which was initiated in 1997 and revized in 2001. 'Consistent poverty' is measured on the basis of an income poverty line set at 70% of median income *and* a 'basic deprivation' index measured by the absence of a number of items from a 'basic possessions' list. 'Consistent poverty' has declined significantly – from 14.5% in 1994 to 10.7% in 1997 and 4.9% in 2001; for children it declined even more steeply, falling from 25% in 1997 to 6.5% in 2001.[74]

Many, however, query the value or relevance of this measurement and focus instead on the data on relative income poverty rates; these have shown a persistent trend upwards since the mid-nineties. At a poverty line set at 60% of median income, 15.6% of all persons were poor in 1994;

18.2% in 1997 and 21.9% in 2001. Among adults, 11.1% were poor in 1994, but 21.3% in 2001. Among children, poverty, on this measure, had declined slightly from 24.5% to 23%.[75]

The increase in poverty as measured by a poverty line set at a percentage of average income reflects the fact that average households' incomes rose so sharply during the nineties. While rates of social security payments increased in real terms, they did so by much less than incomes from employment. The composition of the population in poverty has changed significantly. It now includes far fewer households where the head is unemployed but many more where the head is retired or ill, or is a lone parent, or is in employment but on a low wage. The decline in poverty among children, as measured on the basis of a relative income line, reflects the drop in the numbers of 'unemployed' households and a considerable improvement in rates of child benefit.

In 2001, Ireland's relative income poverty rate (measured at 60% of median income) was, at 21%, the highest in the then 15-member EU. The EU average was 15% and the best performing countries had a poverty rate of less than half that for Ireland. Furthermore, over the past decade as a whole, Ireland has been consistently among a group of countries, which includes the UK, with relative income poverty rates about the EU average.[76] A recent analysis of the factors lying behind the differences between the 'best practice' EU countries and those like Ireland performing relatively badly, has highlighted that, to be effective, anti-poverty policy requires enhanced education and employment opportunities ***and*** improved income supports. 'Both elements are necessary – neither is sufficient on its own to ensure success in combating relative income poverty.' [77] The study concludes that for Ireland to reverse its high incidence of relative income poverty, it would need to complement its achievement of high employment growth with a more comprehensive welfare safety net and higher rates of welfare payments.

Taxation

Lowering taxation has been a key concern of government policy for well over a decade but there is little evidence of a commitment to thoroughgoing reform of all aspects of the Irish tax system in the interests of greater equity. Corporation taxes have been slashed from 40% to 12.5%

to increase Ireland's attractiveness to foreign companies, but there has been limited questioning of whether such a low rate of corporate taxes is equitable or sustainable. Capital gains taxes have also been reduced substantially; this erodes the tax base and benefits solely those who are investors or owners of assets. VAT and excise duties raise proportionately more of the overall tax yield in Ireland than in other EU countries, except Sweden and Denmark, yet these taxes can bear most heavily on the lowest income groups. Recent revelations that the ability to avail of an array of tax relief schemes has enabled some of Ireland's highest income earners to pay no direct tax at all has finally evoked a commitment by the Government to analyse the structure and effect of these schemes. For several decades there has been no taxation on private homes in Ireland. Suggestions that the huge rise in the value of houses and the growth in the number of second homes would now provide scope for the introduction of property tax[782] have met with a Government response which suggests a belief that while a property tax may be feasible in other countries it is a political no-go area in Ireland.

Public expenditure[79]

As personal incomes have grown, public spending has failed to keep pace. Current public spending as a share of GNP has fallen from 44% in 1990 to 31% in 2002. Some of this reflects the fall in national debt interest and the decline in unemployment with a consequent decrease in social security costs. Economic dependency decreased with a fall in the birth rate, an expanded working generation and higher work-force participation. Ireland's older age profile is much more favourable than that of France and Germany who are struggling to pay today's pensions. But even allowing for these factors, Ireland is well behind other European countries in the share of national income it devotes to public services.

Ireland largely missed out on the development of the modern welfare state which was consolidated throughout the rest of Europe after the second world war. Before the 1970s and EU membership, Ireland looked to UK models and rarely beyond. However, it developed only a very watered-down imitation of the post-war UK welfare state – a feeble version of the Beveridge social security system and a two-tier health service. Free second-level education was not introduced until 1967.

The principle of subsidiarity has been a deep-rooted theme of Irish social policy. Early social services were initiated by charitable and religious bodies and later on these services attracted state support. The underlying state philosophy was support for individual and philanthropic effort, not building a social safety net or a network of public services based on the rights of citizens. In general the approach has been selective not universal; what has been termed a 'basic security' model in contrast to the Scandinavian 'encompassing' welfare state.

The expansion in coverage of Ireland's welfare system in the 1970s and 80s partly coincided with the period of retrenchment in the UK as the Reagan/Thatcher ideas about rolling back the state took hold. But while expenditure on social security grew steadily during the recession of the 1980s, expenditure on health and housing were being severely pruned. Ireland arrived into its 1990s economic miracle with underdeveloped physical and social infrastructure, and with public services more poorly developed than the EU norm.

The boom should have offered a unique opportunity to catch up. However, while public spending on the main social services did rise throughout the boom years, the share of national income spent on public services fell steadily.

The core bargain at the heart of the Social Partnership that is regarded as playing such a key role in Ireland's economic recovery involved a trade-off between lower taxes and moderate wages. This helped facilitate a focus of budgetary policy, particularly as the Exchequer began to generate surpluses after 1997, and on the scale of the tax cuts to be offered rather than on enhancing public services. There was a clear ideological view at the heart of Government that favoured cuts in income tax, in corporate taxes, in capital gains taxes. Starting from a philosophy of 'giving people their own money back' rather one built on social solidarity, it has been unsurprising that the detail of tax cuts, particularly in the budgets of the late 1990s, focussed gains on the wealthiest. This approach has been modified somewhat in most recent budgets, particularly that introduced in December 2004, as the Government has sought to answer some of the critics of its policies – and, perhaps more importantly from its point of view, respond to the concerns of its own backbenchers, alarmed at the disaffection with the Government evident in the results of the local government elections held in June 2004.

Housing

An important 'downside' of the economic boom has been the fact that an increasing proportion of the population has found it difficult, if not impossible, to access adequate and affordable housing. Ireland has for several decades had a high rate of home ownership (at one point it had the highest rate in Europe) and enabling people to own their own home has long been a stated objective of public policy. However, having peaked at over 80%, the percentage of households who own their own home has declined in recent years and it now stands at 75%. This reflects the impact of the massive increase in house prices since the mid-90s – in real terms, prices have risen by over 187% since 1995 – so that more and more people on moderate incomes who previously would have assumed they would be able to buy a home have found that this is now impossible. Many others have had to move great distances from their work in the major cities in order to afford a home.

The numbers on local authority waiting lists for 'social housing' have grown sharply. There are currently 48,000 households, with an estimated 50,000 children, on these lists, but this official 'count' almost certainly does not reflect the full extent of need. The number of homeless people (including street sleepers, hostel dwellers and people in bed and breakfast accommodation) has risen significantly.

The scale of house building in Ireland in the past decade is striking, with, in total, nearly 400,000 new homes completed. 2003 was the ninth successive year of record house building and the number of completions in that year was nearly 160% higher than in 1995. Ireland has now by far the highest rate of house building in Europe. The overall figures for house completion, however, conceal some important facts. While the rate of provision of local authority and voluntary sector housing has risen in the past few years, this was from an extremely low basis so that such housing represents only around 9% of total output. Equally significantly, more than a quarter of new houses completed in 2003 were second or holiday homes. To a substantial extent such housing is publicly subsidized through the availability of tax relief schemes for holiday homes in specific areas and by public provision of infrastructure. Already by 2000, 9% of the top decile of the income distribution owned a second home. This has almost certainly grown significantly since then. The huge increase in property values in the past decade has impacted greatly on the distribution of wealth. The obvious beneficiaries are those who purchased homes prior to the boom and have seen their value escalate. Many of these will be among the 40% of householders who own their home without any mortgage. Overall, there is little indication that the Government has been concerned about the distributional effects of trends in housing nor is it apparent that the Government regards what is in fact a serious housing crisis for many as an issue that merits active, substantial and sustained public intervention.

Health

Expenditure on health was a major victim of public spending cutbacks in the late 1980s. Since 1999, there have been significant increases in public health expenditure. At first sight, Ireland now appears to be spending somewhat above the EU average on health, having for so long been significantly below that average. However, the OECD now assesses that 25% of Irish health expenditure is, in fact, social spending that should not be included in comparisons with other countries.

The legacy of years of under-expenditure and the growth in demand for services (part of which is due to an increased population and a growing number of older people), has resulted in increasing pressure on the system, evident especially in the public hospital services. There has been a marked rise in the percentage of the population taking out private health insurance coverage, largely motivated, research suggests, by speedier access to treatment as well as the perceived shortcomings in the standard of public care. Ireland's two-tier hospital system is now deeply entrenched. It is notable that much of the media and public anger about public hospital services focusses on the long delays for services in Accident and Emergency Departments, and on the number of patients who have to lie on trolleys or sit on chairs because no beds are available for them. All patients have to use the Irish hospitals' A&E departments, since private hospitals do not have such departments. Only here does the section of the population that has private health insurance encounter the reality of the public system. This is a group that is largely middle-class and articulate.

The percentage of the population with a 'Medical Card', a provision intended to give access free of charge to all GP, pharmacy and hospital services for the lowest income groups, was by 2004 at its lowest level since the introduction of the scheme in the early 1970s. This entitlement is strictly means-tested and so many still on low incomes but just above the cut-off point, especially families with dependent children, can experience considerable difficulty in affording charges for visits to the GP and for prescription medicines. Following considerable public lobbying on this issue, the Government announced in November 2004 the issuing of 230,000 additional medical cards – but 200,000 of these are to be 'doctor only' cards, with the patient having to bear the cost of prescription medicines. This represented a significant change in the medical card system but was not based on any published analysis or public debate.

Middle-class opt-out [80]

Ireland's welfare state, unlike mainstream European or Scandinavian ones, has struck a relatively fragile bargain with the middle classes. It opted for a model of basic-level provision, where many of the middle class add a privately-funded layer onto their state entitlements, be it in health, education or pensions. It has been argued that it is a system whose effect is to consolidate inequality rather than redistribute resources. Without a strong engagement by middle-class voters with the welfare state, its future may be fragile as Ireland becomes an increasingly prosperous society, heading rapidly towards an 80% middle-class society.

Virtually every child in the state attends a state-run primary school, and people engage with what has been by and large a high quality public service. In contrast, 49% of the public pay into private health care. And in perhaps a signal of what is to come, over half the second-level pupils in South Dublin attend fee-paying schools.

Research across OECD countries shows that universal services tend to be generous ones, but selective services for the poor only get poorly funded. Korpi and Palme using evidence from the Luxembourg Income Study show a strongly consistent link between highly selective welfare systems and poor levels of income support.[81] This finding supports the hypothesis that countries whose middle class have little stake in the welfare state are likely to have a poorly funded and developed welfare state.

Ireland is for the time being a middle-class society with one foot in the past. It is just 150 years, about six generations, from the Great Famine. Today's pensioners typically left school at primary level, and most are heavily reliant on state welfare pensions. They rely, to a much greater extent than their sons or daughters, on the public health services. The prosperous middle-aged retain an important link to the welfare state through their parents. Many of today's home owners were reared as local authority tenants. But while many of today's middle class have a stake, through their parents, in ensuring adequately funded and properly run state services, will that stake survive the passing of that older generation? What future for the welfare state in an era of increasing prosperity, where the culture of contentment is in the ascendancy?

Quality of life

'Every person and every society is at once wealthy ***and*** poor.'[82] The Republic of Ireland may now be richer than ever before but it is also becoming conscious of the ways in which it may have become poorer.

Whether they name it as such or not, a great number of people experience 'time poverty'. Longer working hours for many, lengthy commuting distances, traffic grid-locks that make travelling, be it to work or for leisure or other activities, extraordinarily time-consuming, all serve to eat into people's sense of control over their time. Most people may have more comfortable and better-equipped homes than ever before (in their parents' and grandparents' eyes these homes are like mansions: quite a number are mansions), but too many have little time to spend there.

House price escalation has meant for some being permanently 'locked out' of home ownership and for many others it has meant the taking on of a mortgage that assumes there will be two earners to pay for it; it has also resulted in the phenomenon of parents taking out new mortgages to assist their grown-up children to get a foot on the property ladder.

While the higher incomes from employment are welcome, they are frequently coming at a price of increased requirements to perform, 'to deliver', in the work-place. Parents of young children face particular demands as the pressures of the work-place and of commuting are accompanied by a scarcity of suitable and affordable child care.

Higher standards of living make possible the enjoyment of

consumer goods and activities at an unprecedented level, but the desire to maintain a certain 'lifestyle' involve considerable expenditure for some and this is reflected in record levels of personal debt. The high levels of consumption of alcohol, with binge drinking almost the norm, and the extremely unhealthy patterns of food consumption create a wide range of personal and social costs in Irish society (conservatively estimated to amount to about 2.36 billion euro, or the equivalent of 2.6% of GNP).

Those who are poor or deprived may be less impoverished than before, but their situation is in some ways much more difficult for they are experiencing poverty in the midst of plenty and are faced with at best indifference from much of the population and at worst an attitude that 'there is now no excuse to be poor'.

The stability that characterized marriage and the family in Ireland in the past has now gone. Too often, of course, that stability concealed deep unhappiness and even abuse. Greater respect for personal freedom and choice, together with legislative reform, now enables people to leave destructive and unhappy relationships. But alongside these changes, there is a sense that long-term commitment in relationships is now an 'unrealistic' expectation and that the 'right' to self-fulfilment should take precedence over other considerations. The importance attached to family connections, including wider kin, which was found in urban as well as rural Ireland, has diminished greatly. Identification with and involvement in the local community have lessened, with the springing up of new estates, the demands of work and a reduced sense of being interdependent with others. All these have an impact on the previously strong sense of belonging to and playing a part in a local community.

Ireland's increased levels of industrial output, its record road building and house construction, the phenomenal growth in car ownership and use, and the overall increase in consumption, have impacted enormously on the environment. Irish society as a whole has not even begun to face up to the choices that must be made if its traditional image of being a 'green island' is not to be destroyed forever. It may be unspoken, but for many the environmental damage is a price worth paying for the prosperity now being experienced. A Green Party member of parliament recently commented: 'The definition of sustainable development here is sustained development.'

In summary, the importance now attached to earning and spending, to being 'successful', to getting ahead, have eroded the sense that it is people, good relationships with others and a harmonious relationship with the environment that are what are really important in life.

NORTHERN IRELAND

Northern Ireland economy[83]

There is a widening gap between the picture of the Northern Ireland economy painted by conventional indicators of economic activity and the desired structure of the economy, as set out in economic development strategies.

Taken at face value, the recent economic performance of Northern Ireland – as measured by employment, unemployment, GDP growth and even industrial output – has been relatively good. Employment is at a record level – though there are questions about its composition – and unemployment is low at around 5%. Maintenance of the existing policy approaches in the period up to 2010 will almost certainly see even higher employment levels, lower unemployment and further GDP growth in line with recent trends.

However, these conventional economic indicators do not reflect the core issue concerning the Northern Ireland economy, which is that growth and employment are highly dependent on the public sector. In 1999-2000, public expenditure was £9.2 billion compared with GDP for 1999 of £17 billion; in June 2003 public sector employment was 211,660 or 32% of all employee jobs. In effect, the public sector is the main dynamic in the Northern Ireland economy. The inordinately large public sector is a direct result of the Troubles; the state stepped in as the private sector was getting out due to the political violence from the 70s onwards.

Current UK government policy means that up until 2007/8, public expenditure in key service areas, such as health and education, will rise at an accelerating rate. These higher levels of public spending are dictated by the Labour Government's commitment to delivering improvements in health and education by the time of the next election. Increases in expenditure in Northern Ireland on these policy areas, and on transport and environmental services, as well as the likelihood of additional infrastructural spending, mean that the public sector which is already such a large part of the regional economy will become still greater. Even if the non-public sector element of the economy were to develop in the next few years along the lines envisaged in ***Strategy 2010***,[84] it would have to compete with a hungry public sector for human and other resources. In effect, one of the outcomes of the envisaged increased levels of public spending will be to attract resources away from the private sector – a form of 'crowding out' – especially in view of the rapidity of growth of spending over such a short time. Northern Ireland therefore seems set to become even more dependent on the public purse and on large fiscal transfers from the Exchequer. This is a trend that is not sustainable in the long run.

What can be done to restructure the Northern Ireland economy to achieve more of the aims and objectives of ***Strategy 2010***? Or to put it slightly differently, who are the agents of change that could undertake a more sustainable development strategy?

For Northern Ireland to become a successful economic region, there has to be a huge increase in private sector activity, presumably in knowledge-based enterprises and this means supporting, promoting and encouraging entrepreneurs and risk-takers. Even though it was envisaged that the Northern Ireland Assembly and Executive would have a key role in taking ***Strategy 2010*** forward, there was little evidence in the Assembly that political parties are sufficiently pro-business and enterprise for the task; there was clearly greater appetite for the politically more advantageous equality agenda. It is open to question whether most of Northern Ireland's politicians understand the scale of the external pressures and challenges facing the region's businesses, now and in the immediate future, or have grasped the fact that Northern Ireland can only have a sustainable economic future if business and enterprise are seen as a priority and supported accordingly. It seems unlikely then that even if there is a return to devolved government, the new Assembly and Executive would have the political will to take the decisions necessary to crowd the private sector back into the local economy.

Could the momentum for reform of the Northern Ireland economy come from within the public sector itself? The envisaged review and reform of public administration in Northern Ireland could lead to more efficient central and local governance and a streamlining of supports and resources for developmental purposes. However, it is unclear whether reforms in governance can create the space and momentum for the value-adding private sector growth required to rebalance the economy. In any case, whatever administrative rearrangements are made, they will still have to cope with rapidly rising public expenditure over the latter half of this decade.

The Chancellor of the Exchequer has stated the intention to introduce regional consumer price indices across the UK as the basis for future regional pay bargaining in the public sector. Even if this were to happen, it would be a considerable time before this policy would have any effect in Northern Ireland since it would take time to establish inflation differentials and to put in place the corresponding public sector pay differentials.

In any case, there remains a huge differential in the average earnings between the public and the private sectors in Northern Ireland. In 1992, average non-manual earnings in the public sector were 30% higher than private sector non-manual earnings. Even though this differential narrowed over the following decade, by 2002 it was still 20%. In Britain, the differential is reversed: private sector wages for non-manual adult workers are higher than for the public sector, and the gap has increased from 3% in 1992 to 6% in 2002. In Northern Ireland, then, the normal incentive system has become distorted by the scale and growth of the public sector. It can be argued that there is thus no incentive for young people to become risk-taking and entrepreneurial when the rewards in the public sector are so much greater.

Attracting external investment and promoting indigenous business growth through the development of linkages with the foreign-owned sector are seen as the key pathways to growing the tradable sector of a modern economy. This approach worked well in Northern Ireland in the 1960s but foreign direct investment was problematic throughout the Troubles and even since the ceasefires the recovery of external investment has been disappointing. In the meantime, the nature and scale of mobile international investment has changed and has moved southwards and eastwards.

Even within its immediate neighbourhood, Northern Ireland has to compete against the Republic of Ireland, Scotland, Wales and the regional development agencies of England in the effort to attract investment. In particular, it appears that Northern Ireland cannot now compete effectively with the Republic for foreign direct investment. Apart from its political problems, its higher energy costs, transport costs and additional compliance costs put it at a relative disadvantage. Its traditional strengths, an abundance of well-educated labour and relatively low wage costs, are not as compelling as they once were.

On economic grounds, the argument is stronger than ever for the integration of industrial development efforts on an all-island basis: both Northern Ireland and the Republic would each derive measurable economic benefit from this. Northern Ireland could benefit from developing deeper and stronger supply chain linkages with the foreign high-technology sectors in the Republic, and the North's labour supply could contribute meaningfully to meeting the needs of a modern, knowledge-based industrial mix across the island. While the economics of such an approach make sense, the politics would be unlikely to permit a single industrial development policy for the whole of Ireland in the immediate future. But the proposition of creating a single industrial development effort and a more integrated labour market on the island of Ireland has merit. In any case, in the absence of serious progress towards creating a fast-growing, knowledge-based industrial structure the longer-term outlook for the Northern Ireland economy is not good.

In summary, while progress has been made in the promotion of local economic development, Northern Ireland is still a long way from achieving the aims of ***Strategy 2010*** to 'create an economy which is fast growing, competitive, innovative and knowledge-based...' and to achieve 'a rising standard of living with a skilled, creative and well-paid work-force in modern high-value businesses'. By 2010, the public sector is, in fact, likely to have grown even more important, both in terms of employment and the share of public expenditure in the total economy; the trading element of the private sector will be smaller in employment terms and Northern Ireland will *not* be a high wage, high added-value regional economy.

Poverty in Northern Ireland [85]

The Northern Ireland Executives' ***Programme for Government*** acknowledged the problem of poverty: 'We recognize the inequalities in the life experiences of our citizens in terms of poverty, health, housing, educational and economic opportunity and disability and we are determined to tackle them.' It did not, however, adopt an official definition of poverty. (Likewise the UK Government has not adopted a definition of poverty, despite the commitment to halve child poverty by 2010.)

A study on poverty in Northern Ireland, conducted from late 2002 to early 2003 and published in October 2003, aimed to provide for the first time a 'baseline measurement of poverty and social exclusion' which can be updated periodically.[86] The study adopted a 'consensual' poverty measure: using a random sample of individuals, it sought initially to establish what items and activities respondents considered to be necessities for people living in Northern Ireland at the start of the 21st century. These included new, rather than second-hand clothes, having enough money to pay heating, lighting and telephone charges, being able to afford home contents insurance, the ability to repair or replace household goods, the ability to attend weddings, funerals and other social functions, one week's annual holiday away from home. The study then sought to establish the extent of involuntary deprivation of these items and activities in the population. The final stage of the study was to use a range of statistical techniques to identify the combination of low income and lack of necessities which best distinguished between poor and non-poor households.

By these measurements, 29.6% of households in Northern Ireland were poor in 2002/3 and another 12% could be described as vulnerable to poverty. In other words, at least half a million people in Northern Ireland were poor. Children were particularly at risk of experiencing poverty, with over 37% growing up in poor households. Two-thirds of lone parents were poor; more than half of households including a person or persons with a disability were found to be in poverty, compared to 29% of households where no member had a disability. Women were more likely to live in poor households than men (29% as against 25%). Catholics were 1.4 times more likely to be below the poverty line than Protestants.

The findings of the study indicate that the extent of poverty in Northern Ireland is higher than in Britain or in the Republic of Ireland.

The group identified as 'vulnerable to poverty' seemed to be largely comprized of people who had lost their job or gone through a relationship breakdown with a consequent splitting up of a family home. The population living in poverty is not a static one: at any time around

3% are moving in or out of poverty. An important finding of the study was that a significant number of people were economising on food. The study showed an incidence of poverty among older people that was less than anticipated, but this may have been because respondents in this group were unwilling to admit they could not afford particular items or activities, saying instead that they did not want them.

In the light of the growing volume of evidence that, while poverty blights lives and leads to health and other social problems, it is inequality, the gap between rich and poor, that is even more significant in its consequences, the study considered the extent of inequality in Northern Ireland. In Northern Ireland the Gini coefficient increased from 38 in 1998/99 to 42 in 2002/3. (The Gini coefficient runs from a scale of 0 where there is total equality through to 100 where there is total inequality or where one person gets all the income.) The richest 40% of households in Northern Ireland receive 67% of total income and the poorest 40% receive 17%. In terms of wealth and capital resources, 6.5% of households in Northern Ireland have a second home and over 2% own other houses apart from their own home or a second home. Meantime, one third of households do not own their home and 14,000 people are homeless. The study concluded that Northern Ireland was one of the most unequal societies in the developed world.

In Northern Ireland, discussions in the media and political forums are dominated by issues arising from divisions based on religion and political preference but there are other equally important, divisions that are less visible in the public domain, and are based on class, gender, age and disability. A progressive equality framework, including human rights legislation, is now in place in Northern Ireland. The question is: does the political will and social consensus exist to harness that framework to addressing the issue of poverty? Local politicians face an important constraint in that key policies in the pursuit of such a goal, namely fiscal policies and social security measures, remain the responsibility of Westminster, not Stormont.

Quality of life[87]

Quality of life in Northern Ireland can, of course, be assessed in many different ways. If 'physical and social environment' is an indicator, then it must be noted that Northern Ireland is a place of incredible physical beauty, with 5,500 square miles of land occupied by a population of just 1.65 million. People are on the whole friendly and helpful. There is now a vibrant feel about Belfast and people can move about more freely than before; the ceasefires opened up social space which has greatly improved the quality of life. School leavers in Northern Ireland have higher educational attainments than the UK average and the proportion of young people who go on to university is higher than in any other country in the European Union.

Another indicator of 'quality of life' is physical and mental health status and here it is apparent that the years of sustained political violence have taken their toll on the health of the people of Northern Ireland. It has the youngest population in the UK, with 24% under 16 years compared to 20% elsewhere, yet two in five households report at least one person with limiting long-term illness. Heart disease and cancer, both of which are related to lifestyle factors, are major causes of death. Mental health trends are particularly worrying; it is estimated one person in six suffers from some form of mental health problem (a total of 300,000 people across Northern Ireland). There are 66% more prescriptions for drugs for psychosis and related disorders and 37% more for anti-depressants than anywhere else in the UK.

These figures tell in a graphic way the story of a community that is allowing the effects of trauma to become evident. Violence may have largely ceased, but the memory of it continues to do its damaging work in the psyches of the people of Northern Ireland. It is only now, a decade after the ceasefires, that people dare to acknowledge the extent of the traumatisation – not just for those who were directly affected but for the population as a whole.

Buried in descriptions of disrupted physical and mental health is a key question: how do we heal the past? Therapeutic measures may help individuals and families, but when a whole society is traumatized what kind of process could release enough of the emotions and heal enough of the hurts to allow society as a whole to find stable ground on which to re-build itself?

In Northern Ireland, the factor that indicates most accurately the quality of life is 'community relations'. The region is not yet in a position to experience adequate, let alone positive, cross-community relationships between the two largest traditions. However, there is a movement, albeit a slow movement, in a positive direction. A large number of initiatives aimed at improving cross-community relations exist but there is a sense that the urgency about them has waned in proportion to the lessening in violence.

The breakdown of trust which led to the suspension of the Northern Ireland Assembly mirrors what is going on in a sharper way at local level. In many areas there is an uneasy stand-off. However, the patterns of tension and violence are changing. Violence is becoming more localized – it is shrinking or being contained. But the potential for it to spread is always present. With the absence of large-scale violence, the kind of low-level intimidation and tit for tat attacks which used to be commonplace and hardly remarked upon are coming under close scrutiny: the threshold of notice of and reaction to attacks is getting lower. The message is that violence is not acceptable.

However, people are reporting that they experience the divisions in local areas as being much sharper than before. This is a reflection of the fact that the peace process has thrown many people and communities into identity confusion; it gets expressed this way: 'We knew who we were when we were fighting one another, but who are we now?' The negative 'over against the other' way of constructing identity, which is at the heart of sectarianism, is proving very resistant to change – but at least it is becoming more clearly exposed for what it is. Expressions of resentment against 'the other' community appear in fact to be increasing. At least part of what is happening is that the will to peaceful co-existence is not yet sufficiently developed in local communities.

A further disturbing development is that racial antagonism is increasing with a rise in the number of racially motivated attacks on members of the Chinese and other immigrant communities.

In summary, attaining a better quality of life in Northern Ireland rests on the unstable foundations of an improving but still very dysfunctional state of community relations. The situation is getting better but it is vital that the sense of urgency is not allowed to wane. Two key issues need to be addressed if there is to be a sustained improvement in the quality of life in Northern Ireland. Firstly, there is need to find ways to enable individuals and the community as a whole to heal the past. Secondly, people need to learn to live peaceably with those who are different. This is an educational task as well as a legislative one: criminalising 'hate' elements of crime is one important step in moving beyond sectarianism, but the law on its own cannot effect the required change. What is needed is a conversion of heart and mind. The question for the people of Northern Ireland is: do we yet have the will to work at that conversion personally and communally?

Conclusion

When the economic boom in the Republic of Ireland was still new there were many who felt that 'this cannot last', that economic success and prosperity would recede as quickly as they had apparently arrived. There is now greater confidence that, despite down-turns, there will not be a return to a prolonged recession, and that the economy is on a path to mature development.

Aside from the economy itself, however, there are enormous questions about the use and destination of the prosperity generated during the past decade: about how Ireland has chosen, and is choosing, to 'spend the boom'. There are questions about the distribution of income and wealth: economic success has reinforced an existing highly unequal distribution pattern. Some senior Ministers in the current Government have expressed the view that inequality is not a problem; that it can serve to provide a useful incentive to people. Voices in non-governmental organisations and the Churches continue to strongly challenge such views, but there is no doubt that they are held by many in the population. There are questions too about the balance between private and public spending and the difficulty of persuading people that good quality public services and an adequate infrastructure can only be financed from taxation. Irish people have become used to tax cuts and their sense of having a civic duty to pay taxes, which was never very strong, has been eroded still further by the evidence of widespread tax evasion by large numbers of the well off.

As the Republic of Ireland has been getting used to its status of being one of the wealthiest countries in the western world, it is just beginning to question the ways in which it may have become poorer over the last decade. In a recent speech, the country's Ombudsman and Information Commissioner, Emily O'Reilly, highlighted some of the more unappealing features that have emerged with prosperity – the emphasis on 'success', the preoccupation with materialism, the crass displays of consumerism, the damage to family and community relationships, the decline in spiritual values.[88]

Her speech was notable not just in its analysis but in the fact that it received wide media coverage and generated considerable public debate, suggesting that it resonated strongly with many people. Perhaps this is an indication that Ireland is now ready to explore how its new wealth may serve to allow all its people to prosper in more wholesome ways.

The pattern for future development is fairly clear in the Republic. It is less so in Northern Ireland. The disastrous economic effects of the conflict over the last thirty years are evident – not just in abstract figures but in people's lives. The disruption of life in the Province has prevented its people from enjoying the fruits of prosperity that have been evident elsewhere in the United Kingdom and in the European Union. Businesses have not thriven; very necessary state intervention has left the economy too highly dependent on the public sector for growth and jobs, which inadvertently crowds out private enterprise. That must change if economic development is to be sustainable and prosperity is to be more widely enjoyed. Equally important is the re-establishment of trust within the whole community. It is paradoxical that as something like peace begins to be enjoyed, the politics of the Province are more sharply polarized. The churches certainly wish for a growing degree of trust within the whole community, and a vision of peace and prosperity which will transcend difference.

11

Conclusion and Policy Recommendations

The essays in this collection have a common theme. It is that a modern commercial society is able not only to generate wealth, but also to create genuine prosperity.

The instruments which create modern wealth are not to be despised, especially when they help to achieve widespread prosperity. Work and income provide people with the capabilities that enable them to enjoy and share greater well-being. It is also clear that such success is most easily achieved in an innovative, competitive market economy. This is not to idolize competition, but to see it as an essential means to desirable ends, not least the provision of extensive and expensive public services.

Nonetheless, the effects of the competitive market need to be examined with some scepticism. The market creates an ever-greater abundance of goods and services. But this wealth of possibilities engenders a range of hedonistic values, which inhibit human striving for genuine prosperity. It is possible to enjoy a vision of a society of informed, active and sympathetic citizens, linked together by a variety of common purposes. It is also possible to suffer the nightmare that we shall become simply a collection of consumers, seekers after entertainment, with no shared life or aim. Somewhere, between the priggish vision and the selfish nightmare, lies the possibility of a good life. The achievement of such a life depends on our ability to treat wealth as a means to serve human ends, not an end in itself. Success in the pursuit of interests and in the satisfaction of appetites makes for an impoverished rather than an enriched life.

Many of the features of modern life that diminish our humanity have deep historical and cultural roots. But an important number of them are susceptible to policy solutions. We offer policy proposals under three headings – for social justice in Britain; for global economic justice; and for the repair of the worldwide environmental damage which our pursuit of wealth has inflicted.

UK policy proposals: decency without disincentive.

Niall Cooper makes proposals in five areas, addressing the needs of those who are largely excluded from the benefits of modern prosperity.

The detailed arguments for these proposals are found in the sixth essay. They broadly make the case that modern wealth should be distributed most generously to those who need it most, and that nobody should fall below a given 'decency standard'. But such a redistribution should not reduce the incentive to seek success in the labour market.

1. ***An independent body to establish Minimum Income Standards***

   Different poor households have different needs. Those needs reflect a variety of circumstances, like the receipt of benefits and the composition of the household. No household should fall beneath a decency threshold, and benefit levels should reflect this. There needs to be an independent institutional framework which uses household needs as a measure of public policy. Minimum income standards should be set and published, as a guide to anti-poverty policy. This process would require the creation of an independent body. The Low Pay Commission is a useful model for this kind of institution.

2. ***Low pay and poverty***

   The minimum wage has greatly helped to raise living standards, with no adverse effects on employment. It has been argued that this level should be progressively increased. Such a policy fits the official wish to enable the UK to become a 'high skill, high wage' economy. So it is urged that the minimum wage should be increased cautiously, but more rapidly than has been the case.

3. ***Debt on our doorstep***

   The poorest people find it the most difficult to get credit. Three million people have no bank account. Eight million people have no access to credit, and have to borrow at interest rates from 170% to 800% APR. No public agency has responsibility to encourage access to affordable credit. Two measures are called for.

   First, a ceiling on interest rates and charges. These limits need to be carefully designed to avoid choking off credit.

   Second, more community based credit providers, such as credit unions, need to be encouraged. The scope for this development is considerable; less than 1% of the UK population are members of credit unions, yet almost half the population of the Republic of Ireland are. 'Community Development Financial Institutions', like those in Portsmouth and Salford, provide one model.

4. Pensioner poverty

Poverty and inequality in the UK are at their starkest among the old. One fifth of pensioners have retirement income averaging £45,000 a year, while one fifth live below the level of income support. So universal increases in pension levels will be wasted on the former, and should more usefully be targeted on the latter. That is why the Government has introduced the minimum income guarantee and pension credit to pay more to poorer pensioners. But these means-tested benefits are least taken up among older people. Means-testing for pensioners also offers a serious disincentive to saving. For these two reasons it seems necessary, on balance, to increase the state pension across the board, and to restore the link between pensions and average earnings.

Three measures are proposed.

First, to pay Pension Credit automatically to all aged over 75. In this group, poor people are in a large majority.

Second, to index pensions to average earnings and retail prices, whichever is the greater.

Third, to look at pensioner income in the context of the minimum income standards agency recommended above.

5. Taxation and the common good

Taxation falls unfairly on the poor. A successful economy, from which all benefit to some extent, seems almost inevitably to create inequality in the market-place. That unfairness must not be replicated in public policy, one of whose purposes is to compensate those who are less successful in the market-place. The following proposals are suggested.

First, to reduce the tax burden on the poorest, by raising significantly the tax thresholds.

Second, to introduce a higher tax band of 50 percent for higher earners.

Third, a wider review and rationalization of the tax and national insurance system, both to adjust anomalies and to increase incentives for those in marginal and insecure employment.

Global justice

Our world is now marked by substantial economic growth, which is raising the living standards of many millions of people. That development is enormously uneven, and calls for equally substantial moral and political effort if this aggregate wealth is to be transformed into genuine prosperity. Policy changes in the following four areas of have already begun to create new possibilities of global justice, and need to be pursued, as Ian Linden argues in the fourth essay.

1. ***Regulation of Corporate Power***
   The world's poor need internationally agreed legal rights in order to challenge the activities of transnational corporations in their own countries. A growing body of legislation already exists. The World Trade Organisation should be empowered to act more effectively to achieve these ends. The WTO has moved slowly from being a body designed to serve the rich to a more consistent concern for the interests of all. That movement should be encouraged, and all attempts to reverse this change should be vigorously resisted.
2. ***Regulation of global capital flows***
   Unregulated global capital flows have damaged the newly-industrialized economies of South Asia, Mexico and Turkey. These crises have risen for a wide variety of reasons, but this lack of global regulation has been one of them. Contraction of these economies has affected employment in parts of the UK. It is recognized that capital mobility forms part of the necessary discipline required to control corruption and incompetence. But good economic management will require regulation of short-term capital flows in times of crisis, without inhibiting inward capital flows. The IMF should be empowered to approve the imposition of capital controls on the currencies of weak, threatened economies, for a period no longer than 6 months.
3. ***Reduction in rich country protectionism***
   The United States and the European Union are notorious for the flagrant manner in which they breach the principles of free trade. The harm done to agriculture among the world's poor is deeply unjust, especially in the case of the Common Agricultural Policy of the EU.

Again, the World Trade Organisation has made significant progress in halting the worst offences against fair trade. The Churches and their Aid Agencies have campaigned for reform for many years now, and must continue to do so. The British Government is a strong advocate of fair trade as a means to achieve social justice, and should be supported in that endeavour.

4. Good governance in poor countries

Many of the world's poor suffer under dishonest and incompetent states. Their talents are squandered under these conditions. It is possible for even the poorest people to prosper when economic growth and social justice are properly pursued. Such success depends on many factors, but two are of particular importance.

The first is commercial integrity: the fostering of the virtues and institutions that create a successful economy whose benefits are widely spreads.

The second is property rights for poor people. Bureaucracy and corruption worldwide hugely inhibit the poor from gaining ownership of the modest properties within which they live and work, thus creating collateral against which they can expand their businesses, increasing wealth and employment as a consequence.

The third is that aid and trade agreements are increasingly made conditional on the discussion of these questions of governance, with the view to enabling greater global wealth to be spread more widely; that pattern of change should be encouraged.

Prosperity and the environment

These policy objectives, working together in a renewed institutional setting, offer the best conceivable chance for the wretchedly poor of the world. That is a formidable task to maintain over the generations. But the already headlong growth in global living standards threatens the global environment. Wealth accompanied by environmental degradation is a travesty of true prosperity, and ecological catastrophe has already begun to threaten the wealth and the life of the planet.

It follows that the human economy must be seen as part of the whole created order, and shaped accordingly. This means that the instruments of wealth-creation must be respected as aspects of the whole, and shaped to serve it. This will require a new vision shared between environmentalists and economists. One central future of that vision must be an understanding of how radically greenhouse gas emissions must be reduced if the future is to be viable. This prospect raises challenging questions for our endeavours to create and to share wider prosperity. How are we to make our living in an environmentally sensitive way? What will be the new business opportunities, and what sort of profits will they make? The global economy must be reformed within a framework of ecological concern. In the fifth essay, Jennifer Potter argues for the following policy approaches.

1. ***The Government should embrace the concept of 'Contract and Converge'*** as the most effective and fair global solution to the problem of climate change, and that other policies for a low carbon-emission economy should be set within this wider framework. Such a policy is no less than is necessary, but its establishment is only likely in the medium term. It obviously needs to be preceded by interim measures, as indicated below.

2. ***The Government should develop a new energy policy***, based on a long-term policy of diversity and security of energy sources. This will require a mix of renewables, nuclear power, new cleaner conventional plant and the integration of locally produced power into the National Grid.

3. ***The Government should work with commerce, industry, and the academic and the voluntary sector to set a regulatory framework to limit carbon emissions.*** The tax system should reward companies that reduce emissions and that develop innovative processes. The possibilities for emission trading should be more vigorously explored. In this regard the Carbon Disclosure Project is commended.

Notes

Chapter 3 A Christian Reflection on Economic Change

[1] William Temple was Archbishop first of York (1929-42) and then of Canterbury (1942-44) but his influence survives today. He took the Anglican tradition of social ethics and brought it into dialogue with contemporary society. His mind worked from first principles, through a consideration of society, as it existed at the moment, into conclusions. In his most far reaching and widely read book ***Christianity and Social Order*** published in 1942 Temple argued that the three great principles of Christian social thought were freedom, fellowship and service. What contributed to human freedom, and what might freedom be for? It is interesting, in passing, to note how Temple valued freedom of choice as an absolute. Fellowship included the groupings which made up society: unions, clubs, family and much else. Service or vocation was the way in which individuals might build up society. All Anglican social thought since then has been indebted to this way of arguing. It is a tentative, exploratory argument but at its best it has huge power in setting out a Christian vision for society.

[2] Reinhold Niebuhr 1892-1971) was an American pastor, theologian and social activist in the Reformed tradition. The most lasting of his many writings is ***Moral Man and Immoral Society*** (1932). A Socialist in his earlier thinking, he developed a theology that engaged critically with modern commercial and political society. His thought is generally described as that of 'Christian Realism'. He was sharply critical of liberal Christian assumptions. Human sin brings about the evil which is evident in history, and only faith in the graciousness of God can create moral renewal. But Christian adherence to the ruinous myth of modern progress exposes the Church to Divine judgement. His biblical understanding of human nature acknowledged the deep ambiguity and frequent hypocrisy of modernity. He saw his form of social realism as necessary to the shaping of Christian moral purpose, in the face of cynicism or despair.

[3] Miroslav Wolf, ***Work in the Spirit*: *Toward a Theology of Work,*** Oxford, 1991.

[4] William Temple, ***Christianity and Social Order,*** Penguin 1942

[5] Peter Sedgwick, ***The Market Economy and Christian Ethics,*** Cambridge 1997;Andrew Britton and Peter Sedgwick, ***Economic Theory and Christian Belief*** Peter Lang, 2003.

[6] See Peter Sedgwick, ***The Enterprise Culture***, SPCK, 1992.

[7] S. Pattison ***The Faith of the Managers***, Cassell, 1997; R.H.Roberts ***Religion, Theology and the Human Sciences,*** Cambridge 2001

[8] Graham Ward, ***Cities of God,*** Routledge 2001

[9] John Atherton, ***Marginalization***, SCM Press, 2003

[10] Richard Sennett, ***The Corrosion of Character,*** Norton, 1999

[11] See for example Hilary Russell, ***Poverty Close to Home: A Christian Understanding***, Mowbray, 1995.

[12] For a discussion of what this term might mean in economics and theology see the chapter on this subject in Britton and Sedgwick, 2003.

[13] Nick Donovan and David Halpern ***Life Satisfaction: the state of knowledge and implications for government,*** Strategy Unit December 2002

[14] http://cep.lse.ac.uk. A summary is in the ***New Statesman*** 3 March 2003

[15] Professor Lord Layard, advisor to the Labour administration.

[16] ***Life Satisfaction*** pages 18-19

Chapter 6 The Political Economy of Poverty & Prosperity

[17] ***Inside Out, Rethinking Inclusive Communities***, Demos 2003.

[18] HM Treasury, ***Child Poverty Review***, 2004.

[19] David Darton, Donald Hirsch and Jason Strelitz, ***Tackling disadvantage, a 20-year enterprise***, Joseph Rowntree Foundation, 2003, page 12

[20] Equal Opportunities Commission, ***Gender and Poverty in Britain***, 2003

[21] For up to date statistics on poverty in the UK see: http://www.poverty.org.uk

[22] Polly Toynbee, ***Hard Work***, 2003

[23] David Darton, Donald Hirsch and Jason Strelitz, ***op. cit.***, page 10

[24] Will Paxton and Matthew Taylor, Bridging The Wealth Gap, in ***New Statesman***, 12 July 2002

[25] ***Worth Working For, Job Opportunities in 21st Century Britain***, United Reformed Church, 2002

[26] Nicholas Timmins in ***Overcoming disadvantage, an agenda for the next 20 years***, Joseph Rowntree Foundation, 2004, page 14.

[27] Georgina Klein, ***Life lines, the NCC's agenda for affordable energy, water and telephone services***, National Consumer Council, 2003.

[28] Pat Conaty and Henry Palmer, ***Profiting from Poverty***, New Economics Foundation, 2002

[29] CAP national policy forum participant, 9 July 2001

[30] Church Action on Poverty, ***Speaking from Experience, Voices at the National Poverty Hearing***, 1996, page 25.

[31] See ***Overcoming disadvantage, an agenda for the next 20 years***

[32] ***Taxation for the Common Good***, 2004, page 39

[33] No 10 Policy Unit, ***Strategic Audit 2003***.

[34] JK Galbraith, ***The Culture of Contentment***, 1992

[35] Church Action on Poverty, ***Speaking from Experience, Voices at the National Poverty Hearing***, 1996, page 30.

[36] Nicholas Timmins, *op. cit.* 2004, page 19.

[37] TUC (2003) ***Eliminating Child Poverty,TUC submission to the Treasury Review of Child Poverty***,Trades Union, Congress, London

[38] Parker, H. ed. (1998) ***Low Cost but Acceptable – A Minimum Income Standard for the UK: Families with Young Children***, The Policy Press and Zacchaeus 2000 Trust, Bristol and London; Wills, J. ed. (2001) ***Mapping Low Pay in East London,*** September 2001, UNISON; Ambrose, P. (2003) ***Love the Work,Hate the Job: Low Cost but Acceptable Wage Levels and the 'Exported Costs' of Low Pay in Brighton and Hove***, Health and Social Policy Research Centre, University of Brighton

[39] See Ambrose *op. cit.*(2003)

[40] Scottish Low Pay Unit (2003) ***Earnings and Gender in Britain and Scotland***, Scottish Low Pay Unit, Glasgow

[41] New Policy Institute (2003) ***Monitoring Poverty and Social Exclusion 2003***, NPI, London

[42] TELCO (2003) ***Socially Responsible Contracting in London's Financial Districts,***The East London Communities Organisation, London

[43] Georgia Klein, ***Life lines, the NCC's agenda for affordable energy, water and telephone services***, National Consumer Council, 2003

[44] Datamonitor figures reported in ***Profiting from Poverty***, New Economics Foundation, December 2002

[45] Provident Financial have produced figures to show that their costs are comparable with those of unauthorized overdrafts and home catalogue companies.

[46] Richard Murphy, Fulcrum Accountancy, 'Provident Financial and the case for an interest rate ceiling in the UK', June 2003

[47] New Economics Foundation, ***Profiting from Poverty***, December 2002.

[48] Claire Whyley, Sharon Collard, Elaine Kempson, ***Tackling financial exclusion: an area-based approach***, Joseph Rowntree Foundation, June 2001

[49] For a more detailed critique of Government policies on debt and financial exclusion see: ***Forgive us our Debts***, Church Action on Poverty, December 2002

[50] Paul Johnson, 'Sponging off the poor', The Guardian, 10 March 2004

[51] Will Paxton and Mike Dixon, ***The State of the Nation, an audit of injustice in the UK***, Institute for Public Policy Research, July 2004 page 23.

Chapter 7 Scotland

[52] T M Devine , ***The Scottish Nation 1700-2000***, (Penguin, 1999), p.252

[53] ibid p.249

[54] Ron Botham and Bob Downes, 'Industrial Clusters: Scotland's Route to

Economic Success', in ***Scottish Affairs***, no.29, Autumn 1999, pp.43 f.

[55] Jim Cuthbert and Margaret Cuthbert, 'Can Fiscal Autonomy Improve a Devolved Scotland's Economic Prospects?' in ***Scottish Affairs***, no.41, Autumn 2002, pp 86 f.

[56] ibid p.89

[57] David Webster, 'Scottish Social Inclusion Policy: A Critical Assessment', in ***Scottish Affairs***, no.30, Winter 2000, pp.28 f. David Webster is Chief Housing Officer for Glasgow City Council.

[58] Daniel Mittler, 'Sustaining Edinburgh: The Lord Provost Commission on Sustainable Development for the City of Edinburgh', in ***Scottish Affairs***, no.29, Autumn 1999, pp.104f.

[59] Wilson McLeod, 'Language Planning as Regional Development? The Growth of the Gaelic Economy', in ***Scottish Affairs***, no.38, Winter 2002, pp.51f.

[60] T M Devine, *op.cit.* p.468

[61] Malcolm Anderson, 'Control of Immigration and Exclusion', in ***Scottish Affairs***, no.30, Winter 2000, pp.16f.

[62] Lindsay Paterson, 'Social Inclusion and the Scottish Parliament', in ***Scottish Affairs***, no.30, Winter 2000, p.75

[63] David Heald and Alisdair McLeod, 'Fiscal Autonomy Under Devolution'. ***Scottish Affairs***, no.41, Autumn 2002, pp.5f.

[64] Jim Cuthbert and Margaret Cuthbert, *op.cit.*

[65] SCSIN is co-ordinated by the Scottish Churches Parliamentary Office. This paper owes much of the information on the Scottish Parliament and Executive to the work of this office and its regular Briefings.

[66] John Flint, Rowland Atkinson and Ade Kearns (2003) ***Churches and Social Capital: the Role of Church of Scotland Congregations in Local Community Development***, Department of Urban Studies, University of Glasgow

[67] Chris Baker, ***Towards a Theology of Partnership***, Faith in Partnership Series no 2, William Temple Foundation & others, 2003.

Chapter 9 England's North-West Region

[68] **Gross Value Added**

GVA is an important measure in the estimation of GDP

What is Gross Value Added?

Gross Value Added (GVA) measures the contribution to the economy of each individual producer, industry or sector in the United Kingdom.

What is it used for?

GVA is used in the estimation of Gross Domestic Product (GDP). GDP is a key indicator of the state of the whole economy. In the UK, three theoretical approaches are used to estimate GDP: 'production', 'income' and 'expenditure'. When using the production or income approaches, the contribution to the economy of each industry or sector is measured using GVA.

What is the 'production' approach to estimating GDP?

The production approach to estimating GDP looks at the contribution of each economic unit by estimating the value of an output (goods or services), less the value of inputs used in that output's production process.

What is the 'income' approach to estimating GDP?

The income approach to estimating GDP measures the incomes earned by individuals (e.g. wages) and corporations (e.g. profits) in the production of outputs (goods or services).

What is the 'expenditure' approach to estimating GDP?

The expenditure approach to estimating GDP measures total expenditure on finished or final goods and services produced in the domestic economy.

What is the method used for balancing GDP?

All three approaches to estimating GDP are balanced annually using the Input-Output Supply and Use accounting framework.

How does GVA relate to GDP?

The link between GVA and GDP can be defined as GVA (at current basic prices; available by industry only), plus taxes on products (available at whole economy level only), less subsidies on products (available at whole economy level only), equals GDP (at current market prices; available at whole economy level only), or, in summary:GVA + taxes on products – subsidies on products = GDP

Source: Office for National Statistics: www.nationalstatistics.gov.uk

Chapter 10 Ireland

69 Adele Bergin et al, ***Medium-Term Review2003-2010***, Dublin: Economic and Social Research Institute, 2003, p. 2.

70 International Monetary Fund, ***IMF Concludes 2004 Article IV Consultation with Ireland***, 4 November 2004, p. 2 (www.imf.org)

71 National Economic and Social Council, ***An Investment in Quality: Services, Inclusion and Enterprise***, Dublin: National Economic and Social Council, 2003, p. 392.

72 Helen Russel et al, ***Work-Poor Households: The Welfare Implications of Changing Household Employment Patterns***, Dublin: Economic and Social Research Institute, 2004.

73 Brian Nolan, 'Income Inequality During Ireland's Boom', ***Studies***, 2002.

74 Christopher T. Whelan et al, ***Monitoring Poverty Trends in Ireland: Results from the 2001 Living in Ireland Survey***, Dublin: Economic and Social Research Institute, 2003, Table 5.8, p. 40; Table 5.12, p. 42.

[75] *op. cit* Table 4.13, p. 27; Table 4.16, p. 28.

[76] Tim Callan, Mary Keeney, Brian Nolan and Bertrand Maitre, ***Why is Relative Income Poverty so High in Ireland***, Dublin: The Economic and Social Research Institute, 2004, pp. 7-9.

[77] p. 56.

[78] International Monetary Fund, ***Ireland: Selected Issues***, Washington DC, November 2004 (IMF Country Report No. 04/349).

[79] This section is based on a presentation by Eithne Fitzgerald, economist, to a Consultation organized by the Department of Social Issues of the Irish Inter-Church Meeting, held in Dublin on 27 January 2002.

[80] Ibid.

[81] Walter Kopi and Joakim Palme, 'The Paradox of Redistribution and Strategies of Equality', ***American Sociological Review***, Vol. 63, 1999 (October), pp. 661-687.

[82] Sahr Yambusa, Methodist Minister, Galway, presentation to DSI Consultation, Dublin.

[83] This is an edited version of a presentation by Michael Smyth, Senior Lecturer, School of Economics and Politics, University of Ulster, given at a Consultation organized by the Department of Social Issues of the Irish Inter-Church Meeting, held in Belfast on 8 October 2003.

[84] ***Strategy 2010: Report by the Economic Development Strategy Review Steering Group***, Belfast, March 1999.

[85] Based on a presentation to the DSI Consultation in Belfast by Paddy Hillyard, Professor of Social Administration and Policy, Department of Social Studies, University of Ulster.

[86] Paddy Hillyard, Mike Tomlinson and Eithne McLoughlin, ***Bare Necessities: Poverty and Social Exclusion in Northern Ireland***, Democratic Dialogue, 2003.

[87] This is an edited version of a presentation to the DSI Consultation in Belfast by Cecelia Clegg, staff member of the Irish School of Ecumenics.

[88] Emily O'Reilly, 'Imagining the Future – An Irish Perspective', Address at the Annual Ceifin Conference, Ennis, Co Clare, 3 November 2004

Biographies

Margaret Burns

Margaret Burns has been Social Policy Officer with the Jesuit Centre for Faith and Justice in Dublin since October 2003. She previously worked with the Council for Social Welfare, the advisory body on social issues to the Irish Catholic Bishops' Conference, She is a member of the Department of Social Issues of the Irish Inter-Church Meeting, and was a member of the Working Party which prepared the report, ***Unemployment and the Future of Work: An Enquiry for the Churches***, published in 1997.

Niall Cooper

Niall Cooper has been National Coordinator of Church Action on Poverty since 1997. Prior to that he set up and coordinated the Churches National Housing Coalition for six years. In 1999 he co-founded the Debt on our Doorstep network for fair finance. In 2000 he chaired the UK Coalition Against Poverty's Commission on Poverty Participation and Power and in January 2004, joined the Government Advisory Group on Over-indebtedness.

John Devine

Monsignor John Devine is a priest of the Roman Catholic Archdiocese of Liverpool. In thirty years as a priest John has worked in Skelmersdale New Town, the Peruvian Andes and Huyton. For 10 years he was Director of St Joseph's College, Upholland with additional diocesan responsibility for clergy in-service training, missionary activity and justice & peace. He was appointed Churches' Officer for the North West in 2000 to liaise between the mainstream Christian Churches and regional government bodies. He is based at the Northwest Development Agency in Warrington. He is vice chair of the Economic and Social Partners Group of the North West Regional Assembly, Chair of the North West Stakeholders Forum, Chair of 5050 Vision: the NW Forum on Ageing, and he serves on the board of Voluntary Sector North West and Culture North West.

John Kennedy

John Kennedy is a Methodist minister. He spent 5 years on the East Coast of Sri Lanka, working with the Society of Jesus in technical training and job creation. He worked for nine years in the London Borough of Tower Hamlets. As Secretary for Political Affairs he worked in the Methodist Connexional Team for 11 years, and since 1999 has performed a similar task for CTBI. He has traveled widely in Central America and the European Union. He writes regularly for The Independent.

Ian Linden

Ian Linden is an associate professor in the Study of Religion at the School of Oriental and African Studies. He was director of the Catholic Institute for International Relations (CIIR) for fifteen years, and holds a CMG and an honorary doctorate from Southampton University for work in human rights. His recent study of globalization, *A New Map of the World,* was published by Darton Longman and Todd in 2003.

Jonathan Lomax (editor)

Jonathan Lomax is the Public Affairs Officer for The Salvation Army and deals with political, parliamentary and public policy issues. After studying politics at university he spent time working in journalism and in parliament before moving to The Salvation Army in 2002. The Salvation Army is a Christian Church and the largest and most diverse provider of social welfare in the UK after the Government. Its practical service provision is complemented by campaigning and advocacy on issues of social concern.

Robin Morrison

Revd Robin Morrison is the Church and Society Officer for the Church in Wales. He relates to the national organizations of Wales and supports church specialists working with economic, social or environmental issues. He is Chair of the South Wales Institute of Directors and on the Advisory Board of Common Purpose. He has been a hospital, university and industrial chaplain, a Social Responsibility Officer, an assistant head of a community school and a parish priest.

Mervyn Phillips

Mervyn Phillips CBE is an elder of the Presbyterian Church of Wales and past Moderator of one of its Associations. Since retiring as Chief Executive of Clwyd County in 1992, he has been active in church social and ecumenical affairs in Wales. A graduate in jurisprudence and law and in theology, he is the author of *Wales: Nation and Region*, published by Gomer in 1997.

Jennifer Potter

Jennifer Potter has spent most of her working life in Africa - largely as a Geography teacher in Botswana, where she was active in the National Ecumenical Council. In her later years there she was also very active in the National Ecumenical Council. In 1996 Jennifer became the International Affairs Secretary for the Methodist Church. She has an MSc in Environmental Management, and is deeply engaged with environmental issues. Jennifer trained for the ministry and since 2002 has been a Minister at Wesley's Chapel in London. She is the Moderator of the CTBI International Affairs Liaison Group.

Peter Sedgwick

Peter Sedgwick works as a priest in the Church in Wales and is Principal of St Michael's College, Llandaff which is a theological college training clergy and laity ecumenically. He worked formerly at the Public Affairs Unit in the Church of England and has written several books on Christian social ethics.

David Sinclair

David Sinclair has been the Church and Nation Secretary of the Church of Scotland for the last six years. Before taking up his current position, he was a parish minister in St Andrews, Fife and a social worker in Livingston, West Lothian.

Acknowledgements

The publishers are grateful to the following for their permission to reproduce the extracts below:

Chapter 3 (A Christian Reflection on Economic Change: Peter Sedgwick)
Miroslav Wolf: ***Work in the Spirit: Towards a Theology of Work,*** *Oxford University Press, Oxford 1991*

Chapter 5 (The Environmental Challenge: Jennifer Potter)
Jonathan Porritt: Seeing Green, Blackwell, Oxford 1985
Mark Lynas: **Hot News**, *Granta 83:* ***This Overheating World,*** *editor Ian Jack, 2004*

Chapter 7 (Scotland: David Sinclair)
Extract from ***The Scotsman****, February 2004.*

Printed in the United Kingdom
by Lightning Source UK Ltd.
105067UKS00001B/175-225

9 780851 693095